JOB EVALUATION
Volume 1
a new method

By the same author

MANAGEMENT THEORY

Job Evaluation
Volume 1
a new method

T. T. PATERSON, MA, BSc, PhD (Cantab.). FRSE

Research Professor, Chesters Management Centre, University of Strathclyde
Past-Fellow of Trinity College, Cambridge

London

BUSINESS BOOKS LIMITED

First published 1972

© THOMAS THOMSON PATERSON, 1972

ISBN 0 220 66842 6

This book has been set 10/11 Baskerville
at The Pitman Press, Bath
for the publishers, Business Books Limited
(registered office: 180 Fleet Street, London EC4)
publishing offices: Mercury House, Waterloo Road, London SE1

Made and printed in Great Britain

To

KIRSTY and TARA

Contents

Tables

Figures

Preface

About two thirds of the employed population in the USA are pay-graded by job evaluation schemes [47, p. 79]. Less than half of that proportion is at present graded in the UK, whereas, in Holland, nearly the whole of the employed population is graded by one national scheme. The importance of job evaluation is self-evident, and also the need for it in the UK.

Since the beginning of the 1950's I have been interested in wages because of their importance to industrial relations, and I collaborated with my colleague the late Professor D. J. Robertson in this field. His book *Factory wage structures and national agreements* [59] was a first attempt at studying the reality of wage determination on the shop floor. It became clear to me then that economic theories did not explain the facts and could not predict either (so they were not sound theories), and I turned to behavioral and philosophical approaches, trying to find out, from intensive study of a Glasgow factory, what is meant by the phrase 'a fair day's wage for a fair day's work'. I got so far but not enough to promulgate a theory [49].

By the beginning of the 1960's the general theory, given in this book, had emerged and I applied it in *Reports on the Organization of the Southern Rhodesia Public Services* in 1961 and 1963 [51, 53]. The ideas were adopted and worked. Since that time, with the aid of students and colleagues (for no other aid in this field of research could be had) I continued to experiment and the results were consistently good. Other people, in India and South Africa, independently tested these ideas and found them applicable to the real life of the firm. As a result I am now confident that the theories and the developed method (what my students insist should be called 'The Paterson Method') are sound; they explain facts and they predict. They are simple, like most general theories, easily understood, based on what I have learned from people who live in industrial and other enterprises, and so readily learned for use in the firm.

As I understand it to mean, job evaluation is a complex of job analysis, the study of jobs, job description, the statement of the results of the analysis, upon which follows job grading, the placing of jobs in a sequence or ranking which is the basis of job assessment and the establishment of fair pay based on job grading.

This book is the first of two and establishes the theory and principle of the Method. This is done after existing methods have been analysed and their common denominators isolated. The four long-established methods, Ranking, Classification, Point and Factor Comparison, are joined by three others, Time-Span, already well publicised, Castellion (from South Africa and hardly known in Europe and America) and the Guide-Chart Profile. These three are particularly important since they are linked by the common factor decision-making; and this is the basis of the Paterson Method, the technique of which is detailed in Volume 2: *Job evaluation—manual for the Paterson method*, referred to hereafter as *The Manual*.

The technique of work analysis because of its wide connotations, leads to many 'bye-products', merit-rating, training and development, job enlargement and enrichment, manpower policy and selection, organisation and management strategies, incentives, productivity bargaining and negotiation. It becomes the general theme of the management of men, the utilisation of human resources.

The Method can be applied industry-wide; it can be applied nation-wide as I show in the last Chapter. There lies in this a new concept of control of pay inflation, a possibility of a new incomes policy, a possibility built on the fundamental of distributive justice, a 'fair share of the cake', for everybody. But, naturally, there is still much to do to bring this possibility into being, not least a change of attitude, to believing that men's labour is not bought but rewarded.

Acknowledgements

The Secretarial staff of Chesters Management Centre have been most industrious in getting this material into type for me, above all most patient and understanding of the irregularities of authorship. My friends the management consultants, Inbucon, Urwick-Orr and Hay-MSL, have kindly helped with information ably handled by my good colleague Dr T. M. Husband, Head of the Department of Production Management at the University of Glasgow whose work he has freely given to me to quote, as has Dr Lucien Cortis. I benefited, too, from discussions with Dr D. C. Limerick of the Graduate School of Business Administration, of the University of Witwatersrand in Johannesburg; and an old friend, Mr Basu, of Cobim Limited, Bangalore, India, carried out some tests I found most useful—I quote them. Besides all this I wish to acknowledge the help of all those firms, managers, shop stewards and trade unionists who showed so much active interest.

Chapter one   **Introduction**

The reasons for the introduction of job evaluation schemes are not far to seek. In those firms without job evaluation of some kind confusion of pay structure is rampant. The relativity of pay for one job to pay for another can seldom be explained other than 'it grew like Topsy', or was fixed arbitrarily, or negotiated with a strong trade union and so on. "The overriding impression is that the wage structure develops through a series of *ad hoc* decisions in which one expedient is piled on top of another to raise the earnings of timeworkers . . . relative to those of pieceworkers" [61, p. 149]. Special moneys are given for all kinds of reasons, to keep labour in the firm, to prevent a strike, 'dirty money' for conditions, built in to the wage until it is a chaotic compilation of bonuses and allowances long after the circumstances for these allowances have gone. In the middle 1950's it was estimated that boilermakers' wages in shipbuilding in Clydeside in Scotland were made up of bonuses given in relative antiquity, in one case as far back as 1891. The problem has been worsened by the introduction of new technologies which affect the content of jobs, and require new ways of estimating reward—the old style bargaining of piece rates mainly on the basis of physical effort is being replaced by time rates for mental skill.

Incentive payments, mainly piece rate, in the more automated factories led to situations where semi-skilled staff were earning more than skilled, meaning those with long years of special training and education behind them—"It appears quite common for pieceworkers to have higher standard earnings than timeworkers with a higher level of skill" [40, p. 155]. But there always has been a differential payment between unskilled and skilled to the advantage of the latter, right from the times of the Greeks (see Chapter 12) and this relativity the skilled wish to retain. "Change—always, everywhere, in everything—requires justification: the strength of conservation is that it is held to justify itself. It is not, therefore, surprising that the maintenance of standards, absolute or comparative, should be woven as warp and woof into the texture of wage discussions" [74, p. 162]. So, as one group of staff earns more, by whatever means, other groups require that they are paid more to maintain these relativities, the differentials, even though they may not be working harder or doing more. Pay on the shop-floor 'leap-frogs' and the managers lose control. American managers use job evaluation schemes extensively (for two thirds of employees) and, as one writer has put it, "As a broad generalisation it is suggested that American employers are more concerned to maintain control over internal wage structures than are British and Swedish employers" and that "in Britain . . . some firms have made their wage structures so flexible as to abdicate all effective control" [60, p. 69].

It would appear that these *ad hoc* changes bring about the phenomenon known as 'wage-drift', seen by economists as the rate of increase in earnings which is not accompanied by extra effort. ('Primary' wage-drift occurs when pieceworkers' earnings rise, perhaps due to bargaining or labour shortage, or higher productivity. 'Secondary' wage-drift occurs when the original relativities are restored.) This produces obvious problems on the national scale but managers are naturally more concerned with its effects on the economy of the firm; they are more concerned with the costs of production as these are altered by this drift. To them the secondary wage-drift is the more serious.

Much of the argument about relativities or differential payments is based on the concept of equal pay for equal work but, in the absence of job evaluation, there is no way of establishing what is equal work. The problem is not helped by the economists, who have constantly told managers that they should pay 'the going rate' (what other managers are paying in the local labour market), for the economic theory of supply and demand control of price of labour does not fit the facts (Chapter 12). "Research has shown wide discrepancies in pay for similar jobs at different firms within the same locality . . . it is just not true that firms pay the same wages for specific occupations as are paid by other, competing, firms in their locality. It is therefore difficult, if not impossible, to place any meaning on such phrases as 'the going rate' or the 'local level of wages' " [46, p. 22]. Despite this the UK Civil Service has a Pay Research Unit which spends most of its time searching for the 'going rate' in industry and commerce in order to establish a pay scale in the Service. Some authors on pay administration—especially for managers—exhort firms to look at the markets so as to pay the market rate, whatever that may mean, forgetting that the firm will tend to pay the average of that rate. The result will be cumulative increase of payment in the upper brackets of the market rate, for an average implies upper and lower—and this leads to inflation, another aspect of wage-drift.

Partly as a result of wage-drift, as a result of the failure of the economists to produce a practical theory to account for wage inflation and its control, as a result of the stronger 'institutional pressures' in the firm—"all the evidence suggests that there are factors operating within individual plants which effectively isolate it partially from the external economic forces operating in the local labour market" [61, p. 65]—there is a movement in UK towards a decentralisation of collective bargaining away from national agreements and towards factory-level agreements [59]. But, "unless there is some mutually agreed framework, or set of principles to which appeal can be made, the situation very soon degenerates into power politics and horse-dealing" [Quoted, 46, p. 13]. And job evaluation helps provide just such a framework. "It is thus a potentially important instrument for dealing with one of the main reasons why the growth in incomes tends to outstrip the growth in productivity—namely, the struggle engendered by what are regarded as inequitable, irrational and arbitrary pay structures" [46, p. 15].

Job evaluation has other advantages as a kind of side effect. The information gained in job analysis helps in reorganisation towards a better structure of jobs. Good job specifications form the basis of selection and recruitment, for they are thus geared to the finding of the right men for the available jobs; and the same information is the background to performance appraisal and merit-rating, and so, also, of training and development. In large enterprises, with a large managerial staff spread out over several subsidiaries, the problems of development of managers by transfer from one to the other, without drastic pay disarrangement, can be considerably assisted, if not wholly eradicated, by good job evaluation. To employees on the shop-floor and in the offices it has the advantage of being 'fair', or if not truly so, at least an attempt at being fair in pay distribution.

There are difficulties inherent in the methods now mainly used, and described in Part II. They do not cover all jobs in the firm in the same way and they tend to divide jobs, and so their holders, into 'classes' like 'white collar', 'blue collar', 'lab. people', 'indirect and direct labour' and so on. They sometimes give results which clash with the existing structure to such an extent that they are unacceptable; and this becomes greater when historically determined differentials are affected. There is a tendency in the most popular method, the Point Method, to confuse the job content with the skills and capacities people bring to the jobs, such as apprenticeship, a university degree, examinations passed. Performance appraisal allowances for these skills, and allowances for the results, tend to be built into the rate of pay for the job, and the original confusion is re-constituted. The 'going rates' in the local labour market do have an effect (even though that effect is not yet understood, as already mentioned) and negotiational pressures by trade unions may concentrate on one occupational skill in order to produce changes at isolated points in the pay structure, again disturbing the job evaluated system and bringing about imbalances. Another source of confusion is payments made for conditions of work, one of the main factors in the Point Method. Conditions vary, yet this factor, and the proportion of pay awarded by its presence, remains constant. There are some non-logical aspects of job evaluation methods that may instigate confusion of the kind the methods are devised to eliminate; and there is a rigidity in a job-evaluated pay structure which does not permit of easy reaction to change. What appears to be the fault, and what will be examined later, is the lack of coherent theory.

The problems of pay are worse on the bigger scale of the industry within which the firm is placed. In the USA and Sweden job evaluation schemes for separate industries have been instituted and appear to be acceptable to trade unions representing unskilled, semi-skilled and skilled staff. This is, in the main, due to the trade union structure which is industrial. But in the UK the craft-based trade union structure raises real difficulties. For example, in the chemical industry there is the engineering craft union and the chemical workers' union. The first has a tradition of 'skill' as defined by apprenticeship of at least five years. The second has "skilled" members who have no such apprenticeship, because it is not necessary. The engineering union demands the retention of a 'skill differential'. In the printing industry it is even more difficult—three closely-related unions battle over differentials. In the automobile industry in the UK the craft and general, i.e. non-craft, unions appear to have combined to form a kind of industrial union, but individual union activity upsets differentials established on this combined basis. And throughout any one industry jobs with the same titles vary in job content so that, locally, there has to be adjustment to the industry-determined scheme. Even in one industry such as steel the variations can be very wide (Chapter 6). As for clerical and managerial staff their pay structure is cast back and forth on the waves of technological change and inter-firm competition.

There are lessons to be learned. In Sweden, despite the industry-wide schemes, there is still bargaining at plant level on how much is to be distributed, the firm's ability to pay, the 'wage kitty' and its distribution [46, p. 21]. This is done under guidance from the joint employers' association and trade union confederation. "But even with a common scheme, local evaluation produced such widely differing results for similar jobs in terms of points totals" (a Point Method is used) "that the employers' association decided that local job evaluation required some form of central legislation. This was achieved by experts from the employers' association taking part in all local evaluations, in checking jobs and in vetting results before the presentation of the points total to the union" [47, p. 23]. There are six major schemes differing in construction. "The number of factors in each scheme range from 9 to 19, and have no common definition; neither have they a common pattern of sub-factor or degree breakdown" [47, p. 24]. One must ask the question, therefore, if it is possible that jobs are being compared on a logical basis in such circumstances—there is every indication that they are not. And when it comes to assigning money to these comparative points totals, even if they are similar for similar jobs, "the actual pay grade can vary from plant to plant depending on how the local parties aligned points to pay grades when the scheme was installed" [47, p. 25].

There are benefits despite this somewhat confused system. Job evaluation is cheaper for the individual firm, there are central experts to help with knotty problems especially with change of rating when jobs change—these experts help in union–employer negotiations—and industrial relations are better. Job-evaluated pay structures form an acceptable basis for negotiation and reduce disputes and leap-frogging. Apparently the pay structures are accepted as fair and reasonable (despite the extraordinary variations noted in the paragraph above). This may have its roots in the feeling already discovered in the UK, a job evaluation scheme, whatever it is, is better than none [46, p. 11]. There are also advantageous side effects of the kind already noted.

The problems in an industry-wide job evaluation scheme are greater in a nation-wide. The off-quoted example is the Dutch, again limited to unskilled, semi-skilled and skilled employees. In order, in the first place, to control wage inflation, a *Standardized method of job evaluation* was introduced to cover all industry but not white collar workers. This was a form of Point Method with ten factors and a variety of weightings leading to a structure of 'grades' varying in number and 'points width'. The relation of grade to pay was settled by Government on the basis of two 'key jobs', the unskilled laborer and the skilled engineering mechanic. "Once wages were established for the two benchmark jobs, a straight line was drawn between them giving wage levels for all intermediate points values. Initially the line ran straight on beyond 85 points but was subsequently altered to a curve, so as to yield progressively higher rates for exceptionally skilled jobs" [47, p. 37]. (Note the alteration was made "so as to yield" . . . not because there was any believed theoretical validity for a curved line).

"There was pressure from the shop floor for job evaluation in the early post-war years, since workers, with the exception of those in industries which historically paid higher than average rates, e.g. building, began to believe that its introduction would always increase their wages. This belief was reinforced by an agreement between management and unions that in no case would the application of job evaluation lead to a reduction in pay for individual workers. It has also been said that if wage increases were inevitable and had to be justified, job evaluation was an officially approved means of doing this with considerable incidental advantages, since such increases were channelled to the improvement of the relative wage-structure" [47, p. 38].

There were many problems. There were the difficulties inherent in the job evaluation method itself, weighting of points, the relative importance of different factors. "Since 1963/4 increased weighting has generally been given to the 'inconvenience' factors because dirty and unpleasant jobs have become more and more unpopular" [47, p. 39], i.e. the non-logic of building 'conditions of work' into job content combined with labour market changes forced an alteration of the original, supposedly reasonable factor and its weighting. The failure of the Standardized Method to fit all industries, led to the recognition that it could hardly be used to fix inter-industry differentials—though it could be used for intra-industry and intra-firm differentials.

Because there was no factor which recognised that the forces of labour supply and demand had to be reacted to the scheme was finally opposed by employers paying more than the fixed rate for labour in short supply. This led in 1964 to a 'wage explosion' with increases up to as much as 15 per cent. "These developments heralded a period of inflation, punctuated by Government intervention, and ultimately a credit squeeze and significant unemployment" [47, p. 39]. The role of job evaluation as an instrument of national wage control disappeared.

There was a fundamental principle on which the incomes policy requiring job evaluation was based, i.e. there should be "equal pay for work of equal technological value" as measured by the Method. "The equal pay principle was fundamental to the 'harmonious' wage structure concept which implied that there should be no inter-industry differentials for closely comparable jobs, jobs with similar content thus receiving the same pay irrespective of industry or company profitability" [47, p. 40]. Hence less profitable firms, small firms too, which did not have the ability to pay were penalised. The bigger more profitable firms could then put away profits and not distribute some at least to their employees. So, "on the one hand, workers could not share in the benefits of increased efficiency to which they might have directly contributed, while on the other hand companies were prohibited from paying more wages in order to attract scarce labor" [47, p. 40].

The national job evaluation scheme in Holland is still very widely used, no doubt because employees, unions and firms, find some of the advantages that have been referred to, but it is no longer used to control wage inflation or to set up an inter-industry pay structure for these reasons:

1 The Standardized Point Method has no theoretical validity in application to a wide range of jobs in different industries, and can be distorted.
2 It cannot permit of reaction to environmental changes such as in conditions of work, in the labour market and in technology.
3 It does not recognise that ability to pay must be taken into consideration in establishing a pay structure, that a firm, say a small one, may be unable to pay the same as a large one, and that an efficient firm is unable to reward (except surreptitiously) its staff who have made it efficient—in other words inhibitory of increased efficiency.

The question must be asked "Is there a logical principle that governs occupational differentials throughout a nation? Is there some way by which the incomes of such diverse occupations as dustmen and dockers, unskilled automobile builders and postmen, public servants and engineers, miners, managers and teachers, can be put on a scale, say of worth, of importance, of difficulty, of unpleasantness, whether any of them can be equated as being the same in content, and whether, being so they should be paid the same, and why?"

In the UK as I write this, there is a galloping pay inflation as big as in Holland in 1964, people are recommending a credit squeeze and unemployment rises. Former members of the National Board for Prices and Incomes, from whose Reports I have deliberately quoted above, now say the UK can solve this problem on the lines of the Dutch experiment in job evaluation and they do not talk in terms of economic theory. Perhaps they have forgotten what they reported but, if what they reported is true, then the Dutch example is not for the UK and its troubles. This does not mean to say that job evaluation cannot help as an instrument in control of pay inflation. The Dutch experiment failed because of the three reasons just given. A job evaluation method that is based on some sound theory which is both explanatory and predictive, and is acceptable, may well be the answer. The Dutch government's idea maybe was right, the implementation was wrong in the choice of method.

Part 1

The three chapters of this Part are a recapitulation, a summary of much that is expounded in a previous publication *Management theory* [54]. This is necessary because the terminology used by the many writers on job evaluation varies in meanings often undefined, and confusion is the result. The precise use of words like 'supervision', 'responsibility', 'accountability', 'authority (line and staff)' is essential. It is as essential to know what the difference is between skilled, semi-skilled and unskilled, between middle and senior management, between job, position, and function. Wherever possible the words used are as defined in the Oxford English Dictionary. Only three new words are introduced, sapiential authority, advisability and informability. The first, I now read, is recognised in modern British management literature; the other two are almost self-explanatory.

All jobs, whatever the particular field or function, require people to make decisions, so decision-making is common to all jobs—for which reason decision-making becomes an important factor, if not the only one, by which jobs can be compared.

Decision-making implies a decision process, a sequence of four stages, stimulation which becomes *Information*, assessment of the information to present *Conclusions* or alternatives for action, selection of an alternative which becomes a commitment to action and so a *Decision* proper, and, finally, the stage of *Execution* requiring decision on how to carry out the commitment.

In any enterprise a decision by one person may become the information or the conclusion for another, so requiring further decision-making. Hence each of the four stages of decision-making can be seen to form a decision-system which, in the case of human enterprises, is an open one. The stages or 'units' of the decision system are related one to another, and thus relations can be defined in terms of necessity (for decision-making in a firm implies necessity), and necessity involves 'right to do' and hence authority. All relations can be specified in terms of authority.

There are four forms of authority: structural—the right to command, sapiential—the right to be heard by reason of expertness, personal—the enhancement of structural and sapiential authority by reason of the fitting-ness of personality, and moral—the enhancement of structural and sapiential authority by reason of proven rightness and goodness of action. Job evaluation in this book concerns itself with the content of a job and not with the characteristics of its performer, so the only relations requiring examination are those stemming purely from structural and sapiential authority.

There are six kinds or bands of decision to be found in any enterprise and, theoretically, there are no more possible. So any job can be defined in terms of these decisions and of the authority relations that are involved, under such broad terms as 'supervisor' and 'adviser'. Each job is composed of tasks, and each task can be broken down into decisions required. The top managers have tasks requiring policy decisions; the senior managers have tasks that involve programming decisions, i.e. planning the implementation of policy; the middle managers have tasks that require interpretation of the plan and the choice of what is to be done inside that plan; the skilled workmen decide the processes necessary to do what has been decided requires doing; the semi-skilled men have decisions on the cycle of operations within a process; and the unskilled can decide only on the elements of operation.

A job is what a person contributes towards the achievement of the purpose of the firm. It is composed of tasks which are groups of related processes and operations; a process is a set of logically related operations; an operation is a complete and logical cycle of elements (either as physical movements or mental activities).

Difficulty of a job is a relative term—what is difficult to one person may not appear difficult to another; but relative job difficulty can be expressed in terms of kinds of decision, the higher the decision grade of the job the greater the difficulty. Within a grade of job the relative difficulty can be expressed as job complexity, determined by the number of the constituent tasks and the range of difficulty of these tasks.

Chapter two   **Relations in decision-making**

A person makes a decision when he reacts to a stimulus, which may be of many kinds although all of these can be placed under the one title *Information*. He analyses this information, perhaps breaks it down into constituent parts, he may synthesise it and categorise it. As a result he discovers whether a problem has been established, so that he, therefore, has to consider how he must react, or not react. He then looks over possible reactions and their effects and comes to a *Conclusion*, an assessment of the information, that one or more reactions are possible and are relatively right or not so right, good or not so good.

He has still to decide what his reaction has to be; he selects one of the alternatives upon which he has concluded and commits himself to it. This, as distinct from conclusion, is the essence of *Decision*, the commitment to action and responsibility for the result. He then plans how he will implement the decision and selects one of several ways, thus deciding on the *Execution* of the decision.

An example of the decision-process can be taken from the production line. The production manager's progress-chaser reports that there is a slowing down at the final position of the assembly line. The manager analyses the information, times, loading of the line, kinds of product, and concludes (assesses) that there is a problem to be solved. He then analyses the possible actions, such as slowing down at the input and or at some point along the line, or stopping the line altogether. He comes to the conclusion (assessment) that the best thing to do, in terms of pressure on production and answering sales demands, is to slow down at the input end for a certain length of time. He decides to act on this conclusion and then proceeds to decide on the right way to go about it, what kind of order to give, to whom, and at what moment. Willy-nilly, he has to go through this whole decision-process.

The *decision-process* can be reduced to the four, broader, sequent stages which are of universal application for all systems; see Figure 2.1:

1 INFORMATION, reception and categorisation of stimuli.

2 CONCLUSION, assessment of the problem, if any, and appreciation of possible courses of action.

3 DECISION, selection of a course of action and decision to act on it.

4 EXECUTION, analysis of the possible methods of carrying out the selected course, and the decision to act in the chosen method.

In a firm many people are making decisions and the decision of one may become the information for another. For example, a sales clerk may receive

———► Information ———► Conclusion ———► Decision ———► Execution

Figure 2.1   Decision-process

a form of order from a customer. He sees that it is a standard form for a standardised product, concludes the order can be filled, decides to take action by passing the order as proper to the despatch clerk, and executes this decision by sending the form, duly initialed as dealt with, to the despatch clerk. This form, with the conclusion of the sales clerk that it is proper, becomes information to the despatch clerk who recognises it as requiring action. He has other information, state of inventory, next mail out, and such like, concludes the order can be met by despatch at either of two times and decides on one. He then executes it by giving orders to the packer and the transport section.

It is also possible for each of the four stages to be carried out by different persons. For example, a junior may collect data and sift it out, passing it on to a senior who concludes upon it and then makes recommendations to another person (or to a group), who decides what is the right thing to do, and thereafter passes the decision on to another person for action. This is fairly common in the public service where a junior, as an assistant, provides information to a senior.

When this happens, however, it should be recognised that in each stage of the process a decision is required by the person who handles the information or the conclusion, or the decision, or the execution. In other words, each individual in the decision system goes through a complete, individual, decision-process himself. For instance, the first person may receive information, concludes that he should hold it, and decides to hold it. He then files it, this being execution. On the other hand, he might conclude that it should be in a particular category, decide to place it in that category, and act by passing it on to somebody further up. This person, receiving the categorised information, concludes that something ought to be done (it is good to be done), and thereafter decides that this conclusion should or must go to the Board (for instance). He thereupon acts by preparing a report, and this is passed to his Board. The Board receives this as information, discusses it in coming to a conclusion, and decides what should be done as action; it then passes this policy decision to a senior manager. He receives the policy as information, concludes on the possible alternatives in carrying this out, decides on which alternative must be used, and then acts by issuing a command for programming this alternative.

Whether there are one or four persons in the process, the four stages must exist, and the four units involved in these stages together can be called a *decision-complex*; which can then be defined as the system of relations between the units of a decision-process for any one decision. But the process flow is not all one way. There is a form of *feedback*. In the example given above, sales and despatch clerks, the despatch clerk, having sent off the ordered material, sends to the sales clerk for his files a report that the order has been filled. There is also a form of *feedforward*. If the sales clerk receives an order about which he has doubt that it can be filled, doubt about the size of stocks say, he rings up the despatch clerk to find out about stocks before he sends the

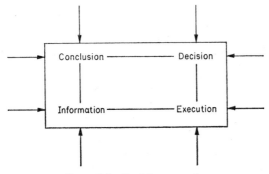

Figure 2.2 Decision-complex

order form to the latter as proper to be filled. So the decision-complex can be portrayed as in Figure 2.2.

The complex is an *open system* for each unit can receive stimuli from outside the system itself (arrows). Each unit, a person, can be a sensory mechanism in himself, each going through the decision process in his function as part of the complex. The *decision-system* in a firm is a mass of such complexes reducible to one broad complex, the firm itself. The relations of complexes are described later, but first it is necessary to define the relations between the units of any one complex.

RELATIONS

An enterprise has purpose towards the achievement of a goal or goals. In a modern firm all the members, shareholders, managers and men alike, have one *goal*, survival, through the use of money obtained by cooperation in the *purpose* of the firm (say, making bicycles). To achieve that purpose there are *functions, jobs* that have to be done, and when a man does a job in a firm, fulfills his function, this is his *contribution towards the achievement of the purpose*. These functions must be coordinated, related, and the system of relations of functions constitutes an organisational *structure*. A function can, therefore, be said to have a *position* in this organisational structure. A person fulfilling the function is then said to have a *role*, the part he plays in the achievement of the purpose, defined in terms of his function and of his relations to others fulfilling their functions. (Role is thus defined as in the drama). *Role behaviour* is the expected (but not obliged) behaviour of a person in a given role. (An actor does not 'create a role'—the author does that—he interprets the role behaviour as he uniquely apprehends it). In organisational literature, as well as in ordinary speech, we say manag*ing* is a function and manag*er* is the appropriate role.

A *relation* can be defined, in universal terms, as that abstraction of the nature of a bond set up when two entities have any form of contact, electrical, mechanical, chemical, visual, verbal or otherwise. In human, social organisms, such as a firm, the kinds of human relation depend upon the differences between persons filling roles since the contact is human communication and this communication is governed by the differences of the persons in their roles. All men are different, in that each man is unique, and it is this difference which governs the kind of communication that passes between them. There are four main categories of difference:

1 Difference in *position*, i.e. in the vertical and horizontal framework of an organisational structure of the functions that men fulfil, which means the difference in the kinds of function and the decision-making involved. For example, a manager is said to be 'superior' to an operative, a 'vertical' relation, one being subordinate to the other who has the right to give commands.
2 Difference in *knowledge*, i.e. each man is unique in having different upbringing, capacities and experience, hence his relative knowledge or expertness governs his communications with others.
3 Difference in *personality*. Each man has a unique personality and this affects the way in which communications are made and received.
4 Difference in *mores*. Because of the way a man behaves in society, conforms to the mores of society and its rules of going about doing things, conforming to 'what is done', so people will react when he communicates with them.

Since we are here concerned with jobs and not the people in the jobs, the way in which personality and mores affect communications need not be considered, although all four differences are intricately intertwined. The differences of position and knowledge are intimately concerned with the decision-system—position is involved with ordering and coordinating, and knowledge with the way in which information is handled and conclusions drawn—and these can now be considered separately.

THE SYSTEM OF STRUCTURAL AUTHORITY

When several men come together to achieve a common purpose they agree each to contribute a function, that is, they contract or oblige themselves to do so. But these functions must be coordinated and so there must be another function, that of coordinating. This is of necessity, otherwise the purpose would not be achieved. Hence the person fulfilling the function of coordinating is given the *right to command and so to expect obedience*. This is *Structural*

Authority, for authority implies the 'right to do something or other of necessity'.

Thus, when a person enters a firm and contracts or obliges himself to contribute a function, implicitly he obliges himself to obey the commands of the person having the function of coordinating, having the right to command. Structural authority is vested in the coordinator by those coordinated; and, since the function of coordinating is a position in the structure, the authority is *vested, in the first place in the position,* and only secondarily in the person fulfilling the function, hence the term 'structural authority', sometimes called 'formal' or 'legal' authority. (Should a manager leave the position, his successor is vested with the same structural authority).

It has been argued that the right to command is vested in a manager by the owners of the means of production, a belief that stems from our dominating laws of property. This cannot be so. A person may own a factory stuffed with machinery but he cannot go to any one on the street and order him to work a machine. The man chooses and contracts of his own free will to join the firm and work the machine, and chooses also to vest the manager with structural authority, otherwise the man could quite well be doing work without contributing anything towards the common purpose, towards profitability, value added, and so reward.

Since a person 'taking on a job' not only agrees to do it but contracts to do so (reward being the other side of the bargain) he obliges himself to carry it out. Being so obligated, should he fail he may suffer retribution of some form—retribution is the negative of reward. Similarly, since he contracts to obey the rightful commands of one who has the function of coordinating, failure to obey such commands will also involve retribution. Punishment on a member of a group is inflicted by the group—the whole has the right to punish the part.

In modern complex societies the group cannot act as a whole so the right to impose retribution is usually vested in one who has structural authority. The President is authorised and empowered by the People to impose retribution. He delegates this authority and power to the judiciary. In a firm the most senior manager is like the President in that he is authorised to command—and he, too, can delegate his authority. So a manager may not only have the right to command and to expect obedience, he may also have the right to enforce it. He is authorised and empowered. He is entitled to use the *categorical imperative* (for the command is 'of necessity') being *words to the effect,* "You will do so-and-so otherwise I shall punish you". (The use of the imperative 'will' in this fashion is a Scottish and Irish manner of speech, not English).

The persons to whom the senior can give such commands and on whom he can visit retribution for failure are said to be responsible to him. *Responsibility is a relation* between two persons one of whom has the right to command the other and to enforce obedience. We often use the word 'responsibility' to mean the function for which a person is responsible to another. It is thus a loose expression implying that a person is 'responsible for his responsibility'! We are referring to the relationship and properly so when we talk of 'a sense of responsibility'.

This relation is two-way. If the junior is responsible 'upwards' to the senior the latter is also responsible 'downwards'. The senior is responsible for providing the junior with the facilities necessary for the latter to carry out what the former orders. Otherwise the junior cannot be held responsible for failure. Indeed, in some cases juniors can impose retribution on seniors. A factory not provided with enough heating for the operatives is a failure in responsibility downwards, and the operatives may come out on strike.

Another aspect of responsibility downwards lies in *delegation*. If a manager gives a supervisor some operatives to carry out a job, i.e. a facility for getting a function fulfilled, he must also add another facility, the right to command. He delegates structural authority since he cannot hold the supervisor responsible if the latter is unable to exercise the right to command. Where the manager delegates not only the right to command but the right to enforce obedience as well, he is saying to the operatives (in the *sphere of authority* of the supervisor) that they are responsible to the supervisor. In Fig. 2.3 the

Figure 2.3   Structural diad

relation of responsibility is indicated by a solid triangle with the apex towards the superior. This straight delegation of authority and power is sometimes called 'line authority'. The structure is a *diadic*.

At this juncture an important point—for the purpose of job evaluation—must be made clear. If a manager orders a subordinate to do something, i.e. *the function*, and if he also orders the way in which it is to be done, i.e. *the procedure*, and the function is not fulfilled, retribution cannot be visited on the junior—he did not decide the procedure. For example, if a supervisor orders a skilled turner (whose function is turning) to use his lathe in a particular fashion, and the product is faulty, it is the supervisor who is held responsible and not the turner. For a person to be held responsible for a function he must have freedom or discretion to decide the procedure; provided he is capable of deciding on a procedure that will get the job done. This proviso must hold since a person cannot be held responsible for doing something that he cannot do—a senior should never give an order to a junior that he cannot carry out. For example, a semi-skilled man cannot be given an order to set up a lathe, but a skilled turner can be.

Another proviso to this dictum of freedom to decide procedure is that the senior can order certain procedures that are *necessary for coordination* of one function with another. A junior cannot have complete freedom to choose a procedure that will interfere with the functions of his colleagues. Such procedures are known as *procedures specific to function*. It follows that if these, ordered by the senior, lead to failure the senior is responsible not the junior.

Given these definitions *responsibility is the immediate concomitant of a decision on procedure*. If a person has responsibility he must be given the right to make a decision. For a simple example, a plant manager may give the weekly production schedule to a departmental manager, the schedule specifying the production to be obtained. The departmental manager is responsible for obtaining this and he does so by deciding what men and machines are to be used, their coordination, and what is to be done by the operatives. One of the operatives is told that he is to make a particular product and he is given a machine, materials and power (as facilities). He decides his procedure, how to set up the machine and operate it, and he is thus responsible for producing the part.

Where, in the Point and Factor Comparison Methods of job evaluation to be described, 'responsibility' is used as a factor this is an implicit recognition of the decision to be made. In the classical case of the night-watchman believed 'responsible' for a store containing a million dollars worth of materials, he is not responsible for the safety of the materials for he did not decide they would be so stored. All he can decide is the way he goes about his guard duties, patrolling, locking up, testing locks, windows and the like. He is responsible only for these; the manager who decided the storage and the placing of the night-watchman, provision of locks and alarms, etc., is responsible for the safety of the million dollars.

Responsibility cannot be delegated. It is a relation between two people and this cannot be cut-up and parcelled out. What can be delegated or assigned are the functions ('responsibilities') for which a person is responsible. To take the example of the departmental manager in the preceding paragraphs —he is responsible to the plant manager for meeting the weekly schedule, and for this he is given the facilities of a department, men, machines, power, materials and structural authority. He assigns to operatives (perhaps through supervisors) the job of making parts to a specified quality, quantity and time. He still remains responsible to the plant manager for meeting the schedule. He cannot blame failure to meet it on the operatives' failure; *he* has been given the facilities to meet the schedule. Of course, if the men given him are not capable of making the parts he has not been given a necessary facility and so cannot be held responsible; the plant manager who supplies inadequate facilities, remains responsible. If, however, the departmental manager gives the appropriate order to the skilled technician, along with the necessary facilities, and the technician fails in making the right kind of decision on procedure, the manager is not responsible for the outcome. He is responsible only for the decision he makes, in this case a proper one.

Delegation implies, therefore,

1 Assigning a function, loosely called 'delegating responsibility'.
2 Delegating authority (and, perhaps, power) as a facility necessary to fulfilling the function, 'authority commensurate with responsibility'.
3 Specifying decisions to be made, and so establishing responsibility.

For the purpose of job evaluation the last is the most important. If the departmental manager tells the technician to set up the machine in a particular fashion, i.e. making a skilled man's decision for him, and then tells the technician to operate it, the latter is no longer making a skilled but a semi-skilled decision, he is working as a semi-skilled member yet being paid a skilled man's pay.

Responsibility cannot be measured. A human relation, by its very nature, cannot be measured. A skilled operative may feel as great a sense of responsibility (for his product) to his supervisor as the latter does (for coordinating his section) to the departmental manager, or as the last does (for meeting the production schedule) to the plant manager. A clerk, who is very conscientious, that is, has a "strong sense of responsibility", may feel more responsible for the accuracy of his accounts than a senior clerk or accountant who is not so conscientious. A supervisor may feel his responsibility for expenditure of 100 dollars more than the departmental manager for expenditure of 1,000 dollars. In other words, character cannot be gauged, feeling cannot be

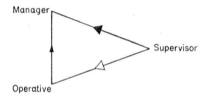

Figure 2.4   Structural triad

measured. But differences in kind can be defined and observed, differences in kind of decision and so of responsibility—see later.

In delegating, a senior may delegate the right to command but not the right to enforce obedience; the junior is authorised but not empowered. The system of relations between a manager, supervisor and operative when the supervisor is not empowered becomes a *triadic* (see Figure 2.4). It is exactly like the system in the military services, the commissioned officer is authorised and empowered, the non-commissioned officer (the sergeant) is authorised and not empowered. An NCO cannot punish a private—he must report him 'on a charge' to the commissioned officer. (This may be one reason why the supervisors in firms are sometimes called 'the NCOs of industry').

It will be clear from Fig. 2.4 that the relation of responsibility holds between the operative and manager and between supervisor and manager, but not between supervisor and operative. The supervisor can give an order to the operative, in effect saying "You must do so-and-so or else the manager will force you to obey". This is not the categorical imperative which implies the right of the one who is ordering to enforce obedience, yet it is of necessity rightful, it is 'must-ness' invoking 'will-ness'. It is still structural authority and the most common system in mid-twentieth century industry.

As the private reports to the sergeant so the operative reports to the supervisor. The operative is obliged to so report although he may, in the absence of the supervisor, report direct to the manager—as in the military system. "Bound to render an account or report" is the dictionary meaning of the word accountability. (The other meaning is synonymous with responsibility

—but why use two words for the same concept!) Thus the relation between supervisor and operative can be called *accountability*, and is defined as the relation between two people one of whom has the right to command the other, both of them being responsible to a third person. The accompanying imperative, "You must or else", is called the *parenthetical imperative* to distinguish it from the categorical. The symbol of the relation is a triangle with the point 'downwards'. The relation of responsibility between the operative and the manager who normally does not give orders direct to the operative is symbolised by an open triangle pointing 'upwards'.

This open triangle implies *nominal control*;
the accountability triangle implies *actual control*;
the responsibility triangle implies *full control*,

the word *control* indicating the use of structural authority. All those controlled by a person are said to be in that person's *sphere of authority*.

THE SYSTEM OF SAPIENTIAL AUTHORITY

A person who is expert in a subject is, sometimes, referred to as 'an authority' on that subject. In a firm, different persons are relatively expert in different subjects, i.e. relative to the other members of the firm, they are, so to speak, 'authorities'. This authority is *sapiential authority*, the right to be heard by reason of knowledge or expertness. (It is sometimes loosely referred to as 'staff' authority or 'the authority of confidence').

Authority, the 'right to do', as already said, stems from necessity. The right to be heard stems from the necessity to make the best decisions possible. The existing work system, and the firm as a whole, may be functioning well enough on decisions that have already been made and are repeated as a standardised set of rules. 'Everything is all right', the purpose is being achieved, the decisions are proper and appropriate to the achievement. But the firm exists in a constantly changing environment, its decision system is 'open', so what is proper or 'all right' will require to be changed in order to react to environmental change. Decisions have to be 'bettered', even the purpose of the firm may have to be 'bettered'. To do so knowledge is required, it is necessary to make the best (the superlative of good and better) decisions. Hence the 'right to be heard'.

This right to be heard is *vested in a person*, not in a position as is structural authority; for knowledge is individual not positional. Everyone has sapiential authority of some kind, meaning that each unique person, by reason of his unique experience, has knowledge that may better a decision. But everyone does not have sapiential authority for every decision.

In mid-twentieth century this right to be heard has been much misconstrued. Trade unionists want to 'have a say' in the management of firms, which means they believe they have the right to be heard. Some believe that this applies to all of management whether trade unionists are knowledgeable or not; some believe this means 'making the decisions' (to which subject we shall return later). But the right to be heard is limited, the right stems only from knowledge.

This knowledge can relate to an extraordinarily wide variety of subjects and experience but, for the purposes of the subject of job evaluation, it can be classified under two headings, (1) knowledge relating to function and (2) knowledge relating to procedures for carrying out the function. These can best be analysed by example.

1 KNOWLEDGE RELATING TO FUNCTION

A production control manager knows about the state of the order book, the production schedule, inventory, work-in-progress, specifications and such matters. He is, therefore, relatively expert on the matter of the production line loading. He has the right to say to the production manager that if the latter does not make some particular change he will be unable to carry out his function of producing according to the schedule to meet customer requirements.

The production control manager says, in effect, "You must do so-and-so if you are to fulfil your function". He does not say "You will", the categorical

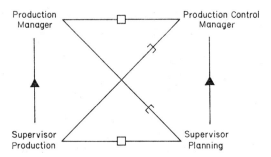

Production
Manager

Production Control
Manager

Supervisor
Production

Supervisor
Planning

Figure 2.5   The functional quadratic

imperative, nor "You must or else", the parenthetical imperative, for he has no structural authority over the production manager. He does not invoke force, merely his knowledge. The production manager, knowing the expertness of the production control manager pays close heed to this *advice*, but he is not obliged to act accordingly, although he knows that if he didn't, he would probably fail to fulfil his function.

The imperative "You must . . . if" is the *hypothetical imperative, advice* defined precisely, is a communication containing the hypothetical imperative, and the relation between the managers is called *advisability*. It is symbolised by a square (see Figure 2.5).

Just as the production control manager can advise the production manager, the latter can advise the former—the relation is reciprocal. Because of his knowledge of the production line, the production manager can use the hypothetical imperative to the production control people saying, for instance, what limits the production control manager must set for production of specific items.

In the same way as their respective managers can advise each other so can the production and planning supervisors. The control manager can say to all those in the sphere of authority of the production manager that his planning supervisor will give advice on planning for the production line; that is to say he, in effect, assigns the function to his supervisor who is then responsible to him for the quality of advice given to the production people. But the control manager cannot hold him responsible for giving advice to the production manager, for the planning supervisor cannot know enough concerning the production manager's decisions which encompass reports, departmental budgets, labour relations and the like. The *degree of sapiential authority* of the planning supervisor is not high enough. The two managers must retain their mutual relation of advisability.

Since both managers have a high degree of sapiential authority they are entitled to advise members of each other's sphere of authority even though they may have assigned such advisory functions to their juniors who are, in the case of the supervisors, in a relation of advisability. The managers are said to be *actual advisers* to each other (the complete square) and *nominal advisers* (the broken square) to each other's juniors. The structure is thus quadratic, in this case a *functional quadratic.*

2 KNOWLEDGE RELATING TO PROCEDURE

An industrial engineer engaged on work study knows about procedures; an organisation and methods expert knows about office techniques. Both are concerned with procedures which, as we have already seen, are decided by a person if he is to be held responsible for his function.

The industrial engineer, having worked out a *better* method for using a machine, cannot command the operative to use the method (using either the categorical or parenthetical imperatives). Nor can he advise the operative to change (where 'advice' is used here in the sense of containing a hypothetical imperative), for the operative is already fulfilling his function by procedures decided by himself and so is under no obligation to act on the advice or even to pay heed to it. The industrial engineer can *expect* him to change since it is for the better, either in reduction of physical effort or increase in productivity.

The engineer can say to the operative "You ought (or should) try this new method for these reasons". This is the *injunction* or injunctive imperative. The operative has complete freedom to act on it or not to heed it. Since there is neither control nor use of the hypothetical imperative the relation between engineer and operative is neither responsibility, accountability nor advisability; and since the communication is essentially one of information the relation is called *informability* and is symbolised by a circle. The communication can range from a mere statement of fact or opinion, through what 'can be done' to 'should be done' to 'ought to be done'.

There are degrees of sapiential authority relating to procedure, and the structure, Fig. 2.6, is similar to that for the functional quadratic.

The industrial engineer and production manager are *actual informants* (full circle) to each other on work study problems on the production line, as are their respective operatives. The production manager is a *nominal informant* to the work study operative (broken circle) and the industrial engineer to the production operative.

All those to whom a person is entitled to give advice (as defined here) constitute that person's *field of influence*. He is then said to *direct* (as distinct from control in structural authority), or *instruct* (meaning to teach or advise) those in his field of influence. 'Direct' has the connotation of 'pointing out'.

The relation informability is universal—every person may have information for other persons, of use in decision-making. An operative may have some facts of use to the Vice-President Manufacturing, the Head of Research

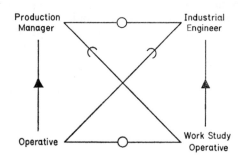

Figure 2.6   The procedural quadratic

and Development may have some useful information for the cleaner in the electrical shop.

If a senior advises a junior responsible to him, i.e. saying in effect "You must do so-and-so if you are to fulfil your function" (for which the junior is responsible) the latter can only take this to mean the categorical imperative. If he did not act on the advice and there was failure the retribution would be much heavier. If it did succeed that success would be regarded by both as the result of the senior's sapiential authority and not of the junior's decision. *A senior cannot advise a junior* on the function for which the junior is responsible to him.

Conversely, if a junior tells the senior that he "must do so-and-so if he is to fulfil his function", which function includes control of the junior, the latter will be regarded by the senior as 'getting a bit above himself', vesting himself with a higher degree of sapiential authority than that he is entitled to. Nevertheless, a junior can advise his senior about an activity which is outside the senior's sphere of authority or the immediate structural line above. And a *junior can always inform his senior*, using at the most the injunction, without incurring a negative reaction. Too often, for example, young graduates do not make the distinction between 'must' and 'ought' believing their sapiential authority is so great they can advise their non-graduate seniors. They learn the hard way.

Chapter three   **Decision-structure**

We are now in a position to set out the relations between the units of the decision-process (see Fig. 3.1).

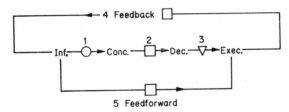

Figure 3.1   Decision-process

Referring to the numerals in Fig. 3.1:

1 There must be a relation of informability between the Information Unit and the Conclusion—the communication is "this is", "this can, should or ought to be done". The Conclusion Unit, in order to do its job, must be able to command the Information Unit to produce the necessary information—accountability.

2 The relation between the Conclusion and Decision Units must be advisability—the communication contains the hypothetical imperative, "you must adopt one of these alternatives if you are to answer your problem".

3 The relation between the Decision and Execution Units involves structural authority; the alternative having been selected—the decision made—the Execution Unit is ordered to carry it out and is left the discretion in procedure of carrying it out. The communication is either the categorical "do this" or parenthetical imperative "you must do this or else", or "you've got to do this". In general, these days in industry and commerce, it is the parenthetical (∇).

4 The effect of carrying out the decision is fed back to the Information Unit so that, in case of need, adjustments can be made by modifying the decision. The relation must be one of informability, "this ought to be done", or advisability "this effect implies that a change must be made if a better decision is to be obtained".

5 Before a conclusion or decision can be made there should or must be knowledge of whether it can be carried out by the Execution Unit. Therefore, there must be feedforward from the Information Unit to the Execution, the communication being, "You must give me information on what can be done, for the Conclusion and Decision Units say that this information must be obtained if the best possible decision is to be made".

In effect, feedforward and feedback are reciprocals of the communication in the relation advisability between the Information and Conclusion Units. The Decision-complex now becomes as shown in Fig. 3.2.

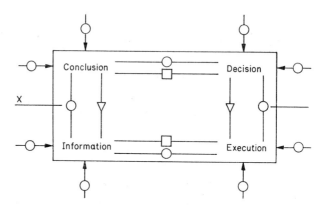

Figure 3.2   Decision-complex

The relation accountability (∇) and advisability ($\square$) entail informability ($\bigcirc$) since a junior can inform a senior, using the injunction upwards, and a member can inform a colleague laterally. (This is, in effect, a combined functional and procedural quadratic.)

For the purposes of job evaluation the important point is that a person who is in the Conclusion Unit, who has the right to tell a colleague that he "must do if", giving the hypothetical imperative in advice, is on the same level (above the line X) as the decision-maker, Decision Unit. Similarly the Information and Execution Units are on the same level but below X.

For example, referring to Fig. 2.5, the Production Control Manager, knowing customer demand and the loading of the production line, can give advice to the Production Manager, who would regard this communication as a conclusion, an alternative upon which he makes his decision. The Production Control Manager is 'on the same level'. If, however, the Supervisor Planning gave advice to the Production Manager, told the latter what he "must do if", the Production Manager is almost certain to regard the Supervisor as 'getting a bit above himself', in other words equating himself with the Production Manager and with his own senior. It is all right if he informs the Production Manager, tells him what the schedule is and what the latter should or ought to do about it, informs upwards. (Note the difference in 'weight' between "must" and "ought".)

KINDS OF DECISION

A firm is a living social organism and, like all living organisms, it has six primary functions (using the word 'function' in its second meaning of an activity, as in management literature):

1 INGESTION, e.g. the purchasing of raw materials for processing, or buying of machines.
2 PROCESSING, e.g. manufacture and selling of goods.
3 REACTION TO ENVIRONMENT, e.g. acting on the markets, implementing a marketing strategy for selling so as to be able to get more for ingestion.
4 SUPPORT OF THE PARTS, e.g. reward (pay) to members of the firm, provision of management services to the production function, flow of money, 'the life blood of the firm'.
5 REGENERATION OF PARTS, e.g. the maintenance and replacement of human and material resources by the personnel and maintenance departments of the firm.
6 ORGANISATION, e.g. the management of the other five functions. (There is as well another 'life' function—reproduction—which a firm can also do.)

These primary or major functions can be called divisions, departments and the like, and there are secondary sub functions, minor functions.

In the carrying out of these functions decisions are made, decisions about production, about costing, about design and so on. It is clear that the middle manager in the production department is making a different kind of decision to that made by the skilled technician or the unskilled laborer; and it is clear that the middle manager accounting department is making a different kind of decision to that made by the senior costing clerk or the copy typist. What is not clear is the difference in kind of decision made by the skilled turner, the skilled fitter and the skilled pattern-maker, or the difference between the decisions of the middle manager production engineer and the middle manager design engineer. We use these terms throughout business, unskilled, semi-skilled, skilled, middle managers, senior managers, top managers, and they apply to persons working in different functions and sub-functions. There is a very good reason.

Take a one-man firm. (Theory should apply to a one-man firm as well as to a large corporation if it is a valid theory.) He sets out to make a living by manufacturing and selling, say, whistles. He has made a *policy* decision. To carry this out he *plans,* he works out how much money he needs and if and where he can get it, what machines he needs and how much to spend on them, how much for selling expenses, etc. He then gets brochures about machines and timber and goes and sees them. Within the limits of his planned budget he decides on the machines and the timber, and on similar matters. He has made a unique decision in *interpreting* the plan in action—but he still hasn't begun to make whistles. The machine is mounted in the shed at the bottom of his garden and he now works out how it is to be set up in order to drill holes in the wood; he decides the *process* and, having done so, puts in the drills and the timber and operates the machine by a series of *operations* that constitute the process. Carrying out these operations he makes decisions on how fast he works, how his hand movements are controlled, he decides on the *elements* of these operations. (It will be obvious to readers who know work study that I draw upon the ILO handbook on work study and its definitions as given by the late Russell Currie of ICI, a good friend of Chesters Management Centre).

As the firm prospers the owner takes on labourers to operate the machines, clerks to look after the books and stamp letters, typists, and a clerk for sales orders. They make decisions on elements and operations but he still decides policy, plans it, interprets it and decides how machines and books are to be used (process). This is the beginning of the division of labour. He does well and so he gets in a foreman, a skilled machine man, to organise the skilled men working not only wood but metal, because he has now diversified into bassoons and tin whistles. Later he has someone to run the production, a production manager, a sales manager, an accountant, but he still decides policy and plans all five major functions. A big factory is built, he has diversified into wood, plastic and metal furniture, he now has a works manager, a designer, a chief accountant, a chief sales manager, who do all the planning of his policy. And at this point he 'goes public' remaining as chairman and president. There is a board of directors making *policy* decisions (*top management*), there are schedulers and planners (*senior management*) who work out the *programming* of the policy, departmental heads who *interpret* the programme (*middle management*) and *skilled, semi-skilled* and *unskilled* shop floor and office staff.

In a still larger firm it may be necessary to coordinate at an intermediate level these various decision-makers. The president (managing director) organises the executive vice-presidents at Board level; a general manager coordinates the works manager, chief engineer, chief accountant, etc., a departmental manager coordinates department superintendents, a foreman coordinates skilled men, a charge-hand coordinates semi-skilled, an unskilled man who coordinates unskilled men is, automatically, making semi-skilled decisions at least.

Kinds of decision are called *Bands* of which there are six; they are subdivided into two (except the unskilled) and these are called *Grades* of which there are eleven. It is impossible to conceive of any more kinds or Bands of decision or of any more Grades of decision. There are possible subgrades of the grades but the decisions remain the same. Bands are referred to as O, A, B, C, D and E. Grades are numbered 0 to 10. Even-numbered grades involve coordinative decisions, coordinating decisions of the odd number of the same grade. An odd-number grade decision coordinates decisions of the band below. The scheme can be given as shown in Table 3.1.

TABLE 3.1 *Decision structure*

Band	Kind	Title	Grade	Kind	Title
E	Policy-making	Top management	10	Coordinating	President (MD)
			9	Policy	Vice-President (Ex. Dir.)
D	Programming	Senior management	8	Coordinating	General Manager
			7	Programming	Works Manager, etc.
C	Interpretive	Middle management	6	Coordinating	Department Manager
			5	Interpretive	Superintendent
B	Routine	Skilled	4	Coordinating	Supervisor
			3	Routine	Technician
A	Automatic	Semi-skilled	2	Coordinating	Chargehand
			1	Automatic	Machinist
O	Defined	Unskilled	0	Defined	Labourer

The decision bands can be defined shortly in the following fashion.

BAND E   POLICY DECISION (TOP MANAGEMENT)

These are associated with board level management. The word 'director' implies the direction or guiding of the enterprise, which the Board does by taking decisions on corporate policy. The limits set on the decisions are wide and, in many cases, are specified only by the laws of the state.

BAND D   PROGRAMMING DECISION (SENIOR MANAGEMENT)

These are made typically by 'divisional managers', chief accountants, works managers and chief engineers, deciding the plan for execution of the policy which sets the constraints within which the decisions are made. A typical senior management decision is on the master and monthly production schedules. Another is the decision on how to set up computer facilities for the whole firm, the decision to purchase a computer being policy.

BAND C   INTERPRETIVE DECISIONS (MIDDLE MANAGEMENT)

These are usually made by departmental heads such as a machine shop manager, or project research manager, or life assurance department manager. The schedules having been laid out by the senior managers, the middle managers decide how to utilise machines and manpower, etc., in order to meet the schedules. The departmental manager knows 'why' certain people have to do this or that.

BAND B   ROUTINE DECISIONS (SKILLED TECHNICIANS)

Skilled technicians know how to set up machines, they know all the rules that govern 'how' to make something. They can decide which process to be used in order to carry out the Interpretive Decisions. They know the operations, 'what' to do, 'where' and 'when', all of these combined as a process. A senior clerk in an income tax office knows how to complete income tax returns, 'what' and 'where' entries have to be made—he has the book of rules and regulations beside him, if necessary. A chief invoice clerk in a business office may decide how the invoicing is to be tabulated and returns collated, in the light of the needs of the sales accountant making Interpretive Decisions.

BAND A   AUTOMATIC DECISIONS (SEMI-SKILLED)

Each process is a cycle of operations (see in detail next chapter). The machine process having been decided by the technician who sets up the machine, the semi-skilled machinist works the machine. Within the constraints of the process, the 'how', the semi-skilled man can decide 'where' and 'when' he carries out the operations that constitute the process.

BAND O   DEFINED DECISIONS (UNSKILLED)

Where not only the process is specified but also the operations, all that is left to the unskilled man is the decision on speed, the 'when' of the element, a cycle of which constitutes an operation.

The British Institute of Management has officially described similar decision-making grades which it has subdivided into 'Zones' (Table 3.2). The descriptions are here given alongside the Decision Bands and Grades as listed above.

We may take as example, part of a minor function to illustrate those different kinds of decision that may be involved in the fulfilling of this function. The head of a section, having made an Interpretive Decision involving a unique case, decides that this decision should be distributed for information to appropriate departments. This is also a decision of Band C. He then orders his junior to "distribute appropriately". This junior, knowing the rules and regulations governing distribution, that is to say, the rules that prescribe what kind of information should be sent to whom, then gives the order to another person in a phrase such as, "complete Form G with this information, date-stamp, sign, and distribute to X, Y, Z within the next week". He has ordered a particular process and operation, and is held responsible by his senior for the choice of the appropriate medium of communication and of the time for distribution, in view of the fact that he knows the rules and regulations sufficiently well to make this kind of decision. He follows the rules; it is a Routine Decision, Band B.

TABLE 3.2 *Bands, Grades and BIM job zones*

Band	Grade	Zone	Description
E	10	I	The Top Executive—the most senior in the organisation. In some cases a full-time chairman would fill the position, but where the chairman is only part-time on a 'retainer' basis, a managing director, or one of similar title, would occupy this zone.
		II-1	The second-in-command (if any) of the organization—for example, a deputy to a Zone I job holder. In those cases where there is both a full-time chairman and one or more managing directors, the latter would come into this sub-zone.
	9	II-2	Full-time members of the Board of Directors, each in charge of a major function for which he is responsible. A director may be in charge of more than one major function.
D	8	III-1	Heads of major functions where the responsibility is direct to the Top Executive or Zone II-1 job-holder.
		III-2	Heads of major functions including major operating divisions, where responsibility is to a Board member of Zone II-2.
	7	IV-1	Senior managers responsible for the day-to-day running of major functions or divisions and reporting to Zone III job-holders. Responsible for implementation of policy.
		IV-2	Senior managers, as in IV-1, but operating a unit of lower importance either by size or by responsibility. Top-ranking specialists, where the emphasis is on individual contribution rather than on control of others, would be included in this zone. (Here is a clear-cut recognition of sapiential authority.)
C	6	V-1	Middle Management including the next-in-command to Zone IV-1 job-holders, and other specialists with some years experience.
	5	V-2	Middle Management as in Zone V-1, but occupying a position of slightly less importance—probably reporting to a Zone IV-2 job-holder.
		VI-1	Second-line management, normally reporting to a Zone V-1 job-holder, and including qualified specialists on first appointment.
B	4	VI-2	Second-line management as in VI-1, but occupying a position of lesser importance. Would probably include senior foremen who are responsible for chargehands or junior foremen in Zone VII.
		VII	First-line management—the first rung of the management ladder. This Zone will include those supervisors or foremen who control the work of individuals as a team in a section of the office or factory and who are regarded as part of the management structure.

The person ordered to carry out these processes has no choice over the process whatsoever; indeed, he need not know why there should be a rule and regulation for this particular form and for that particular distribution. Suffice it is that a particular process has been ordered to be carried out within a particular time. Since the operations are not completely defined, that is, the order is one concerning the process and not the operations within the process, then this person has the choice of operations in the completion of the process, not only in time (though there is a limit) but also in the way it should be carried out, as long as the end result is that which is ordered. For instance, this person may decide, in view of the width of the time element, that the form should be distributed by post, or by hand, a judgment of the time element and acceptance of responsibility that the particular forms will be delivered within the time limit, as ordered, an Automatic Decision of Band A.

This person may decide that it may go by messenger, and orders a messenger to "take this Form G to X by this afternoon". This order to the messenger is an order that governs only operation, translating a document from one place to another, the kind of operation that can be repeated in a cycle of elements of movement. The person so ordered has no choice in operation, it is ordered. The only choice left to the messenger is in the speed with which he may translate the document. For example, if the time limit is such that it would allow him to, he might decide to walk slowly and stop for a chat with somebody. Or, if the time limit is very tight, he may actually decide to run, so that, after delivery of the document, he would have time to stop and have a chat with a friend. He has choice only over the element of movement and not over the operation, a Defined Decision of Grade o. His senior who had ordered him is responsible for seeing to it that the document is despatched in the proper form within the appropriate time. He, the messenger, is responsible for translating the document, using the appropriate elements of movement and, within the time ordered, to the proper person as ordered. There is here, then, a distinction between discretion in operation and discretion in element of operation.

This cycle involves four people. If there were only one person, that is to say, at the level of Band C, who made the original decision, then he would have to carry out all the other tasks. He would then be responsible for everything to his superior. The fact that there are three other people to carry out the processes and operations which are of different level of difficulty, that is, different level of decision in choice, does not absolve him from the responsibility for the total minor function; but in such a situation he, therefore, has the right to see to it, through supervision, that these three junior people carry out that which is ordered. But he assigns the distribution to his immediate junior and with it, delegates the appropriate structural authority to give orders to those below him, wherefore the junior assumes responsibility, the responsibility for the decision in ordering the processes. The third person becomes, therefore, responsible for the operations, though not for the processes, because the processes have been ordered by his senior. Since this third person is responsible for the appropriate choice of operation, the messenger cannot be held responsible for that particular operation which was ordered— taking that document at that particular time within that particular limit. He can only be held responsible for the movements he employs to carry out the operation. We thus have the appropriate sequence from Band C through Bands B and A to Grade o.

It follows that, in *job description*, the job of the member at Grade o should be described as the elements that are necessary to the operations that constitute the tasks; that is to say, elements specific to the operation, which may also include times and dates. He makes Defined Decisions on those elements that are not prescribed. Similarly, for the member in Band A, the processes should be prescribed with all those operations that are specific to the carrying out of these processes, that is, of operations (procedures) specific to the process, and this may also include times and dates. The job description for the member in Band B would include the minor functions and all those processes necessary to the fulfilment of this minor function and it, too, may include times and dates. The person in Band B needs to have a knowledge of the whole body of law, and regulations, precedents, and the like, which govern the process, so that he can make decisions within this framework upon cases 'thrown up' by the process. This framework usually covers several interlocking processes and constitutes the minor function. The person in Band B is one who 'knows the ropes'—he can give the answer to most any problem if it is covered by the regulations. (Job analysts do not write out these job descriptions since they are concerned with analysis of the actual activities, the decisions made by the member, and so their grading. The analytical process is of a different order from that of the job description though it must be based upon the job description).

As we have seen, any functions of Band A and B are those which are governed entirely by the rule and regulation specified from above. In Band C, however, there appears a form of choice which is not available to those in the lower bands. Within the framework of a programmed policy the person in Band C can have a choice in decision of a kind which establishes a precedent, a rule, within which members in Bands A and B make their own decisions. This kind of choice or discretion is different from that in the lower bands. Whereas, in Bands A and B the discretion is such that whatever happened, the end result would be precisely defined by the rule and regulation, in Band C, a new abstraction comes into being; the thinking is of a different order.

It is in Band C that a new form of judgment is necessary. Here is the beginning of the framework, the establishing of precedent, against which the person in Band B decides what, when and where. It is at this stage that the person in Band C now uses his judgment in a new form. He has to consider 'why' a thing has to be done. Whereas, in Band B and below, by reason of the fact that the rules and regulations are stimulated by an external agency (higher in the hierarchy), then the result of acting according to these rules and regulations becomes the responsibility of the external body making these regulations. In Band C the person making a judgment knows that the effect of his decision will rebound upon him. Thus, in making his judgment, he has to consider a whole series of possibilities of the effect of action based upon his rule-determining decision—whereas, in Band B the person need not consider the effect of following the rule. This is the essence of the difference between the judgment on 'why' and the judgment on 'what': it is the directive form of the whole decision-making process: it is the beginning of the creativeness of judgment, of the use of anticipation and prediction.

This does not mean to say that persons of Bands B and A and Grade 0 are not capable also of using anticipation and prediction. Indeed, it is well-known that people at Grade 0 and Band A level are capable of thinking up new kinds of operation which stems from anticipation and prediction in mental process. And people in Band B are also capable of anticipation and prediction in thinking out new kinds of processes for the good of the whole. Indeed, when we are considering people in terms of promotional possibilities, we use the words 'initiative', 'creative', and the like, to pick out those who are capable of using anticipation and prediction. For we are looking for such persons for promotion to upper levels, where these capacities are essential in this 'creative-directive' function in the Bands C to E. In the normal process of the functioning of the total group, this creativeness and anticipation-prediction is not necessary in work of Grade o to Band B, but it is necessary in these upper Bands, because the decision-making process requires this.

Chapter four   **Job structure**

The job that a man does is his contribution to the achievement of the purpose of the firm. If the firm is small it may be the equivalent of one of the major functions, e.g. he may be making decisions over the whole range of the manufacturing or of the financial function. In a larger firm, because of the need for division of labour, his job may be part of one of the major functions, e.g. he may be a departmental head or an office manager.

A job can be analysed in terms of the activities involved, either by analysing the major function and breaking it down into its parts then grouping some of these parts as the structure of the job, or by directly observing the activities of the job and constructing the job from them.

FIRST METHOD OF ANALYSIS—ANALYSING THE MAJOR FUNCTION AND BREAKING IT DOWN

The five main functions of the organism may be called *major functions*. Decisions on each are made in Band D (Programming) within the over-all, integrative policy of Band E. The job might be called, for example, 'in charge of manufacturing' or 'in charge of marketing'. The major functions are generally divided, even in relatively small firms, into sub-functions or *minor functions*, the decisions being Interpretive, of Band C. For example, the major function manufacturing may be subdivided in 'departments' such as foundry, machining or assembly; but for large firms these 'departments' may be broken down into smaller units, e.g. melting shop, pattern shop, foundry, stamping shop, boring mill, centre lathe shop, etc., each having a departmental manager 'in charge' and making Interpretive decisions.

But the job concerning the major function may not, and generally does not consist wholly of making decisions of Programming nature. There are also 'decisions specific to function', that is decisions may have to be made of the Interpretive kind necessary for integration. For example, a works manager (major function Programming, Band D) may decide that a particular department, say machining, shall utilise more skilled than semi-skilled operatives. It is a decision that could be left to the departmental manager, but the senior prefers to retain this decision because of problems of industrial relations in the whole of the manufacturing function.

Within the departments or sections below Band C come those jobs that are concerned with carrying out what the departmental head has decided, and according to the rules and methods necessary for execution. There is usually a variety of processes that may be used and the skilled operative (or clerk), knowing these rules and processes, decides which is applicable to the particular matter in hand. His job will be of the kind known as turning, fitting, drafting, computer programming, wage costing. Each job itself may involve several processes, e.g. a turner analyses the job specification or drawing deciding how it is to be implemented, selects the sequence of processes, decides how to set up his machine, decides its speed and the like.

He may carry out the whole job of turning, but he may be limited to setting up the machine which is then taken over by a semi-skilled machinist (Band A) who selects the operations within the process decided in the setting up of the machine. And, if the machine is of a nature that the operations are 'specific to function', that is, are also decided, an unskilled machine operator (Band O) can take over the working of the machine, merely feeding it, starting and stopping it.

An example of the same kind of structure may be taken from the accounts division of a firm. The chief accountant, Band D, acting on a policy decision of the board, programmes the system of authorising mileage payments for members of the firm travelling on its business. He decides which sub-department of the accounts division shall look after this minor function and the head of that department, Band C, decides which senior clerk will be given the job, at the same time specifying in broad outline the methods by which it should be implemented. He retains the right to interpret and decide on unique situations not covered by the methods he specifies.

The senior clerk decides the details and assigns to clerks in his section the various processes that will be involved, such as dealing with particular types of documents, their signing, their transfer from one place to another, cross-references, recordings, each such process made up of a number of operations. Depending upon the amount of work involved and their complexity the total job can be assigned to one clerk or the processes distributed among several. Each operation within a process can be broken down into a series of movements as, for example, picking up a form, entering a number, replacing the form.

The person who decides on the major function, say the chief accountant, uses procedures for making his decisions, procedures over which he has control since he is responsible for their outcome. He will, therefore, use techniques of computing, analysing and the like, especially at the information stage of the decision process. Each procedure can be broken down into processes and operations. Thus, a senior will include in his job decisions of lower bands similar to those of his juniors.

These definitions are best given by illustration. To take a clerk involved in mileage payments—his job may include a task 'date-stamping documents'. This can be broken down into several kinds of movements, called elements, each easily distinguished as a unit of movement (almost a therblig, to use Gilbreth's terminology).

Left hand	Right hand
	Reach (15 in)
	Grasp document
	Position document (15 in)
Hold document	Release document and reach 12 in
	Grasp date stamp
	Position stamp (12 in)
	Strike document
	Return stamp (12 in)
	Position stamp on pad
	Return hand to rest
Place document on tray (18 in)	

This portrays a complete cycle, and the operation of date-stamping can begin again. *A logical cycle of elements constitutes an operation.*

This particular operation involved almost nothing but physical activity, but an operation could also involve elements of mental activity, e.g. computing the number of running totals of mileages performed. This is part physical, part mental, in that it may involve a series of elements of noting down figures, and elements of arithmetical computation, simple addition and subtraction; but there would be a cycle of such elements constituting the one operation.

It is possible to conceive that each element, or several, of one operation could be carried out by different persons, and, in some production systems, work is reduced to elements to such an extent that members' activities are confined to parts of one operation. But in nearly all cases, on the shop floor or office, this breakdown is uneconomic from the organisational point of view and people are given at least one operation as their job. Even so, it is also found to be uneconomic to confine a person to one operation (quite apart from the psychological effect of monotony of repetition) and so most people have jobs that consist at least of several operations.

These are almost always logically related and such *a group of related operations is called a process.* The cyclical nature of a process stems from the logic of causality, one operation must precede another so that the end result can be achieved. For example, there might be an operation 'computing running totals', another of 'reading running totals', and a third 'allocating running totals'. These three, as a consecutive cycle, constitute a purposive sequence of operations, the process of 'calculating departmental mileage'. It is vertical specialisation or division of labour, 'departmentalism'.

This same specialisation can be continued—*a group of related processes can be brought together as a minor function.* A series of processes such as recording details of each claim on an annual schedule of claims, calculating departmental mileage, comparing and checking against authorised allocations, and certification, constitute the minor function of authorising mileage payments. Similarly a related group of *minor functions constitute a major function.*

It may be better, for three reasons, not to organise jobs in the way described, reasons which will be treated more fully in *The Manual* which follows this volume.

1 It has been found that a person may be motivated to work harder if his *'job is enlarged'*. This does not necessarily mean increasing quantity of work but variety of work. He may be given processes or operations that are not logically related and their differences constitute variety.

2 His *job* may be *enriched*, i.e. he may be given the right to make more decisions of a higher band or grade. Thus a machinist may be taught how to set up (decide the processes) for a particular machine unlike the skilled man who can set up several.

3 A person, as will be shown, is paid according to the kinds of decisions he makes; the more decisions of a particular band the more he is paid. The organisation of work to utilise people to the full in making decisions is known as the *economy of grading*. It may be necessary to allocate unrelated or not closely related operations, or processes, or minor functions in order to achieve economy of grading.

So it may be inadvisable to bring together as the work of one person all the related operations and processes—they may be unrelated. A *group of*

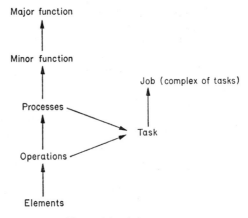

Figure 4.1   Job structure

related operations and processes, not necessarily constituting the whole of a minor function, is called a task (see Fig. 4.1).

It may well be that one task is not sufficient to keep one person occupied and, therefore, he may be given a group of tasks again not necessarily closely related except in so far as they fall within the major function of the department. *Such a complex of tasks, related within the major function of the department, constitutes a job.* Hence, in describing a job, the tasks are described and then the processes and operations in these tasks.

SECOND METHOD OF ANALYSIS—OBSERVING THE ACTIVITIES AND CONSTRUCTING THE JOB FROM THEM

I take an example described by my colleague Dr T. M. Husband [20] who was originally an engineer and is now Head of the Department of Production Management in the University of Glasgow.

An operator on a pillar drilling machine drills $\frac{1}{2}$-inch diameter holes in a 4-inch diameter steel flange. He makes the following movements or *elements*.

1 Lift the flange from the bin adjacent to the machine and place it in the opened vise on the machine table.
2 Tighten the vise until hand-tight.
3 Lift a copper mallet from the adjacent bench.
4 Strike with the mallet to further tighten the vise.
5 Put the mallet back on the bench.
6 Press the start button of the machine.
7 Bring the machine spindle down to the workpiece and feed the drill through.
8 Reverse the drill back up through the drilled hole.
9 Lift the copper mallet.
10 Strike to release the vise.
11 Put the mallet back on the bench.
12 Lift the workpiece from the vise and put it in the finished bin next the machine.

This *complete and logical cycle of elements constitutes the operation* of drilling the hole.

The man is told to move to a radial drilling machine in the same workshop in order to drill and tap a gearbox casing. There he carries out several operations of drilling holes, then he performs another series of operations of tapping the holes. Together these drilling and tapping operations are related, referring to the same holes on the same piece on the same machine, and the sequence, drilling followed by tapping, is logical. They constitute a simple *process, a logically related set of operations*, drilling and tapping gearbox casings.

There is a drilling shop as a separate department of the machine shop where all drilling, reaming, tapping and boring is done. In the drilling shop there will be a related group of processes of radial drilling and tapping, pillar drilling, jig drilling, horizontal boring and tapping, etc. Such a *logically related group of processes constitutes a minor function*. The drilling shop is one of several others, like the milling shop, in the machine shop, and these *minor functions being related* in this way the machine shop itself becomes a *major function*.

The driller who does nothing but 'drilling and tapping gearboxes on a radial drilling machine' has that as a *task* which is defined as 'a group of related processes or operations not necessarily constituting the whole of a minor function'. Since he does nothing else but this task, since this is his contribution to the achievement of the purpose, this one task is also his job, and since he does not decide this one process and the operations, since he has control only over the elements, his task and so his job is unskilled.

A machine setter, on the other hand, is the person who sets up the machine which the driller operates, and he is also called upon to set up machines in the milling shop, the planing shop and so on, within the major function of the machine shop. In the process of setting up he has, of course, to go through many series of operations, each with its cycle of elements. The structure can then be seen as shown in Fig. 4.2. Thus his job, a series of tasks, does not

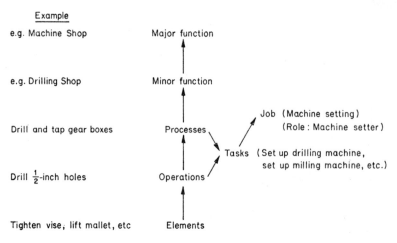

Figure 4.2   Job structure—machine setting

constitute a minor function, but it lies within the major function, machine shop.

Another example in order to illustrate this method of analysis which is the basis of the job evaluation method to be described later is as follows.

In the department of Personnel Management a Personnel Officer is engaged on recruitment for the shop floor. In his sphere of authority is a filing clerk who fills up hiring and firing forms (merely transferring data from other forms) and files them in a specified order. She has no control over the kind of filing system or the operation of filing, she can only decide on the elements of the operation and whether they should be fast or slow, which hand to use and so on. Her decisions are Band O, Defined. The Personnel Officer's secretary makes appointments for interview, and she decides 'how' she is going to do this—by telephone, by letter, or by telegram. She can also decide on the order in which interviewees are seen. In doing these things she not only decides on the speed of the elements of operations but she decides on the sequence of these elements and so on the operations. She has been told "bring these people in for interview on such-and-such a day at that time and arrange that I see them at intervals of half-an-hour", but she does not take part in the actual process of interviewing of which arranging interviews is one of the related operations.

The Personnel Officer decides on all the related operations that constitute the process of interviewing and selection. He is expected to use his knowledge of the techniques of interviewing, his knowledge of types of persons required, of company benefits, bonuses, holiday arrangements, in short he must know the whole framework of rules and regulations governing the employment of

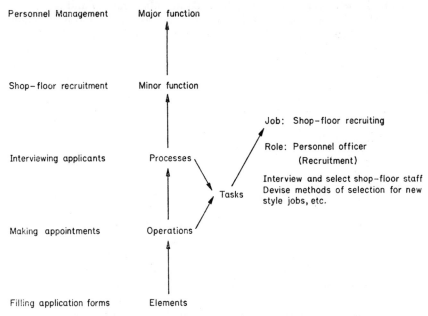

Figure 4.3   Job structure—Personnel Officer

shop-floor employees. All of these constitute the basis for a Routine Decision, a skilled decision (Band B).

But he is also allowed, as a result of his professional education, to pick out trade or other tests for use in recruitment for special jobs. He may even develop his own tests as he learns more about his firm's needs; and he is expected to be able to handle problems of selection of persons for jobs of a new kind, the qualifications for which are not in the rules already established. He would then be deciding 'why' these processes should be used; his decisions would have an anticipatory element, they would be Interpretive Decisions, interpretive of the recruitment programme for unique situations, Band C.

DIFFICULTY

The word 'difficulty' implies a sense of comparison, for what might be difficult to one person may not be difficult to another; a job is difficult only when compared with another job. Hence, in talking of difficulty one is concerned with a range of difficulty.

Physical difficulty refers only to elements within operations and, sometimes

4

when elements of heavy-weight movements or strong-tension movements constitute an operation, that operation is regarded as physically difficult. This is why, when a process includes a physically difficult operation, this is usually extracted and dealt with by a person physically capable, although he may not be mentally capable of other operations or processes. So physical difficulty hardly ever appears in jobs of Bands other than O and A.

Mental difficulty is of a different order, and here we are more intimately concerned with differences in decision-making. The higher in the decision band hierarchy the wider or looser the constraints on the decisions to be made. This may be considered in a para-mathematical fashion. The 'equation' for Automatic Decisions (A) has a very limited number of variables compared with the 'equation' for Routine Decisions (B) which may require the solution of several of the Automatic Decision 'equations'. An Interpretive Decision 'equation', by its very nature, brings in variables that are abstract and much less definite than those for the Routine Decisions, based as they are on fairly fixed rules and regulations.

Similarly the decision of an even-number grade job, which is coordinative of odd-number grade jobs in the same decision band, will be more difficult than the odd-number grade decisions, since it must take into consideration the interaction of those decisions—the coordinative 'equation' is a solution of a set of odd-number grade 'equations'. In that same sense a decision of an upper band, being coordinative of the decisions in a lower band, must be more difficult an 'equation' to solve than that of the lower.

Thus it appears that difficulty is related to the kind of decision in the hierarchy of decisions, the higher the band or grade the greater the difficulty. Hence it takes longer for a person to learn the higher band decisions and almost always a person has to 'go through the mill' of learning to make more difficult decisions by 'working his way up' in the firm. (This is the main reason for including education and experience as a measure of difficulty in the process of job evaluation).

Jobs in Bands C, D and E all require at some time or another decisions of Bands O, A and B. (By definition a job in one grade cannot require decisions of a grade above.) For example a production control manager makes decisions which require calculations. These calculations conform to mathematical processes governed by the rules of mathematics—routine procedures. The process may require arithmetical computations as a sequence of operations, the actual element of the operations being addition, subtraction and multiplication which are themselves Defined Decisions. Of course he could order a clerk to do the arithmetic (Band A) and he might leave the mathematical processes (Band B) to a senior clerk. They would provide him with Information upwards for his Conclusions. But he performs these processes and operations himself, partly because of the economics of time and resources, and partly because they have to be integrated in the totality of conclusion-making. The task is the decision-making and the decision made, as an end result of the Information from such decisions on processes and operations.

To a mathematically minded person such a decision process is relatively easy, to the non-mathematically minded it would be difficult. On the other hand the marketing manager, dealing with abstractions of the human consumer, may be making decisions that are relatively difficult for the production control manager. What we can say is that decisions of the same band or grade would tend to be regarded as relatively of the same order of difficulty to the person capable of handling both definitive systems and indeterminative systems.

COMPLEXITY

This concept is of use in *comparing jobs of the same grade*. A job with more tasks of the same grade and band is relatively more complex; but complexity requires attention to difficulty of tasks. A job may have fewer tasks than another but these tasks may be more difficult because they involve more of higher decisions. The management services specialist of Band C may need to use more complicated mathematical processes than the departmental production manager (Band C) who may use only arithmetical operations within standardised mathematical processes for say, maintenance scheduling —but the production man may have and usually has more tasks to perform in the same unit of time. To balance out number and difficulty is subjective, it does not lend itself to definitive statements. We can say then, that *job complexity* is determined by the number of the constituent tasks and the range of difficulty of these tasks. Similarly *task complexity* is determined by the number and range of difficulty of constituent processes and operations.

Henceforward in this book Band and Grade as defined in this Part will be given the capital first letter to distinguish them from those not so defined.

Part 2 JOB EVALUATION METHODS

There are many texts on job evaluation most of which are listed in the bibliography here. There are three main categories of method.

BY QUALITATIVE JUDGMENT ALONE

JOB RANKING METHOD

Jobs are compared one with another and arranged or valued in the order of their importance or their difficulty or their value to the firm. It is a highly subjective method and depends upon the experience of the people doing the ranking; a committee usually carries out the procedure. These people should be familiar with all the jobs and, therefore, there are few people available to serve on such a committee.

JOB CLASSIFICATION METHOD

This method depends upon a recognition that there are 'differences in the levels of duties, responsibilities and skills required for the performance' of different jobs. These differences, once recognised, can be expressed as grades or levels. These grades can then be defined and jobs classified by the selection of a particular grade for each job to correspond to its worth.

BY QUANTIFYING QUALITATIVE JUDGMENTS

POINT METHOD

Jobs show characteristics which are common to all or most. These characteristics, called factors, generally fall under the four headings of skill, effort, responsibility and conditions. To each factor is arbitrarily attached a number of points (a percentage of a total for all jobs) the number varying according to the 'degree' of the factor involved. The sum of all the points for a job permits of its comparison with other jobs and so a scale of pay.

FACTOR-COMPARISON METHOD

This is associated with the name of E. J. Benge. To each factor (as in the Point Method) is ascribed a money value. Key jobs, representing the various levels or grades (as in the Job Classification Method) are ranked factor by factor, and upon this ranking a scale of factor/money values is prepared. The sum of the values for each factor is taken to be the money value of a job.

BY COMPARING DIFFERENCES IN DECISION-MAKING

CASTELLION METHOD

This is associated with the name of Dr Lucien Cortis. Each job is analysed for the kinds of decisions made (relative difficulty in terms of variables taken into consideration), the frequency of decision-making, kinds of computations involved and comprehension required, vigilance exercised, the consequence of errors, experience and controls applied. To each of these factors is assigned (arbitrarily) a number of points as a percentage of a similar total for all jobs. The sum of the points permits of comparison and hence a scale of pay. It is a form of the Point Method with accent on decision-making.

TIME-SPAN METHOD

It was discovered by Professor Jaques that the higher in the hierarchy of organisational structure of jobs the longer the period (time-span of discretion) before the results of a decision are scrutinised for adequacy. This time-span appears to have a correlation with that pay felt by the incumbents of jobs to be 'fair pay'. Hence an analysis of time-spans for different jobs yields a scale of pay felt to be fair.

GUIDE-CHART PROFILE METHOD

This is associated with the name Dr E. N. Hay. Three factors, Know-how (Education/Experience), Problem-solving, and Accountability (meaning Responsibility) are each divided into eight degrees or levels and these qualified by a second, or 'breadth' dimension, each factor and breadth being concerned with some aspect of decision-making. The Problem-solving 'dimension' is given as a multiplier of Know-how which further accentuates the decision-making nature. Points are awarded for each degree as it is qualified, and the sums for different jobs are compared.

Chapter five **Job ranking and job classification methods**

"Job ranking was the first of the conventional job evaluation methods to be devised. It is a procedure whereby jobs are compared on the basis of the whole job—jobs are not broken down into job factors as in the quantitative methods—one with another and arranged or ranked in order of their importance, their difficulty, or their value to the company" [6, p. 108]. The method is now seldom used in American or British industry although some writers [38, p. 34] regard this method, and the Job Classification Method, as preferable to the Quantitative and the Time-Span methods.

Belcher's description is typical [3, p. 241]. There are several stages:

1 Job descriptions are prepared and set out on cards to be used in the ranking process.

2 Factors are selected which form the basis of the ranking. Special factors most useful in one department may be useless in another, e.g. arithmetical facility important in the accounts department may not be so important on the production line. Education and experience may be the major criterion for differentiation in a technical department. Belcher [3, p. 242] points out that it is difficult to compare directly shop floor jobs and clerical jobs but, if one factor is selected for all jobs, comparison in terms of this factor is possible.

3 The jobs are ranked. This is first of all done in each department preferably by people who are as unbiased as possible. This is difficult and Brennan [6, p. 109] feels the choice should land on "a foreman, shop steward, personnel staff or industrial engineer"; but even they will be biased.

The procedure may be carried out in two ways, card sorting and paired comparison. In the cord sorting technique each ranker is given a duplicate set of the job description cards and these he arranges in a pile sequence of 'highest to lowest' (difficulty, or importance, or value). If the department is big this may be a difficult thing to do, so it is then best done by each section of the department. The section sequences are arranged alongside each other, then tied by lining-up jobs in each section of approximately equal value, e.g. foreman with foreman, chief clerk with chief clerk. This provides a departmental list with the beginnings of bench mark levels of jobs of equal 'weight'.

In the paired comparison techniques each job is ranked against every other job. A count is made of the number of times a job is ranked higher than another, whence the job with the highest number comes highest in the sequence, and the job with lowest number, i.e. nil, is lowest in the sequence. This cannot be done readily for a large number of jobs, but lately a large consultancy firm has put a computer to use, and apparently the technique works [21].

4 This stage is one of combining departmental lists. Here an evaluation committee of departmental heads is recommended. Since the series of ranks for any one department does not constitute a scale of equal units this committee has to decide on key jobs in each department which are equivalent, and on this basis extend the departmental ranks horizontally. The members move the jobs upwards and downwards, without disturbing the vertical order, until they agree there is some kind of equivalence. Those departments or sections most easily related in terms of one or more selected factors are grouped as a class with ranks grouped as grades. (If the grades are defined in general terms around the basic differentiating factor this method becomes a job classification method.) Table 5.1 gives some idea of the end result of such an 'inter-class' ranking.

There are several disadvantages of this method. It is difficult to counteract bias among the rankers who cannot know much about all departments and

TABLE 5.1   *To illustrate inter-departmental ranking*

Grade	Class and department			
	Chemical	*Technical*		*Clerical*
	Analytical Laboratory	*Drawing Office*	*Production Control Office*	*Accounts Office*
1	Senior Analytical Chemist	Design Draftsman	Planning Clerk	Chief Accounts Clerk
2			Progress Clerk	Invoice Clerk
3	Analytical Chemist	Senior Tracer		
4		Tracer	Despatch Clerk	Accounts Clerk Costing Clerk
5	Laboratory Technician		Specification Clerk	
6	Laboratory Cleaner	Technical Clerk		Filing Clerk

so must rely upon the sapiental authority of others. The grades do not constitute equal units and so correlation of grades and pay can have no logical basis. In the example given it is impossible to say whether Rank/Grade 1 is twice, or ten or twenty times more difficult than Rank/Grade 6. Lastly it is doubtful if a questioning member of staff will automatically accept a low ranking if he thinks his job should be higher, even though his shop steward, foreman and manager have ranked it so. His questions can hardly be given a rational answer since there is no record of the way in which his job has been ranked; there are only the highly subjective opinions of the rankers. For that same reason the process cannot be checked. Some believe it should be repeated two or three times at intervals of a week or two [31, p. 63].

Its main advantage is simplicity. Nevertheless its failure to be widely accepted, despite that simplicity, suggests that it lends itself to too much disagreement.

JOB CLASSIFICATION METHOD

There are, according to Brennan and many others, "differences in the levels of duties, responsibilities and skills required for performance". These differences can be defined and expressed as classes or grades or levels. Jobs, having been analysed, can then be fitted into these various grades—and almost all people classify jobs (as well as other phenomena) into such groups. Indeed all methods of job evaluation lead to a taxonomy of grading of this nature, even the job ranking method with a relatively continuous series of jobs ends up as a series of discrete grades by which a pay structure can be developed.

The stages in classification are few but complicated. Jobs are first classed as shop-floor jobs, clerical, research, marketing/sales, middle manager and the like, sometimes called job clusters. These constitute major groupings or families within which jobs are graded. Up to this point the procedure is relatively uncomplicated.

The next stage is selection of factors by which jobs in each class are to be graded. These are the 'compensable factors' which are recognised to be what the pay is for or, at least, differences in these factors justify differentials in pay. These factors may be different for each family; the factor appropriate to the clerical class may be inapplicable to the shop-floor class. The committee given the task of grade description then decides how many grades there will be in each family. There may be as few as eight or ten in shop-floor jobs, as many as fifteen in the clerical class. The committee begins by writing the grade description of the two extreme grades, and of the jobs assigned to these grades. The extreme grades for the jobs remaining are next written and the corresponding jobs extracted from the pool of descriptions; and the process continues until the middle grade (or grades) is described.

There are two major job classification systems in use today; one for the US Public Service (described later), and the other for the clerical class of jobs only, expounded in the Institute of Office Management *Manual on clerical job grading and merit rating*, London, 1961. This IOM Manual lends itself to quotation.

"The clerk's salary can best be judged in relation to the importance and difficulty of the job. In any office, however large or small, there are a number of clerical tasks to be performed. In the smallest office one clerk may do them all and in the largest each may be done by a different clerk. In any event they must be assigned singly or in groups to be carried out by suitable people; the office manager must select a number of tasks to form a job and then he must choose a clerk to do it, having regard to the calibre and experience required. Thus a job normally consists of a number of tasks. The same tasks in different offices may be grouped to form jobs in different ways. Thus, although the tasks are common, the jobs are not. For this reason it is more convenient to grade tasks and jobs subsequently."

"A means has to be found for classifying the many and varied tasks in an office according to the calibre of the clerk required to do them. Although the experience and type of skill required for one task will be different from those required for another, it is desirable, if possible, that the same method of classification shall be used for all. This makes for simplicity and flexibility for it enables a common salary scale to be used and avoids difficulty when a clerk is transferred from one type of work to another. In the last resort it is a practical decision that must be made; the manager must decide what kind of clerk is really needed in all the circumstances, that must be the ultimate criterion for any grading." Yet the IOM Manual states that the manager would first get to know what is involved in each job that had to be done. Here is the tacit admission of the difference between what is involved in the job and the skills required in the person to do it. To mix these two is to make the problem much more difficult.

Returning to the first quotation that the clerk's salary can best be judged in relation to the importance and difficulty of his job, note should be made of the distinction between importance and difficulty. A third term that enters into this is the word 'calibre' of the clerk to do the job. Calibre seems to be related to the experience of the clerk. For example, tasks are described "that do not require fully fledged clerks", i.e. which require little previous clerical experience. By a 'fully fledged clerk' is meant "one who has had sufficient experience in clerical work to carry out a responsible clerical job with little supervision. The work to be done may involve typing, machine operation, or any other type of operation, *but this is not of prime consideration* so long as it is work which requires significant experience of clerical work and a reasonable aptitude for it." The italicised phrase is the important one, for the calibre of the clerk and the experience of the clerk, appear to be synonymous, and are taken as defining the job, even though 'importance' of the work itself defines, or helps define the salary, as stated in the commencing sentence above.

Moreover, in the IOM Manual (p. 77 onwards) operations are described which are clearly listed in terms of increasing difficulty, and are then ascribed to grades which are based upon the experience (calibre) of the clerk to do them. The mere fact that they can be listed in stages of increasing difficulty means that the job itself can be described without any reference to the calibre (experience) of the person to do them. That is to say, this is a listing of content of the job, and the word 'difficulty' then becomes related to the content, and not to the calibre (experience) of the person who would be required to do the job. If there is to be a rate for the job, then this rate should have no relationship to the person required to fill the job, only to the difficulty of the job itself. Admittedly, experience of the person to fill the job is necessary as difficulty increases, but this experience is not the criterion of the difficulty of the job, but is secondary to the definition of difficulty. It is the definition of the word 'difficulty' which becomes one of the key points to the evaluation of the job.

In considering the grading and classification of jobs, the IOM Manual uses experience as the basis of their sub-division. "There are those tasks that require only a limited amount of experience and skill and can be closely supervised, work which follows a daily routine with someone there to see that it gets done and to deal with any difficulties." Then, "there are tasks that can be done by those with little experience of clerical work. Such tasks are governed by a limited number of simple and well-defined rules. The work is closely directed and checked and carried out to a timetable. Finally, there are the tasks that require application but not experience, such as messenger work or elementary sorting."

There are three kinds of job that require the 'fully fledged clerk' to do it. One, already mentioned, where the clerk "*follows a routine* laid down and is not expected to show more than a minimum of initiative". Then there is the type which "involves *exercising discretion* and giving day-to-day direction to the work of a limited number of other clerks. The clerk performing such tasks is *concerned more with principles than routine*. He must be capable of taking initiative and deciding on a proper course of action in given circumstances." The italicised phrases are more indicative of content, but their significance is overlain by calibre required. Note here that the concept of control, of the use of structural authority in 'day-to-day direction' is creeping into this. Then there is the task that "needs the exercise of an extensive measure of responsibility and judgment or the application of some professional technique such as accounting". These last two tasks are included in jobs often distinguished by being called 'senior clerk' and 'chief clerk'.

As a result of this kind of sub-division the IOM Manual finds there are six job grades, as follows:

CLERICAL JOB GRADING

"*A Grade*

Tasks which require no previous clerical experience; each individual task is allotted and is either very simple or is closely directed. For example:

(*i*) messenger work;
(*ii*) the simpler forms of sorting."

"*B Grade*

Tasks which, because of their simplicity, are carried out in accordance with a limited number of well defined rules after a comparatively short period of training (a few weeks); these tasks are closely directed and checked, and are carried out in a daily routine covered by a time-table and short period control. For example:

    (*i*) simple copying work;
    (*ii*) straightforward adding operations using an adding machine."

"C Grade

Tasks which are of a routine character and follow well defined rules but which require either a reasonable degree of experience or a special aptitude for the task and which are carried out according to a daily routine covered by a time-table and subject to short period control. For example:

    (*i*) simple ledger machine operations;
    (*ii*) the checking of B grade work."

"D Grade

Tasks which require considerable experience but only a very limited degree of initiative and which are carried out according to a predetermined procedure and precise rules; the tasks are carried out according to a daily routine which varies but not sufficiently to necessitate any considerable direction. For example:

    (*i*) shorthand-typing of non-routine correspondence;
    (*ii*) certifying straightforward purchase invoices by reference to orders and dockets for incoming goods."

"E Grade

Tasks which require a significant, but not extensive, measure of discretion and initiative or which require a specialised knowledge and individual responsibility for the work. For example:

    (*i*) group supervision of routine work;
    (*ii*) dealing with queries of non-routine character."

"F Grade

Tasks which necessitate exercising an extensive measure of responsibility and judgment or the application of a professional technique (legal, accounting, statistical, engineering). For example:

    (*i*) section supervision;
    (*ii*) acting in close liaison with the management."

"It should be reiterated that this grading is based on a determination of the calibre and experience required of the clerk who is to do each task. For this reason it takes no account of the conditions under which the work may have to be done. The conditions under which some clerical tasks are done are more disagreeable than those for others; some tasks may make the clerk dirtier or even subject him to the danger of injury. In different offices, or even in different parts of the same office, the conditions under which the same task is done may vary. This question has not been considered in the grading and must be allowed for in the wage paid independently of the job grading systems as such."

The IOM Manual then goes on to make a definition of what are known as Procedure and Operation: "It is convenient to consider together all the tasks that comprise a clerical procedure for a specific clerical purpose, e.g. the preparation of wages or the keeping of sales ledgers. The tasks which usually occur in any such procedures must be listed and set out in sufficient detail for them to be identified by a practising office manager. The tasks may then be arranged under the Grades A to F according to the calibre of clerk required to do them adequately. Adequate performance is meant to include a reasonable degree of speed, accuracy and neatness."

"In any specification the tasks have been arranged together under sub-headings corresponding to the different steps in the procedure. The tasks in any sub-heading are arranged in ascending order of grade. The grade of task involving the performance of a particular type of operation is influenced by the complexity of the information handled. Thus, checking different kinds of supplier's invoices, although always involving the same operation, must be graded differently according to whether the invoice is expressed in very simple terms or in very technical terms. In such cases the examples show the task under more than one grade, with an indication under each grade of the degree of complexity that is intended. Although it is convenient to deal with each clerical procedure as a self-contained one, quite a number of operations are common to more than one procedure: examples are sorting, filing, machine operation and typing. These common types of operation, though varying for different procedures, are very similar in nature. It is therefore convenient to be able to see them in a single statement so they may easily be compared even though this involves listing the same task for the clerical procedure and for the type of clerical operation."

"It is clearly desirable that, as far as possible, all tasks of a job shall be at the same grade." (This is what I have called economy of grading.) "It is also desirable that the variety of skills and experience required for different tasks of a job shall not be too great and that the distinct tasks to be performed shall not be too numerous. When it is possible to limit the complexity in this way the grade of the job is the same as the grade of the component tasks, for a clerk who is able to do one of the tasks should be able to do them all." Note here that the word 'complexity' is different from the meaning in the paragraph above; here it is a matter of variety, and above it is a matter of difficulty.

"There are however many reasons why, in a given case, it may not be possible to minimise the diversity of the tasks that comprise a job. In such a case, the grade of that job will be higher than the grade of the component tasks for it needs a clerk of higher calibre to do them all than it would to do a limited number of them. How much higher the grade must be depends on the degree of complexity that has been introduced. The decision must depend on the individual case, though it should be exceptional for the grade of the job to be more than one level higher than that for the tasks." (Here complexity is the equivalent of diversity. All this means is that the rate for the job should be dependent on the highest grade of task in the complex of tasks.)

Although this IOM Manual is primarily concerned with the grading of clerical work rather than of clerks, the two are inevitably related. Almost invariably the grade of a job becomes attached to the clerk who does it; in the eyes of his supervisor and manager he becomes, say, a 'D Grade clerk'. The Manual then recognises that a clerk may be a 'starter' in this particular job, then he may become 'qualified' through experience, then he may be still further regarded as 'experienced'. These are three merit ratings for the same person doing the same job. He has increased his calibre and his calibre is his merit rating.

Having become experienced, he is promoted to a job in the next higher grade, at which he again becomes rated as a starter, but: "If his capacity develops while he is still doing his job in the lower grade, he ought to become noticeably superior to the ordinary run of experienced clerks in that grade, and if he does become so superior he again warrants a higher merit rating which he may refer to as 'superior'." Even though he may be superior and there is no room for him in terms of promotion to a higher grading of job, he "may become so outstanding as to deserve a yet higher rating" and this becomes designated as 'superlative' ".

"The management must decide, for each grade, the increment to be paid as the clerk progresses from one merit level to the next. Starting from the minimum grade, minimum rate, for any grade and adding on successive increments it is possible to arrive at scale rates for qualified, experienced, superior and finally for superlative clerks, the rate for the latter representing the maximum for the grade." In effect, this is saying that the clerk is paid for better work in the same job. The increment is pay for this, and is not the rate for the job.

The most widely known job classification system is that used in the Public Services of the USA embodied in the Classification Act of 1949. The Act applies to all civilian positions, officers and employees in most of the departments of the Public Service, and the definitions in the Act may usefully be repeated:

Position means the duties and responsibilities assignable to an employee.

Class (class of position) includes all positions which are sufficiently similar with respect to kind of work, level of difficulty, and responsibility so as to warrant similar treatment in personnel and administration.

Grade includes all classes of position which are sufficiently equivalent as to level of difficulty and level of qualification requirements to warrant the inclusion of such classes within one range of rates of basic compensation.

The following is the list as set out in the Act of 1949 which governs most of the jobs in the United States Public Service. There are two schedules:

1 A General Schedule (GS) covering professional and scientific service, clerical and administrative positions.
2 A Crafts, Protective and Custodial Schedule (CPC).

GENERAL SCHEDULE

Grade GS-1 includes all classes of positions the duties of which are to perform, under immediate supervision, with little or no latitude for the exercise of independent judgment, (1) the simplest routine work in office, business, or fiscal operations, or (2) elementary work of a subordinate technical character in a professional, scientific, or technical field.

Grade GS-2 includes all classes of positions the duties of which are (1) to perform, under immediate supervision, with limited latitude for the exercise of independent judgment, routine work in office, business, or fiscal operations, or comparable subordinate technical work of limited scope in a professional, scientific or technical field, requiring some training or experience, or (2) to perform other work of equal importance, difficulty and responsibility, and requiring comparable qualifications.

Grade GS-3 includes all classes of position the duties of which are (1) to perform, under immediate or general supervision, somewhat difficult and responsible work in office, business, or fiscal operations, or comparable subordinate technical work of limited scope in a professional, scientific, or technical field, requiring in either case (A) some training or experience, (B) working knowledge of a special subject matter, or (C) to some extent the exercise of independent judgment in accordance with well-established policies, procedures, and techniques; or (2) to perform other work of equal importance, difficulty and responsibility and requiring comparable qualifications.

Grade GS-4 includes all classes of positions the duties of which are (1) to perform, under immediate or general supervision, moderately difficult and responsible work in office, business, or fiscal operations, or comparable subordinate technical work in a professional, scientific, or technical field, requiring in either case (A) a moderate amount of training and minor supervisory or other experience, (B) good working knowledge of a special subject matter or a limited field of office, laboratory, engineering, scientific, or other procedure and practice, and (C) the exercise of independent judgment in accordance with well-established policies, procedures, and techniques; or (2) to perform other work of equal importance, difficulty and responsibility, and requiring comparable qualifications.

Grade GS-5 includes all classes of positions the duties of which are (1) to perform, under general supervision, difficult and responsible work in office, business, or fiscal administration, or comparable subordinate technical work in a professional, scientific, or technical field, requiring in either case (A) considerable training and supervisory or other experience, (B) broad working knowledge of a special subject matter or of office, laboratory, engineering, scientific, or other procedure and practice, and (C) the exercise of independent judgment in a limited field; (2) to perform, under immediate supervision, and with little opportunity for the exercise of independent judgment, simple and elementary work requiring professional scientific or technical training equivalent to that represented by graduation from a college or university of recognised standing but requiring little or no experience; or (3) to perform other work of equal importance, difficulty and responsibility, and requiring comparable qualifications.

Grade GS-6 includes all classes of positions the duties of which are (1) to perform, under general supervision, difficult and responsible technical work in a professional, scientific, or technical field, requiring in either case (A) considerable training and supervisory or other experience, (B) broad working knowledge of a special and complex subject matter, procedure, or practice, or of the principles of the profession, art, or science involved, and (C) to a considerable extent the exercise of independent judgment; or (2) to perform other work of equal importance, difficulty and responsibility, and requiring comparable qualifications.

Grade GS-7 includes all classes of positions the duties of which are (1) to perform, under general supervision, work of considerable difficulty and responsibility along special technical or supervisory lines in office, business, or fiscal administration, or comparable subordinate technical work in a professional, scientific, or technical field, requiring in either case (A) considerable specialised or supervisory training and experience, (B) comprehensive and thorough working knowledge of a specialised and complex subject matter, procedure, or practice, or of the principles of the profession, art or science involved, and (C) to a considerable extent the exercise of independent judgment; or (2) to perform other work of equal importance, difficulty and responsibility, and requiring comparable qualifications.

Grade GS-8 includes all classes of positions the duties of which are (1) to perform, under general supervision, very difficult and responsible work along special technical or supervisory lines in office, business, or fiscal administration, requiring (A) considerable specialised or supervisory training and experience, (B) comprehensive and thorough working knowledge of a specialized and complex subject matter, procedure, or practice, or of the principles of the profession, art, or science involved, and (C) to a considerable extent the exercise of independent judgment; or (2) to perform other work of equal importance, difficulty and responsibility, and requiring comparable qualifications.

Grade GS-9 includes all classes of positions the duties of which are (1) to perform, under general supervision, very difficult and responsible work along special technical, supervisory, or administrative lines in office, business or fiscal administration, requiring (A) somewhat extended specialised training, and considerable specialised, supervisory, or administrative experience which has demonstrated capacity or sound independent work, (B) thorough and fundamental knowledge of a special and complex subject matter, or of the profession, art, or science involved, and (C) considerable latitude for the exercise of independent judgment; (2) with considerable latitude for the exercise of independent judgment, to perform moderately difficult and responsible work, requiring (A) professional, scientific, or technical training equivalent to that represented by graduation from a college or university of recognised standing, and (B) considerable additional professional, scientific or technical training or experience which has demonstrated capacity for sound independent work; or (3) to perform other work of equal importance, difficulty and responsibility, and requiring comparable qualifications.

Grade GS-10 includes all classes of positions the duties of which are (1) to perform, under general supervision, highly difficult and responsible work along special technical, supervisory or administrative lines in office, business, or fiscal administration, requiring (A) somewhat extended specialised, supervisory or administrative training and experience which has demonstrated capacity for sound independent work, (B) thorough and fundamental knowledge of a specialised and complex subject matter, or of the profession, art or science involved, and (C) considerable latitude for the exercise of independent judgment; or (2) to perform other work of equal importance, difficulty, and responsibility, and requiring comparable qualifications.

Grade GS-11 includes all classes of positions the duties of which are (1) to perform, under general administrative supervision and with wide latitude for the exercise of independent judgment, work of marked difficulty and responsibility along special technical, supervisory or administrative lines in office, business or fiscal administration, requiring (A) extended specialised, supervisory or administrative training and experience which has demonstrated important attainments and marked capacity for sound independent action or decision, and (B) intimate grasp of a specialised and complex subject matter, or of the profession, art or science involved, or of administrative work of marked difficulty; (2) with wide latitude for the exercise of independent judgment, to perform responsible work of considerable difficulty requiring somewhat extended professional, scientific or technical training and experience which has demonstrated important attainments and marked capacity for independent work; or (3) to perform other work of equal importance, difficulty and responsibility, and requiring comparable qualifications.

Grade GS-12 includes all classes of positions the duties of which are (1) to perform, under general administrative supervision, with wide latitude for the exercise of independent judgment, work of a very high order of difficulty and responsibility along special technical, supervisory or administrative lines in office, business or fiscal administration, requiring (A) extended specialised, supervisory or administrative training and experience which has demonstrated leadership and attainments of a high order in specialised or administrative work, and (B) intimate grasp of a specialised and complex subject matter or of the profession, art or science involved; (2) under general administrative supervision, and with wide latitude for the exercise of independent judgment, to perform professional, scientific or technical work of marked difficulty and responsibility requiring professional, scientific, or technical training and experience which has demonstrated leadership and attainments of a high order in professional, scientific or technical research, practice or administration; or (3) to perform other work of equal importance, difficulty and responsibility, and requiring comparable qualifications.

Grade GS-13 includes all classes of positions the duties of which are (1) to perform, under administrative direction, with wide latitude for the exercise of independent judgment, work of unusual difficulty and responsibility along special technical, supervisory or administrative lines, requiring extended specialised, supervisory or administrative training and experience which has demonstrated leadership and marked attainments; (2) to serve as assistant head of a major organisation involving work of comparable level within a bureau; (3) to perform, under administrative direction, with wide latitude for the exercise of independent judgment, work of unusual difficulty

5

and responsibility requiring extended professional, scientific or technical training and experience which has demonstrated leadership and marked attainments in professional, scientific or technical research, practice or administration; or (4) to perform other work of equal importance, difficulty and responsibility, and requiring comparable qualifications.

Grade GS-14 includes all classes of positions the duties of which are (1) to perform, under general administrative direction, with wide latitude for the exercise of independent judgment, work of exceptional difficulty and responsibility along special technical, supervisory or administrative lines which has demonstrated leadership and unusual attainments; (2) to serve as head of a major organisation within a bureau involving work of comparable level; (3) to plan and direct or to plan and execute major professional, scientific, technical, administrative, fiscal or other specialised programmes, requiring extended training and experience which has demonstrated leadership, and unusual attainments in professional, scientific or technical research, practice, or administration, or in administrative, fiscal or other specialised work of equal importance, difficulty and responsibility, and requiring comparable qualifications.

Grade GS-15 includes all classes of positions the duties of which are (1) to perform, under general administrative direction, with very wide latitude for the exercise of independent judgment, work of outstanding difficulty and responsibility along special technical, supervisory, or administrative lines which has demonstrated leadership and exceptional attainments; (2) to serve as head of a major organisation within a bureau involving work of comparable level; (3) to plan and direct or to plan and execute specialised programmes of marked difficulty, responsibility, and national significance, along professional, scientific, technical, administrative, fiscal or other lines, requiring extended training and experience which has demonstrated leadership and unusual attainments in professional, scientific, or technical research, practice, or administration, or in administrative, fiscal or other specialised activities; or (4) to perform consulting or other professional, scientific, technical, administrative, fiscal, or other specialised work of equal importance, difficulty, and responsibility, and requiring comparable qualifications.

Grade GS-16 includes all classes of positions the duties of which are (1) to perform, under general administrative direction, with unusual latitude for the exercise of independent judgment, work of outstanding difficulty and responsibility along special technical, supervisory, or administrative lines which has demonstrated leadership and exceptional attainments; (2) to serve as the head of a major organisation involving work of comparable level; (3) to plan and direct or to plan and execute professional, scientific, technical, administrative, fiscal, or other specialised programmes of unusual difficulty, responsibility and national significance, requiring extended training and experience which has demonstrated leadership and exceptional attainments in professional, scientific, or technical research, practice, or administration, or in administrative, fiscal, or other specialised activities; or (4) to perform consulting or other professional, scientific, technical, administrative, fiscal, or other specialised work of equal importance, difficulty and responsibility, and requiring comparable qualifications.

Grade GS-17 includes all classes of positions the duties of which are (1) to serve as the head of a bureau where the position, considering the kind and extent of the authorities and responsibilities vested in it, and the scope, complexity, and degree of difficulty of the activities carried on, is of high order among the whole group of positions of heads of bureaus; (2) to plan and direct and execute professional, scientific, technical, administrative, fiscal, or other specialised programmes of exceptional difficulty, responsibility, and national significance, requiring extended training and experience which has demonstrated exceptional leadership and attainments in professional, scientific, or technical research, practice, or administration, or in administrative, fiscal, or other specialised activities; or (3) to perform consulting or other professional, scientific, technical, administrative, fiscal, or other specialised work of equal importance, difficulty, and responsibility, and requiring comparable qualifications.

Grade GS-18 includes all classes of positions the duties of which are (1) to serve as the head of a bureau where the position, considering the kind and extent of the authorities and responsibilities vested in it, and the scope, complexity, and degree of difficulty of the activities carried on, is exceptional and outstanding among the whole group of positions of heads of bureaus; (2) to plan and direct or to plan and execute frontier or unprecedented professional, scientific, technical, administrative, fiscal, or other specialised programmes of outstanding difficulty, responsibility, and national significance, requiring extended training and experience which has demonstrated outstanding leadership and attainments in professional, scientific, or technical research, practice, or administration, or in administrative, fiscal, or other specialised activities; or (3) to perform consulting or other professional, scientific, technical, administrative, fiscal, or other specialised work of equal importance, difficulty, and responsibility, and requiring comparable qualifications.

CRAFTS, PROTECTIVE AND CUSTODIAL SCHEDULE

Grade CPC-1 includes all classes of positions the duties of which are to run errands, to check parcels, or to perform other light manual tasks with little or no responsibility.

Grade CPC-2 includes all classes of positions the duties of which are to handle desks, mail sacks, and other heavy objects, and to perform similar work ordinarily required of unskilled labourers; to pass coal; to clean office rooms; to perform regular messenger work with little responsibility; or to perform other work of equal difficulty and responsibility and requiring comparable qualifications.

Grade CPC-3 includes all classes of positions the duties of which are to perform, under immediate supervision, custodial, or office labour work with some degree of responsibility; to operate paper-cutting, cancelling, envelope-opening, or envelope-sealing machines; to fire and keep up steam in low-pressure boilers used for heating purposes, and to clean boilers and oil machinery and related apparatus; to operate passenger automobiles or light-duty trucks; to pack goods for shipment; to work as leader of a group of charwomen; to perform messenger work and do light manual or office-labour tasks with some responsibility; to carry important documents from one office to another, or attend the door and private office of a public officer; or to perform other work of equal difficulty and responsibility and requiring comparable qualifications.

Grade CPC-4 includes all classes of positions of which the duties are to perform, under general supervision, custodial work of a responsible character; to guard office or storage buildings; to supervise and direct a force of unskilled labourers; to fire and keep up steam in high-pressure boilers and to operate other equipment used in connection with such boilers; to perform general, semi-mechanical, new, or repair work requiring some skill with hand tools; to work as craft or trade helper; to operate heavy-duty trucks, semi-trailers, or tractor-trailers: to operate a passenger automobile for a department head or officer of comparable rank; to attend the door of a private office of a department head or officer of comparable rank; or to perform other work of equal difficulty and responsibility and requiring comparable qualifications.

These grades fall into the five Decision Bands O to D thus:

Grades CPC-1, CPC-2, CPC-3 and GS-1, all come under the description of Grade 0. It should be noted that under CPC-3 there are operations which would come under grade GS-1, in the clerical grouping, such as paper-cutting, envelope-opening, and so on. The words 'immediate supervision' and 'little or no latitude for the exercise of independent judgment' are the definitive words.

The description of grade CPC-4 includes the expression 'general supervision' and 'to supervise and direct a force of unskilled labourers'. The other operations of this grade are of Grade 0 but, since there is no immediate supervision, and, moreover, it involves 'supervision' of people and, therefore, involves freedom in operation in the handling of people, this must be of Grade 1.

Grades GS-2, GS-3 and GS-4 appear to come roughly under Band A being grades of increasing difficulty in this band from 'limited latitude for the exercise of independent judgment'—associated with routine work—to 'independent judgment in accordance with well-established policies, procedures and techniques'. Grade GS-4 also involves 'a moderate amount of training and minor supervisory or other experience' which suggests that this may well be Grade 2 of Band A.

Grades GS-5, GS-6 and GS-7 appear to come under Band B for the following reasons. Unlike the jobs in grades GS-2 to 4, which are under 'immediate supervision' all of these jobs in grades GS-5 to 7 are under 'general supervision'. The four grades GS-5 to GS-8 are distinguished from grades GS-9 upwards in that the lower group requires a working knowledge as distinct from a fundamental knowledge in the higher group, and that the capacity for independent judgment is in terms of the working knowledge in the lower group, and in terms of the fundamental knowledge in the upper group. The concept of 'working knowledge' means that there is a knowledge of the rules and procedures, principles and regulations, and it is within this working knowledge that the judgments are made. It does not imply the knowledge of a fundamental nature, upon which prediction and anticipation are based.

Grades GS-5 and 6 are distinguished from GS-7 and 8 in that the word supervisory enters in the latter descriptions, suggesting that they come into Grade 4 as distinct from Grade 3 of Band B. Grade GS-5 is distinguished from GS-6 in the expression "exercise of independent judgment in limited fields" and "to a considerable extent the exercise of independent judgment". Grade GS-7 is distinguished from grade GS-8 in the use of the words "work of considerable difficulty" and work which is "very difficult", a distinction which seems to be, in itself, very difficult.

Grades GS-9 to GS-13 are distinguished from grades GS-14 and upwards in that the latter are concerned with planning and directing, or planning and executing specialised programmes, corresponding to Band D, programming in executing of policy. We can assume, then, that Grades GS-9 to GS-13 represent Band C. Again, there appears a differentiation in difficulty, with words that are quite subjective, such as "very difficult and responsible work" through "highly difficult and responsible work", "difficulty and responsibility" etc. (see below). However, the last two grades can be distinguished from the first three in that they require "demonstrated leadership", and GS-13 clearly indicates a supervisory function in "assistant head". These two, then, may be taken as roughly comparable to Grade 6, and the other three comparable to Grade 5.

Grades GS-14 to GS-17 appear to be concerned with functions of Band D, planning and direction of execution of programmes. Again there is a distinction in the description of difficulty and responsibility (see below). Grade GS-17 is distinguished from the other three in that it involves the headship of a bureau, whereas the other three involve the headship of organisations within a bureau. Presumably this grade GS-17 is approximately equivalent to Grade 8, and the other three to Grade 7. Grade GS-18 also involves the serving of a head of a bureau and is distinguished from grade GS-17 in that the bureau would be "exceptional and outstanding" among the whole group of positions of heads of bureaux, whatever exceptional and outstanding may mean. It is, then, also of Grade 8.

In Grades GS-15 to GS-18 there appear the functions of "to perform consulting or other professional, etc. work". These, then, must be regarded

TABLE 5.2 *Correlation US classification and Bands/Grades*

US Public Service Grades	Grade	Band
CPC-1, 2 and 3, GS-1	0	O
CPC-4, GS-2 and 3	1	A
GS-4	2	A
GS-5 and 6	3	B
GS-7 and 8	4	B
GS-9, 10 and 11	5	C
GS-12 and 13	6	C
GS-14, 15 and 16	7	D
GS-17 and 18	8	D

as concerning the exercise of sapiential authority. Since a comparable function does not appear in grades of lower level in Bands C and D, we may assume that these functions are exercised in terms of 'nominal advising' and 'nominal informing', i.e. their juniors would be 'actual' advisers and informers.

The functions of Band E are not mentioned in this list since the grading under the Classification Act apparently does not concern the heads of ministries or their deputies in the terms defined here.

Table 5.2 summarises this correlation (which will be referred to in *The Manual*).

COMMENT

The Institute of Office Management Manual states that "The subject of job grading usually arises in connection with salary rates, as the appropriateness of a clerk's salary can best be judged in relation to the importance and difficulty of his job. It is therefore desirable to classify jobs so as to indicate the level of pay that is appropriate for each, that is, to apply job grading. If the individual chosen should fall short of the real requirements, the job will suffer and the individual is not likely to develop as well as if he were doing a more appropriate job. On the other hand, if the individual is too good for his job he will either have to be paid more than it is worth or less than he is worth, judged according to what he might do". The editors of the IOM Manual admit that "neither of these possibilities is economical and neither is likely to lead to the best use and development of the clerk. It is therefore important that the office manager should try to match the calibre and experience of the clerk as closely as possible to the requirements of the job. In order that he may do this, each job must be graded according to the difficulties, responsibilities and experience it entails."

"The main reasons for adopting a job grading scheme are therefore (1) To staff the office economically and efficiently; (2) To use the analysis of jobs under grades in order to set up lines of promotion that will lead to the best development of clerks; (3) To ensure that the clerks are paid fairly for the jobs they do." In expressing these very desirable objectives it has been tacitly assumed that some means can be found of measuring the degree of competence that is required to do different clerical jobs.

Having made this statement the IOM Manual later goes on to say:

"A means has to be found for classifying the many and varied tasks in an office according to the calibre of clerk required to do them. Although the experience and type of skill required for one task will be different from those required for another, it is desirable, if possible, that the same method of classification shall be used for all. This makes for simplicity and flexibility for it enables a common salary scale to be used and avoids difficulty when a clerk is transferred from one type of work to another. In the last resort it is a practical decision that must be made; the manager must decide what kind of clerk is really needed in all the circumstances, *that must be the ultimate criterion for any grading*." That is to say the IOM Manual distinguishes jobs

mainly by the experience required to do them rather than by the content—
the importance and the difficulty.

The language employed in the IOM Manual is vague and the grade
definition must surely lead to much disagreement. For example B Grade,
to repeat, is defined as:

"Tasks which, because of their simplicity, are carried out in accordance
with a *limited* number of *well defined* rules, after a *comparatively* short period of
training (a few weeks); these tasks are *closely* directed and checked, and are
carried out in a daily routine covered by a time-table and *short* period
control."

The words italicised can be interpreted in many ways, by as many as
there are members of a job grading meeting, and different meetings could
find still more different meanings. Such vagueness, disguised in apparently
clear terminology, appears all the way through the Classification System
for the US Public Services. For example, five grades are distinguished in
part by the following differences:

GS-11   needs "demonstrated important attainments",
GS-12   "attainments of a high order",
GS-13   "marked attainments",
GS-14   "unusual attainments",
GS-15   "exceptional attainments".

This is excelled by the following differentiations:

GS-7   "work of considerable difficulty and responsibility"
GS-8   "very difficult and responsible work"
GS-9   "very difficult and responsible work"
GS-10 "highly difficult and responsible work"
GS-11 "marked difficulty and responsibility"
GS-12 "a very high order of difficulty and responsibility"
GS-13 "work of unusual difficulty and responsibility".

It is not to be wondered that Brennan [6, p. 122] says that "there are, in
most cases, some differences of opinion, but an earnest attempt should be
made to resolve them in open discussion. Inability to reach agreement
indicates that the content of the job and/or grade description, has not been
fully accepted by all committee members." He recommends a 'democratic
majority' ruling.

But the main disadvantage is the inapplicability of these methods to a
wide range of jobs. The IOM Manual is precisely described—it can be
applied only to clerical jobs. In the Classification Method the mere act of
'classification' into families, and the selection of 'compensable factors'
appropriate to each family as the basis for grading, limits its coverage—and
there are several families in every firm of any size.

These disadvantages must be the main reason for the finding that ranking
and classification methods are used much less often than the others [3, p.
240]. Yet McBeath and Rands [38, p. 34] point out the simplicity and
economy of these methods and recommend them, mainly job ranking, and
in their books they 'concentrate mainly on the use of these techniques'. And

even the Fulton Commission on the UK Civil Service recommends the adoption of the US Classification—despite the appalling lack of accuracy and objectivity quoted above.

The *Assessment* of jobs under these methods, that is, the dollar values ascribed as pay, is relatively simple. The selected key jobs are also selected because their pays are regarded as 'fair' or acceptable. If they are not, other jobs in the ranking, whose pays are so regarded, are chosen as representing anchor points for the distribution of pays. The sequence of individual jobs produced by the Ranking Method would thus show a fairly continuous series with such fixed points, the pays for jobs between being settled by negotiation. However, there is a strong tendency to reduce a large series like this to a number of *grades*, a pay grade being "a grouping of jobs of approximately equal difficulty or importance as determined by job evaluation" [3, p. 315]. The upper and lower limits of each grade are negotiated or agreed, depending on how this pay structure is decided. The Classification Method lends itself at once to this grading—indeed the classes are called grades. Again the key jobs indicate the pay distribution, and limits are negotiated or agreed.

The disadvantage of these Methods outlined above are increased by this assessment. There is no indication that the pay differential between each job in the series of the Ranking Method, and between each grade in the Classification Method should be equal or even nearly equal. There is every indication in the US Public Services that the differential between grades is progressively greater the 'higher' the grades; but not even this can be said of Ranked jobs in business enterprises. It is not to be wondered that these Methods are not much used, or if used are adjunct to negotiation.

Lastly there is a disadvantage that some proponents do not recognise. There is no 'measure' of relative difficulty and importance hence there can be no 'measure' of relative value and so pay. Having described job evaluation McBeath and Rands [38, p. 86] state quite explicitly: "There is not, in our view, an absolute set of value relationships between jobs, so that the changing pattern of market values is a fundamental which must be constantly studied and adapted to"; and "individual rates covering jobs in this category (of manual occupations) should directly reflect the immediate local supply and demand situation and be strictly related to the local market rate in the truest sense of that phrase"; and finally [38, p. 63] "the local market rate of each job is really the main criterion of where it should be graded". To do this they rely on job descriptions and job titles for wage and salary surveys of all kinds of firm. This attitude is essentially a recognition of the failure of these job evaluation methods—then why use internal job grading!

Chapter six   **The Point Method**

Since the quantitative methods emanate from the USA, it seems logical to use in these next two chapters American definitions of task, job, and related words, especially those used by the War Manpower Commission [72, p. 7]. "A *task* exists whenever human effort must be exerted for a specific purpose". When sufficient tasks accumulate to justify the employment of a member of a firm a position exists. Thus "*a position is an aggregation of duties, tasks and responsibilities requiring the services of one individual*". It follows that there are as many positions as there are individuals in the firm. Because many positions are identical a *job may be defined as a group of positions which are identical* or so closely similar with respect to their major or significant tasks that they justify being covered by a single analysis. In a one-man firm all functions are carried out by one individual. In a large firm "the necessary functions and duties are divided among individuals, each individual being given a set of duties to perform. That set of duties constitutes a job."

The word 'duty' is not defined, the word 'responsibility' is that for which a person is responsible (his function, as defined in Chapter 2). In the last sentence quoted 'set of duties' is the same as 'aggregation of duties', which is synonymous with position as earlier defined; therefore job is the same as position. Undoubtedly some jobs (and positions) are similar enough to merit the same title and so can be analysed by a single analysis.

Belcher [3, p. 201] clarifies this by example. "A local retail store employs 18 people consisting of the manager, two office employees, ten sales people, three people involved in receiving, marking and stocking merchandise, and two people involved in delivery. Let us assume that the tasks are so aligned that the positions involved in each of the functions are identical. Thus the store contains 18 positions, but only five jobs. The five jobs might be titled as follows: (1) manager, (2) bookkeeper, (3) salesman, (4) stockkeeper, (5) deliveryman. It is seen from this example that analysing each position would be uneconomical. All that is necessary is to analyse the five separate jobs. At higher levels in the organisation, however, each position tends to differ from other positions. In this case, each position is a 'job' ". This is sufficiently close to the definition of job used here, an aggregation of tasks, without the need to complicate the issue with the concept of position. (But it should be noted that Belcher uses the role suffix '-er' rather than the function '-ing', another aspect of the confusion of person, role and job.

Occupation is used to describe a profession or trade such as medicine, teaching, turning, fitting. These are not jobs as defined above since a job normally does not include all the possible activities or tasks that are circumscribed by occupation.

To return to quantitative methods—these are the job evaluation methods most frequently used, in particular the Point Method with its variations appropriate to the firms using it. The Factor Comparison Method "may be thought of as a refinement of the ranking method because jobs are directly compared in both. Similarly, the Point Method is similar to the classification method in that jobs are compared indirectly through a written scale" [3, p. 257].

The Point Method is the first quantitative method to have been devised—by Lott in 1924 [35]—and it appears to be the most widely used method in the USA [31, 55], in the UK [46], and in Holland where it is the basis of a national wages structure policy.

As its title indicates the intention is to assign to each job a numerical or points value by which comparison can be made of relative value, the greater the number of points the more the worth of the job to the firm. The method can be summarised thus:

1 A number of job factors are selected, e.g. skill, effort, responsibility which are believed to be common to all or nearly all the jobs in the firm, and failing that, to a cluster of related jobs, e.g. machine shop, office, laboratory. These are the factors it is believed the firm is paying for, called 'compensable factors'.
2 A 'committee' agrees on definitions of those factors that are suitable to the jobs in the firm.
3 Each factor is assigned a percentage weighting to indicate its relative importance (and so value) in the job.
4 Each factor weighting is divided into parts or degrees to which are allocated numbers or points, the sum of the degree numbers equalling the weighting.
5 Each factor in each job is analysed and awarded degree points; the sum of points for a job represents its relative value.

STAGE 1

There are many variations of the method but the procedure is roughly the same for all of them and the principle is identical. Again it is recognised that not all job factors can be applied to all the jobs in the firm, so job clusters are selected and from each cluster *key jobs* are chosen for analysis and description. "Data obtained from these key jobs will be used for rating every job in the firm; they are the bench marks on which the accuracy of the whole plan will be based" [27, p. 25]. Brennan [6, p. 147] says there are six criteria governing the choice of these jobs.

1 They "must represent the entire range of jobs", meaning range in grades from the highest to lowest and not range in class.
2 They "must be stable", that is unlikely to change in content—although this presents difficulties in a rapidly changing technology.
3 They "must be well recognised jobs, known both to labour leaders and management", meaning not only that they are stable but they are long established and in continuous use.
4 They "must be clearly and exactly defined with respect to skills, responsibilities and requirements" although this is progressively more difficult upwards from the simplicity of the repetitive assembly of Band O.
5 They "must be acceptable to all in regard to description and rate of pay; must not be subject to criticism by any committee man, labour leader or by management", a most rare occurrence.
6 They "must stand out distinctly from other jobs so that there will be no misunderstanding among the raters", meaning that the job title is precisely understood.

These criteria can seldom, if ever, be met but (1), (2), (3) and (6) are those generally used. The jobs provide the necessary base for selection of factors that can best be used for describing the jobs of a job cluster, for subsequent definition of the factors and, later, for testing the accuracy of the choice and its application. 10 to 15 key jobs are usually adequate.

STAGE 2

The *factors usually chosen* fall under the headings already mentioned, and are kept to a minimum. There are four main headings, subdivided to give 10 or more different factors. Some schemes have as many as 50 but are cumbersome and vague because of overlap. The usual procedure is for the committee to choose a large number of appropriate factors (there are lists in most textbooks on job evaluation) and then to whittle these down. "No successful plan has had more than 22 factors. From 8 to 11 has proved the most successful range for jobs with no supervisory responsibilities" [27, p. 16]. But Professor Bloch of Zurich has a successful method involving 31 factors!

The NEMA (National Electrical Manufacturers Association) scheme is the most widely known and practised (an example is given in detail later). The four headings are subdivided into 11 factors thus:

Skill	Education
	Experience
	Initiative and ingenuity
Effort	Physical
	Mental and visual demand
Responsibility for	Equipment or process
	Material or product
	Safety of others
	Work of others

Job conditions   Working conditions
                                Unavoidable hazards

STAGE 3

For use in the firm these *factors are defined* by the committee as the basis of
their job evaluation manual. "It is easy to understand why many committees rapidly become bogged down in endless argument over factor
definitions. It is vitally important, however, that all committee members
understand and accept the definitions. This is no mean task. Many shop
floor representatives find great difficulty in handling terminology which
may be elementary to management. Interpretation of terms differs widely
between shop floor and management.

In one of the projects explored the job evaluation committee met for two
hours every fortnight for a period of 50 weeks and never managed to progress
beyond factor definitions. The simple rule of keeping the number of factors
to a minimum is, therefore, vitally important" [64, p. 47].

The aim of the definitions is to "express in phrases, meaning exactly what
they say, what the factor is to measure so that each member of a group
reading the definitions will have the same concept as to what the factor is
trying to measure" [6, p. 134]. Dr Husband [19, p. 59] takes a definition
of skill quoted by Lytle [37, p. 68] from the Southern California Aircraft
Industry job evaluation plan to illustrate this.

"Skill is the technique acquired through training and experience. The
amount of skill required for different jobs varies considerably. However, the
amount of skill necessary for the satisfactory performance of any job can be
measured with *reasonable* accuracy in terms of the length of time *normally*
required for an *average* individual of *normal mental capacity* to acquire the
necessary trade knowledge and training". The words underlined can hardly
be called exact and certainly can be interpreted differently. (In the example
of a NEMA plan given below the definitions are less subjective but still lay
themselves open to differential interpretations).

STAGE 4

Each factor is divided into degrees so that the raters can estimate the 'amount'
of the factor in a job, "a crucial step in the point method", [3, p. 279].
"These are the inch marks on the ruler, and unless they are clearly marked
and meaningful, resulting scales will produce unreliable and inaccurate
readings". Belcher refers to Otis and Leukart [48, pp. 131–133] who give
this guidance:

  1 The number of degrees (there can be as many as eight or as few as three)
    should be no more than is necessary to distinguish adequately and fairly
    between jobs.
  2 Unless one or more jobs fall at the level specified by a certain degree,
    it should not exist.
  3 The applicability of the degree to the job should be apparent.

4 Terminology should be understandable by employees.

5 Examples should be used wherever possible.

Brennan [6, p. 136] says that the definitions of degrees should be couched in "objective rather than subjective terms" and that "ambiguous phrases and such phrases as may be misinterpreted must be avoided". It is virtually impossible to do this especially where confusion exists between the job content and what the man brings to the job. One example only need be quoted [27, p. 54], a suggestion that factor degrees of required education can be found by looking up "the records on the educational backgrounds of the people" at that moment the incumbents. This information, plus the use of aptitude tests, "will reveal quite specifically how much education is required for the key jobs that are placed in each degree on the chart".

STAGE 5

Factors and degrees are weighted and assigned points. Each member of the committee is furnished with the definitions and separately ranks the factors in order of importance. Together they come to agreement on this ranking. Each member, again individually, assigns a percentage as a 'weight' to each factor; and again the committee comes to agreement. This weighting can vary from committee to committee, from firm to firm in the same industry (see later).

A total number of possible points, i.e. 100%, is selected. It is common to use 500 as in most forms of the NEMA method. Therefore each factor will have its appropriate 'weighting' percentage of 500. This portion is then divided among the degrees; either in arithmetical progression (that is, equal number difference from degree to degree such as 20, 40, 60, 80) or in geometrical progression (that is, each degree is greater than its predecessor by a constant percentage or multiple, e.g. 5, 10, 20, 40, 80). "Actually, where the plan has been developed for a specific job cluster rather than for the entire organisation, it matters little which method is followed; few point plans apply to all the jobs in the organisation" [3, p. 282]. Apparently there is no theoretical basis for using either method—each should be tested to see whether it gives a result approaching what is 'felt' to be correct or, more important, what is acceptable.

"The above discussion assumes that degrees have been defined with sufficient precision to permit the assumption that they represent equal steps along a scale. Where it is believed that this is not the case the committee must decide how the total points allocated to a factor should be divided up among the degrees. Most plans, however, assume that each degree of a factor represents a step equivalent to other degrees" [3, p. 283].

STAGE 6

These definitions of factors and degrees, and the points assigned to them are consolidated as a JOB EVALUATION MANUAL. An example of a Manual for a fairly simple NEMA-type plan follows.

AN EXAMPLE OF THE NEMA POINT METHOD
APPLIED TO HOURLY PAID MANUAL STAFF

Factors	1st degree	2nd degree	3rd degree	4th degree	5th degree
Skill					
1. Education	15	30	45	60	75
2. Experience	20	40	60	80	100
3. Initiative and ingenuity	15	30	45	60	75
Effort					
4. Physical demand	10	20	30	40	50
5. Mental or visual demand	5	10	15	20	25
Responsibility					
6. Equipment or process	5	10	15	20	25
7. Material or product	5	10	15	20	25
8. Safety of others	5	10	15	20	25
9. Work of others	5	10	15	20	25
Job conditions					
10. Working conditions	10	20	30	40	50
11. Unavoidable hazards	5	10	15	20	25

JOB GRADING

Definitions of the factors used in grading jobs
Hourly rated occupations

FOREWORD

Job Grading is the process of analysing a job to determine the degree of skill, effort, responsibility and working conditions in relation to other jobs in the same plant, for the purpose of ranking jobs for scientific wage negotiations or for determining wage differentials. It is a means of establishing occupational wages on the basis of a detailed analysis of the minimum requirements of each job.

Job Grading, while simple, cannot be done by everyone. In order to grade jobs properly, the person doing the grading should be thoroughly familiar with shop operations and the requirements of each job.

The interest and cooperation of the foremen are essential to the success of any Job Grading programme. Much of the information needed to grade the jobs properly can only be supplied by them. Particular care is necessary to see that they thoroughly understand the Job Grading plan.

I   EDUCATION OR TRADE KNOWLEDGE

This factor appraises the requirements for the use of shop mathematics, drawings, measuring instruments, or trade knowledge.

1st Degree

Requires the ability to read and write, add and subtract whole numbers.

2nd Degree

Requires the use of simple arithmetic, such as addition and subtraction of decimals and fractions: together with simple drawings and some measuring instruments such as caliper, scale.

3rd Degree

Requires the use of fairly complicated drawings, advanced shop mathematics, handbook formulae, variety of precision measuring instruments, some trade knowledge in a specialised field or process. Equivalent to short term trades training.

4th Degree

Requires the use of complicated drawings and specifications, advanced shop mathematics, wide variety of precision measuring instruments, broad shop trade knowledge. Usually equivalent to 4 years HG school plus 5 years formal trades training.

5th Degree

Requires a basic technical knowledge sufficient to deal with complicated and involved mechanical, electrical or other engineering problems. Equivalent to 4 years of technical college training.

2 EXPERIENCE

Experience appraises the length of time usually or typically required by an average individual, with the specified education or trade knowledge, to learn to perform the work satisfactorily from the standpoint of quality and quantity under normal supervision. Do not include apprenticeship or trades training, which has been graded under Education. Include under Experience only the time required to attain production standards.

1st Degree

Up to three months.

2nd Degree

Over three months up to one year.

3rd Degree

Over one year up to three years.

4th Degree

Over three years up to five years.

5th Degree

Over five years.

3 INITIATIVE AND INGENUITY

This factor appraises independent action, exercise of judgment, the making of decisions or the amount of planning which the job requires. This factor also appraises the degree of complexity of the work.

1st Degree

Requires the ability to understand and follow simple instructions and the use of simple equipment where the employee is told exactly what to do.

2nd Degree

Requires the ability to work from detailed instructions and the making of minor decisions involving the use of some judgment.

3rd Degree

Requires the ability to plan and perform a sequence of operations where standard or recognised operation methods are available and the making of general decisions as to quality, tolerances, operation and set-up sequence.

4th Degree

Requires the ability to plan and perform unusual and difficult work where only general operation methods are available and the making of decisions involving the use of considerable ingenuity, initiative and judgment.

5th Degree

Requires outstanding ability to work independently toward general results, devise new methods, meet new conditions necessitating a high degree of ingenuity, initiative and judgment on very involved and complex jobs.

4   PHYSICAL DEMAND

This factor appraises the amount and continuity of physical effort required. Consider the effort expended handling material (the weight and frequency of handling), operating a machine or handling tools, and the periods of unoccupied time.

1st Degree

Light work requiring little physical effort.

2nd Degree

Light physical effort working regularly with light weight material or occasionally with average weight material. Operate machine tools where machine time exceeds the handling time.

3rd Degree

Sustained physical effort, requiring continuity of effort working with light or average weight material. Usually short cycle work requiring continuous activity. Or the operation of several machines where the handling time is equivalent to the total machine time.

4th Degree

Considerable physical effort, working with average or heavy weight material. Or continuous strain of a difficult work position.

5th Degree

Continuous physical exertion working with heavy weight material. Hard work with constant strain or intermittent severe strain.

5 MENTAL OR VISUAL DEMAND

This factor appraises the degree of mental or visual concentration required. Consider the alertness and attention necessary, the length of the cycle, the coordination of manual dexterity with mental or visual attention.

1st Degree

Little mental and only intermittent visual attention since either the operation is practically automatic or the duties require attention only at long intervals.

2nd Degree

Frequent mental or visual attention, where the flow of work is intermittent or the operation involves waiting for a machine or process to complete a cycle with little attention or checking.

3rd Degree

Continuous mental or visual attention; usually short cycle repetitive work or diversified operations requiring constant alertness.

4th Degree

Must concentrate mental and visual attention in closely planning and laying out complex work; or coordinating a high degree of manual dexterity with close visual attention for sustained periods.

5th Degree

Concentration and exacting mental or visual attention, usually visualising, planning and laying out very involved and complex jobs.

6 RESPONSIBILITY FOR EQUIPMENT OR PROCESS

This factor appraises the responsibility for preventing damage through carelessness, to the equipment or process used in the performance of the job. Consider the probable amount of damage resulting from carelessness in handling, set-up, operation, etc., for any one mishap. Process relates to operations, such as plating.

1st Degree

Probable damage to equipment or process is say $20.

2nd Degree

Probable damage to equipment or process is seldom over $80.

3rd Degree

Probable damage to equipment or process is seldom over $800.

6

4th Degree

Probable damage to equipment or process is seldom over $3,000.

5th Degree

Probable damage exceedingly high, reaching $5,000.

7   RESPONSIBILITY FOR MATERIAL OR PRODUCT

This factor appraises the responsibility for preventing waste or loss of raw material or partially finished product through carelessness. Consider the *probable* number of pieces which may be spoiled before detection and correction in any one lot or run, the value of the material and labour, the possibility of salvage. Do not use either maximum or minimum, but an average based on normal expectation.

1st Degree

Probable loss due to damage or scrapping of material or product is seldom over $30.

2nd Degree

Probable loss due to damage or scrapping of materials or product is seldom over $300.

3rd Degree

Probable loss due to damage or scrapping of materials or product is seldom over $800.

4th Degree

Probable loss due to damage or scrapping of materials or product is seldom over $1,500.

5th Degree

Probable loss of material which may be damaged or scrapped is very high, reaching $5,000.

8   RESPONSIBILITY FOR SAFETY OF OTHERS

This factor appraises the care which must be exercised to prevent injury to others, and the *probable* extent of such injury. Injury to the employee on the job being graded is to be considered under Unavoidable Hazards. Consider possible accidents to others resulting from careless operation of machine or handling of materials or tools. Can other employees be injured by carelessness on the job? If so, how?

1st Degree

Little responsibility for safety of others. Job performed in an isolated location, or where there is no machine involved and the material is very light.

2nd Degree

> Only reasonable care to own work necessary to prevent injury to others, and accidents, if they should occur, would be minor in nature, such as cuts, bruises, abrasions, etc.

3rd Degree

> Careless operation of machine or performance of duties may cause lost time accidents to others, such as crushed toes, feet, fingers or hands, eye injuries.

4th Degree

> Constant care necessary to prevent serious injury to others, due to inherent hazards of the job, but where such other employees may act to prevent being injured.

5th Degree

> Safety to others depends entirely on correct action of employee on job being rated and carelessness may result in fatal accidents to others.

9   RESPONSIBILITY FOR WORK OF OTHERS

This factor appraises the responsibility which goes with the job for assisting, instructing or directing the work of others. It is not intended to appraise supervisory responsibility for results.

1st Degree

> Responsible only for own work.

2nd Degree

> Responsible for instructing and directing one or two helpers 50% or more of the time.

3rd Degree

> Responsible for instructing, directing or setting up for a small group of employees usually in the same occupation, up to 10 persons.

4th Degree

> Responsible for instructing, directing and maintaining the flow of work in a group of employees up to 25 persons.

5th Degree

> Responsible for instructing, directing and maintaining the flow of work in a group of over 25 persons.

10   WORKING CONDITIONS

This factor appraises the surroundings of physical conditions under which the job must be done and the extent to which those conditions make the job disagreeable. Consider the presence, relative amount of and continuity of exposure to dust, dirt, heat, fumes, cold, noise, vibration, wet, etc.

1st Degree

Ideal working conditions. Complete absence of any disagreeable elements.

2nd Degree

Good working conditions. May be slightly dirty or involve occasional exposure to some of the elements listed above. Typical machine shop working conditions.

3rd Degree

Somewhat disagreeable working conditions due to exposure to one or more of the elements listed above, but where these elements are not continuous, if several are present.

4th Degree

Continuous exposure to several disagreeable elements or to one element which is particularly disagreeable.

5th Degree

Continuous and intensive exposure to several extremely disagreeable elements.

II   HAZARDS

This factor appraises the hazards, both accident and health, connected with or surrounding the job, even though all safety devices have been installed. Consider the material being handled, the machines or tools used, the work position, the possibility of accident, even though none has occurred.

1st Degree

Accident or health hazards negligible.

2nd Degree

Accidents improbable, outside of minor injuries, such as abrasions, cuts or bruises. Health hazards negligible.

3rd Degree

Exposure to lost-time accidents, such as crushed hand or foot, loss of fingers, eye injury from flying particles. Some exposure to occupational disease, not incapacitating in nature.

4th Degree

Exposure to health hazards or incapacitating accident, such as loss of arm or leg.

5th Degree

Exposure to accidents or occupational disease which may result in total disability or death.

Belcher [3, p. 290] quotes from the *NEMA Job Rating Manual*, 1946, a similar point system for salaried employees, meaning white collar and managerial. The factors are:

Education	(6 degrees)	120 points
Experience	(8 degrees)	200 points
Complexity of duties	(5 degrees)	100 points
Monetary responsibility	(5 degrees)	60 points
Contacts	(5 degrees)	60 points
Working conditions	(5 degrees)	25 points

Monetary responsibility "evaluates the responsibility for profit or loss to the company as a result of actions or decisions which involve items such as equipment, material, labour, cost estimate, prices, forecast, purchase commitments, investments;" that is to say discrimination among decisions in terms of their effects—it would follow that a poor 'higher level' decision is likely to involve more loss to the company than one of 'lower level'.

Stage 7

Assessment on the Point Method is conversion of the sum of points to a money value. It is possible to envisage a dollar value for each and every job but the

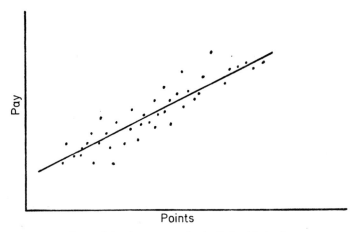

Figure 6.1   A pay curve in the Point Method

tendency is to reduce this large spectrum of values to a simple *pay structure* by grouping similar jobs into *grades*. In the Point Method the usual practice is to set up grades of equal point spread, the number of grades varying from single figures to double, up to as many as 60. There may be few grades for each cluster of jobs, in which the factors and their weighting are the same. The 'imbrication' of all clusters and their final 'integration' for the whole firm may produce a large number of grades.

The usual method is to plot points along an *X*-axis and dollars along a *Y*-axis to produce a scatter diagram of existing pays (see Fig. 6.1). A 'pay curve' is then drawn to give a 'best fit' to this diagram and, say Belcher and Brennan and others, *this curve may be straight or curved*, an assumption being that points represent equal steps along the X-axis. No reason is given anywhere in the literature for deciding the form of the pay curve. The curve can be drawn free hand, or by the mathematical technique of 'best fit', or even more simply, joining two points one at the upper 'level' and the other at the lower, provided these jobs are accepted as 'fairly paid'.

How these grades are decided appears to have no theoretical basis but Belcher [3, p. 316] gives a summary of the broad considerations:

"(1) Place jobs of the same general value in the same pay grade,
  (2) insure that jobs of significantly different value are in different pay grades.
  (3) provide a smooth progression, and
  (4) insure that the grades fit the company and the labor market".

He finishes by saying "Since large numbers of employees are affected by manipulation of pay grades, great care and fairness must be used in final

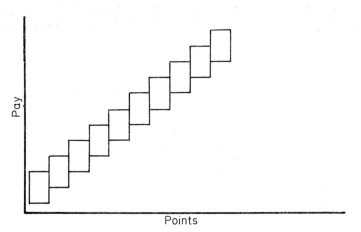

Figure 6.2   Overlapping Grade boxes for a straight-line pay curve

determination of pay grades. Grievances can be avoided by seeing that pay grades with large numbers of employees are not affected adversely."

The grade cut-off points having been selected, the next stage is to express the coverage of each grade so as to include as many pays as possible. For a straight-line pay curve, the structure can be represented as in Fig. 6.2, and for a curved line pay curve as in Fig. 6.3. Each bar I shall henceforth refer to as a *grade box*. Where pays lie outside the grade boxes they are adjusted to bring them inside (or the jobs are altered to justify the pay). This is done by negotiation.

Before going on to describe variations of the Point Method some general comments can be made.

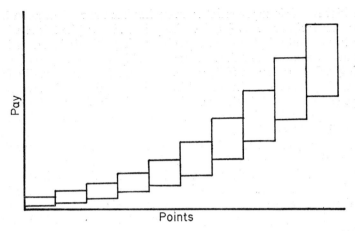

Figure 6.3   Overlapping Grade boxes for a curved-line pay curve

COMMENT

The mere act of assigning numbers to factors and degrees appears to give the Method a semblance of being 'scientific' and so 'objective'—and hence more acceptable than the Ranking and Classification Methods. Admittedly the recognition of factors such as conditions of work and effort will suggest to the manual worker on the shop floor that the Point Method takes more cognisance of aspects of his job that he regards as important for determining reward. But when the numbers are thought to be indicative of 'real' differentials then the Method is abused. It has been reported that, in Holland where there is a national job evaluation scheme based on the Point Method, a demand has been made that all pay should be based on so many guilders per point!

As already mentioned it is generally assumed that each degree of one factor represents a step equivalent to the degree in another factor but, if each factor is weighted differently, i.e. each has a different number of points to be distributed among its constituent degrees, then the number of points assigned to degrees in the various factors must be of different value as ordinate numerals. Says Belcher [3, p. 283], "Where factor weights and the resulting point values for factors and degrees have been determined by committee rather than statistically, it is advisable to evaluate a number of key jobs to determine if the plan achieves the desired relationship between jobs. At this point adjustment in point values may be called for to insure that the plan is acceptable to the parties." In other words the point values are negotiated and are not objective.

The distribution of the factor points among the constituent degrees is either arithmetical or geometric. "It matters little which method is followed" if the plan is for a specific job cluster and not for the whole firm [3, p. 282]. Yet when the total points are plotted against pay during the assessment stage the relationship is assumed to be always linear. It is known that for the whole firm the differential increases exponentially from the lowest grades to the highest. This exponential increase has been remarked upon by Zipf and Rucker [76]; and Hay [15] has also pointed it out (the arithmetic increments in 'job difficulty' are accompanied by logarithmic increases in pay). So it must be assumed that the linear relationship applies only to a job cluster covering a few grades; *or*, if there are many grades, they must be of small intervals. So, apart from the difficulties of choosing factors that can properly be applied to every job in the firm, the methods of point distribution do not permit of application throughout the firm. Kershner [29] studied the 'discriminability of factors' and came to the conclusion that the levels or degrees are, in general, too many—there is considerable difficulty in making the differentiation. He regarded some of the distinctions as 'word figments', reminiscent of the distinctions used in the Classification Method.

The limitation of the Point Method to clusters of jobs is matched by the limitation of any one scheme of factors and their weightings to particular firms. Belcher [3, pp. 295–6] quoted several researches which show the superiority of 'custom-built' plans over 'ready-made' and concludes:

"1. Applicable compensable factors vary from one organisation to another and one job cluster to another.
2. A limited number of factors can provide a workable system.
3. Sufficient factors to satisfy the desires of the principals appear desirable", and "job evaluation plans can be much less complex than many now in use".

One must then ask about the validity of the economists' claims that pay is dependent upon local labour markets. It is reasonable to suppose that pay for different occupations may be dependent upon the market, but that different constellations of factors—so to speak—are required for different firms to match existing pay structures, cannot be explained by economic theory.

In most applications of the Point Method relative factor weights are decided by committee. Scott [64], a former consultant engaged in applying the Point Method, writes: "On the surface it would appear relatively simple to establish agreed weighting within the committee. In practice this can be extremely difficult. Distinct patterns of prejudice emerge, and each category of employees will favour a weighting likely to produce a high points value for their own jobs. Two committees from the same industry can produce phenomenally different weightings." Elliot [12] tried an experiment of influencing rating committees by putting into them personnel officers with instructions to try and change opinions. They did; which confirms Scott's experience.

Apart from the inordinate time consumed by committees on job grading (see already a reference to Scott's experience), the committee can be affected not only by internal, inter-personal pressures, but by the material on which they base their grading. Rupe [63] studied twelve analysts using different approaches to their analysis of the same twelve jobs and found that their job descriptions—on which grading was to be carried out by a committee—varied considerably. Whereas Trathner and Kubis [69] studied eight analysts and a grading committee and found the members of the committee were more consistent than the analysts in their grading. It would seem that the analysts, by reason of their close contact with the jobs, are aware of and are more affected by variations in importance of the different factors, and are more liable to be individually biased by this experience than are the members of the grading committee who see only the written descriptions. The latter tend to be very consistent (Chesler [9]). Again there is reason to believe (and here I write from my knowledge of colleagues' experience) that an analyst/ evaluator accustomed to using work study methods (MTM, etc.) for analysing unskilled jobs finds difficulty in analysing and grading skilled jobs which do not permit of complete analysis by work study.

An International Conference on job evaluation at Geneva in 1950 [22] found that there were two major ways of determining weighting of factors:

1 Deducing them from the existing pay structure.
2 Assessing the relative scarcity of the required abilities.

The Conference concluded the first was better because "job evaluation is not normally acceptable to the workers if it results in major changes in the existing hierarchy of wage rates". The Conference believed that, in any case, the existing pay structure reflected the supply/demand structure of the labour market and so was already established on scarcity of abilities, i.e. (2).

This conclusion does not accord at all with the variations in factor weightings that are to be found in a wide variety of firms some of them in the same industry (see Table 6.1).

There are bound to be jobs in these firms of almost exactly the same kind, especially if they are in the same industry, yet they are to be analysed on the basis of variant importance of factors. Stieber [66], analysing the wage structure in the US steel industry, shows the effect of such differences in factor weightings in determining the hierarchy of similar jobs (see Table 6.2).

That there is no consistency in factor weightings, or even in the choice of factors themselves, is, methodologically speaking, non-logical. It is a fundamental law of measurement that only one dimensional scale may be applied at any one time to the same object. Thus one would not measure length in inches and breadth in centimetres in order to compare areas as in square inches or square centimetres [41]. It is as if the job content (and all authors claim the Point Method analyses job content) were composed of numbers of different items, but the numbers alone summated. To put this in the form of a crude analogy:

Job A	Job B	Job C
20 Bananas	40 Bananas	50 Bananas
60 Oranges	30 Oranges	20 Oranges
50 Lemons	20 Lemons	10 Lemons
40 Apples	50 Apples	80 Apples
170	140	160

All one can say is that Job B is less acid than Job A, and Job C is sweeter than the other two. The totals of numbers have little differential meaning.

TABLE 6.1   *To illustrate range of factor weightings*

Enterprise	Country	Skill	Effort	Responsi-bility	Condition
Volks Wagen	Germany	23·3	24·3	19·0	33·3
Paper Industry	Germany	17·7	24·3	19·8	38·2
Baumann	Germany	33·3	33·3	33·3	—
Massey Ferguson	Germany	30·0	18·0	48·0	4·0
Metal Industry	Germany	21·0	21·0	19·6	38·4
Shell	Germany	23·0	43·0	20·5	14·5
Shell	USA	45·0	16·0	24·0	15·0
National Automatic	USA	78·5	11·2	4·6	5·7
Steel Co. Penn.	USA	24·4	11·8	52·2	11·6
Steel Corp. III	USA	19·0	26·0	49·0	6·0
Eastern Gas/Fuel	USA	70·0	10·0	20·0	—
Arkansas Light/Power	USA	37·5	7·5	45·0	10·0
Pacific Gas/Elect.	USA	20·7	40·2	34·5	4·6
Minnesota M+M	USA	34·0	17·5	46·0	2·5
Pratt and Whitney	USA	58·0	15·5	22·0	4·5
General Electric	USA	62·5	12·5	12·5	12·5
General Motors	USA	28·5	36·3	28·5	6·7
Westinghouse	USA	60·5	22·5	13·5	3·5
Nat. Metal Trades A.	USA	40·0	5·0	50·0	5·0
Loc. Govt. Neuchatel	Switzerland	77·5	7·5	10·0	5·0
Metal Industry	Sweden	35·3	18·9	25·4	20·4
Tele mecanique	France	46·0	12·4	37·0	4·6
Dutch National Standard	Holland	44·4	15·6	36·1	3·9
Electrical Industry	UK	48·6	21·5	13·3	16·6
Imperial Chemicals	UK	40·0	32·0	—	28·0
National	Czechoslovakia	57·5	21·2	11·7	9·6
National	Rumania	50·0	20·0	18·0	12·0

* Extracted from Abbildung 28. *Gehaltsfestsetzung in Wirtschaft und Verwaltung*, I. H. Sauer-Verlag, Heidelberg, 2 Aufl., 1968, by kind permission of the author, Dr Ernst Zander.

TABLE 6.2   *To show the effect of different factor weightings on job relationships*

Light Industry Plan	Heavy Industry Plan
	Roller, blooming miller
	First helper, open hearth
Toolmaker	
Roller, blooming miller	
	Toolmaker
Machinist ——————————	Machinist
First helper, open hearth	
	Assembler, light bench work
Common labourer ——————————	Common labourer
Assembler, light benchwork	

(There is one item common to all these 'fruit' factors, that is, calories. If each factor number were multiplied by the factor calorific content the totals would then be significant. This analogy will be referred to later.)

It may well be that the near correlation of some job gradings with existing pay structure is due to some element common to all the factors or to some of them. Belcher [3, p. 295] reports that Lawshe and his associates at Purdue University, who have made the most extensive series of studies on job evaluation, mainly on the NEMA system, concluded, as a result of factorial analysis (Thurstone centroid), that the skill factors accounted for 77·5 per cent to 99 per cent of the distribution.

Lawshe and Satter [32] found that "skill demands and job characteristics" (the latter meaning conditions) would give the same answer as the eleven factors of the NEMA system. But later work [33] increased the minimum of factors to five—skill demands, supervisory demands, responsibility, conditions and danger. Stieber [66] found that "pre-employment training", "employment training and experience" and "mental skill" were so highly inter-correlated that they could be taken as a measure of the same thing.

However, other research has shown that, although the use of different systems (few factors—many factors) may show a fairly high correlation, the grading results may be different. Gray and Jones [14] studied the application of two methods, abbreviated and long, and found "If the three-items abbreviated scale were employed . . . 62% of the jobs would remain in the same labour grade, 37·2% would be displaced one labour grade, and 0·8% would be displaced two labour grades". Since there is no way of finding out the most important factors, so as to establish an abbreviated scale, without having an intensive analysis by a non-abbreviated, it seems hardly worth while considering the value of using an abbreviated.

At this juncture and, in a way anticipating later chapters, it seems worth showing how a Point Method correlates with the one-factor method of decision-making. Table 6.3 shows a sequence of roles in an engineering firm rated by the NEMA Method which illustrates this Chapter above. Alongside it are placed the Grades and subgrades [19].

The planer's job (K) has a lower points score than the similar job of grinder (F) because of an union agreement, that only 5-year apprenticeship gives a score, under Education, of 60 against 45 for the 3-year training of the planer; the difference of 15 added to the planer's score would bring it properly into Grade 3a. The welder (G) scores more than the other roles in Grade 3a because of extra points given for 'working conditions', just as the window cleaner (U) scores 35 more than the labourer. Otherwise there is a good correlation of points and grading/subgrading.

Despite subjectivity of the Point Method, despite its lack of logical method, there is evidence that firms using it are 'substantially satisfied'; but they are just as satisfied using any of the other methods, though less so with the Classification and Factor Comparison. "There is a uniformly high degree of satisfaction with each of the four basic methods. This suggests that companies have been generally successful in choosing the job evaluation method best suited to their own particular circumstances" [47, p. 13]. In other words job evaluation is better than no job evaluation. The main reason for acceptability

TABLE 6.3 *To illustrate Point Method correlation with decision grading*

	Role	Points Total	Grading
Grade 3			
A	Die miller	345	3c
B	Jig borer	340	3c
C	Maintenance fitter	325	3b
D	Toolroom inspector	325	3b
E	Universal miller	320	3b
F	Universal grinder	320	3b
G	Welder	325	3a
H	Plumber	305	3a
I	Painter	300	3a
J	Joiner	295	3a
K	Planer	285	3a
Grade 1			
L	Centre lathe operator	280	1c
M	Tool and cutter miller	280	1b
N	Tool and cutter grinder	275	1b
O	Radial driller	275	1b
P	Tool storeman	260	1a
Q	Progress man	250	1a
Grade 0			
R	Fork truck driver	210	0c
S	Drill press operator	210	0c
T	Production miller	190	0b
U	Window cleaner	210	0a
V	General laborer	170	0a

appears to lie in the opportunity for changing factors and weighting in order to adjust to existing pay structures, or in order to answer the pressures of those with, as they say, vested interests, in other words to allow 'horse trading'. This negotiating is constantly recurring as technologies and markets alter and jobs with them—and the time-wasting on committee work is consequently increased. For a large firm engaged in a modern technology the time consumed and resources utilised are inordinately large.

There are many variations of the Point Method not only according to different factor selection and weighting for different job clusters and different firms, but in the application of the Method itself. One variation which includes Ranking and Classification techniques is given the name *Profile Method* which uses the factors of Responsibility, Environment (Conditions), Physical Demands, Mental Demands, and Social Skills (capacity to communicate with different colleagues). These, it is believed, are the characteristics for which job incumbents feel they should be rewarded.

Each factor is divided into a few degrees (at the most four) as a scaling, the idea being that the recognizable difference between one degree and another represents something of the order of 50–100 per cent. (Factors are not weighted initially.) Key jobs are selected (a matter of agreement in a committee) and the degrees for each factor marked by the members who then agree on these 'profiles'. These jobs, with the aid of the profiles, are then Ranked by the committee which may decide to weight a factor or factors. A team of raters then 'profiles' the remaining jobs which again have to be agreed by the committee. The jobs are then Classified into like activities and a grading structure designed, also requiring agreement. The appropriate pay structure is finally negotiated. The subjective element is strong, the method can be applied only to classes and not to the whole firm, but it allows great flexibility for negotiation with unions.

The National Board for Prices and Incomes in the UK reports a case of a large firm [47, p. 48] which used a profile method, and based the scheme on 56 'bench-mark' jobs, ranking them by paired-comparison in terms of 'over-all worth' to the firm. The final "points rankings were known only to members of the Central Review Committee and to members of a committee which devised the new wage structure. For a number of reasons . . . the company did not disclose the actual weighting used to the employees, trade union representatives or any other persons, and in spite of union protests this secrecy has been maintained." "Job evaluation was a 'fact-finding' stage, to be carried out with union participation at all levels, but the task of using the 'facts' which emerged was seen as a management responsibility." Apparently the unions agreed to adoption of the new wage structure when a "general award of at least 3d per hour" was awarded, "attractive wage increases which were offered in return for acceptance of the new structure and the completion of productivity bargains at each factory". The trade unions 'participated' only at the Information stage of the decision-process. The 'secrecy' suggests doubt about the subjectivity of the weighting.

Chapter seven **The Factor-comparison Method**

This method, which first appeared in 1926, is associated with the name Eugene J. Benge [4]; but there are variations [15]. In general the method, widely used at all levels, compares jobs using one of five factors at a time, mental requirements, skill requirements, physical requirements, responsibilities and working conditions, or combinations of these factors, these seemingly considered to be the 'universal factors' found in all jobs. The scale of comparison is based on analysis (by these factors) of key jobs which set the standards, and, in variations of the method, the scale of money values. The major difference from the Point Method is that points are not assigned to the factors; a money value is ascribed directly.

During job analysis, and in job description, the factors upon which stress is laid are reduced to as few as four although Benge himself recommends five. He deprecates the use of more than seven since the Method then becomes very unwieldy. These factors are:

1 MENTAL REQUIREMENTS, the mental abilities brought by a person to his job, judgment, patience, capacity to get on with others (and personality traits of a like nature) intellect, acquired knowledge about the job to be undertaken, and, with that, education.
2 SKILL REQUIREMENTS, of a variety of kinds based on learning by doing. There are sensori-motor skills, e.g. manual, acquired by practice. Similarly, experience in doing a job develops a skill such as decision-making which is a mental exercise. Sub-divisions are time required to gain skill and also prior experience necessary to take on the job.
3 PHYSICAL REQUIREMENTS, those bodily efforts necessary in the performance of a job, such as lifting heavy weights, carrying, bending, and so forth. Sub-divisions are time spent on each kind of effort.
4 RESPONSIBILITIES which refer to responsibility for equipment, purchases, money, stores, safe-keeping of documents, and the like; and it includes management of other people.

5 WORKING CONDITIONS, those environmental factors that make the performance of a job dangerous, disagreeable, safe or pleasant.

The Method is applied in several stages, here only roughly outlined.

Stage 1. Some 15 to 25 key jobs are selected for detailed analysis and description in terms of these factors. The selection of these key jobs is critical since they form the cornerstones of the comparison scale; and, moreover they are also selected because it is believed that their existing pay is regarded as fair.

Stage 2. Each member of the ranking committee individually ranks these jobs in a series of difficulty, a rank for each factor at a time. A top ranking for, say, mental requirements is a relatively intensive education combined with knowledge of the work speciality. A member might rank according to each sub-factor, e.g. under responsibility he might rank on the cash sum involved in equipment used, then responsibility for safety, then put these sub-factor series together as a factor series. The chairman of the committee consolidates these vertical rankings in a table such as is shown in Table 7.1.

TABLE 7.1 *Individual ranking of key jobs by factors*

Key jobs	Skill	Mental requirement	Physical requirement	Responsi-bility	Conditions
Invoice clerk	8	7	6	9	4
Departmental secretary	6	10	4	10	3
Copy typist	3	2	5	2	6
.	.	.	.	.	.
.	.	.	.	.	.

The committee must agree, which it does by discussion. If disagreement continues the committee may adjourn for several days (presumably to forget their original rankings) and repeat the process. An intransigent member of the committee may be removed; or a key job on which disagreement remains may be eliminated.

Stage 3. Again individually, members take each job and assign to each factor a percentage of its importance in getting the job done; and again this has to be agreed by discussion.

Stage 4. Each member breaks up the pay for each job into the amounts he considers represent the importance of each factor. Some authors, e.g. Lanham [31, p. 115], believe that Stage 3 can be bypassed, but the percentages agreed are a help to members in corroborating their distribution of pay which is vertically expressed. Thus for a skilled fitter with a basic pay of $200 per week the breakdown may be given as shown in Table 7.2. The members then meet and agree, perhaps using averages or merely discussing.

Stage 5. The committee now has two sets of factor hierarchies, the original difficulty ranking, D, and the money ranking, M, according to amounts ascribed to each factor (see Table 7.3). If the two rankings agree then the

TABLE 7.2 *Job: skilled fitter*

Skill	80
Mental requirements	60
Physical requirements	10
Responsibility	40
Conditions	10
	$200

key jobs are acceptable as such. If they disagree (as in the case of the Departmental secretary illustrated) then two decisions are possible:

1 Adjustment of the money values may be made which, of course, if too large will affect the rankings of other jobs—a difficult procedure.
2 Rejection as a key job.

TABLE 7.3 *Ranking by factor and factorial worth*

Key job	Skill		Mental requirement		Physical requirement		Responsi- bility		Conditions	
	D	M	D	M	D	M	D	M	D	M
Invoice clerk	8	8	7	7	6	6	9	9	4	4
Departmental secretary	6	7	10	10	4	4	10	10	3	2
Copy typist	3	3	2	2	5	5	2	2	6	6
.	.		.	.	.	.	.	.	.	.
.	.		.	.	.	.	.	.	.	.

Stage 5. A Job Comparison Scale is devised. One column registers dollars in an appropriate scale of intervals, and alongside are the columns for each factor. Into these columns are placed the key jobs. The sum of the amounts for each factor is the pay. Lanham [31, p. 118] thinks that additional key jobs should be found if there are large gaps in the scale, and there will be additional checks on the key jobs already accepted. This may lead to some difficulties if there is failure in correlation.

Stage 6. More jobs are analysed and compared to the key jobs, one factor at a time. The committee agrees on how each job is slotted into each factor column, according to this comparison. For any of these jobs the amount for each factor is read off and the sum of these amounts is the pay. The end result is a complete sequence of job pays undivided into grades.

COMMENT

Like the Point Method this is highly subjective, probably even more so because of the need for committee agreement at all stages. Moreover key jobs which are generally regarded as paid fairly are hard to come by, and the scheme depends wholly on key jobs, in terms of factors and equitable pay. This is a serious weakness which the Point Method does not face, which also requires less time-consuming, expensive committee work. The fact that there is no grading scheme makes the problem of change of job structure a matter for more and more committee work, not counting the complexities of pay accounting.

Chapter eight   The Castellion Method

This method gets its name from the products of the South African Breweries where the method was first developed, and is associated with the name of Dr Lucien Cortis. It is based essentially on the differentiation of kinds of decision in terms of the thinking required. "Decision-making involves the exercise of a choice between alternative lines of action. This choice is the central point of decision-making." (This definition is the same as that used in this book.)

There are several 'factors', the kind of decision itself, how often it is exercised ('pressure of work'), the kinds of computation involved, and the comprehension required, vigilance exercised, the consequence of errors, experience, and controls exercised (equivalent to time-span). The kind of decision—the decision-making scale, is 'the major grouping'.

FACTOR 1. DECISION-MAKING

SIMPLEST OF DECISIONS

Compares against rough standards with broad limits, e.g. is the floor clean? Alternative lines of action—simple and very limited. Brief induction to learn essentials of the job.

SIMPLE DECISIONS REQUIRING A LITTLE KNOW-HOW

Needs to take into account a few simple facts—applies one or two checks; action simple in essence but requires a modicum of industrial know-how, e.g. sorting bolts, filing alphabetically.

SIMPLE DECISIONS BASED ON CATEGORISED DATA

Data needed for decisions is categorised arbitrarily and simple—no concern with whys and wherefores—restricted use of verbal material, e.g. copy typing, selecting tools in store from given list.

DECISIONS REQUIRING BROAD ESTIMATES

Estimates involve limits which cannot be stated precisely but which are quickly derived. Critical information may have to be found through a small number of checks, by using a set of simple tools or techniques. Needs to know the consequence of a poor estimate—shows limited concern therefore in whys and wherefores. Compares an over-all impression against a pattern of cues which he has memorised, e.g. garage attendant, checking invoices.

SIMPLE AND VARIED DECISIONS

Simple decisions taken in a wider set of circumstances—each situation requires its own type of simple decision. A number of broad estimates, some require a superficial appreciation of how people act. Planning at the elementary level hardly goes beyond the current day. Use of simple forms and check lists—some trial and error to find cause of events, e.g. 3–4 checks to disengage a jammed machine.

DECISIONS REQUIRING THE COORDINATION OF DATA

Varied input of data, making coordination necessary, e.g. operating a motor car; abstracting, summarising from prime documents. Simple chains of decision-making—a decision generates information which is built into subsequent decisions.

Analysis of human behaviour involves brief enquiries into the interpretation of straight-forward policy items.

DECISIONS WHICH FOLLOW FROM A REASONED ESTIMATE

Has as a rule more information than he needs—must become selective *before* he can *reason out to an estimate*. Specific instances relate, among others, to:

1 Reasoning in two stages:

   (i) reasons out how to categorise data.
   (ii) uses categorised data for final estimate.

2 Uses incomplete information—possible, however, for him to get additional information within a brief period of time.
3 Some evaluation of performance. Reasons out how performance of semi-skilled workers can improve.
4 The choice of the best way to do a job with a number of semi-skilled or unskilled workers.

DECISION REQUIRING PRACTICAL KNOW-HOW

Reasoned estimates are quite complex—they go to form an *assessment*. The man knows how to spot critical cues—their meaning is extended by practical experience, i.e. rule of thumb, what happens in practice. Understanding of principles as they apply to concrete situations.

The action which he takes after his decision is complex, and involves in itself a series of subsequent decisions. The need to take subsequent decisions can be anticipated, however, and so lead to the first stages of definite planning. Some decisions need to be taken in a context of uncertainty, which may last a couple of days.

DECISIONS INVOLVING SYSTEMATIC SEARCHES

Decisions typified by a systematic search for cause of events from a limited number of variables. Area of search and search strategy determined by verbal reports which the decision-maker interprets. Decisions are taken sequentially—on the form of a decision tree. Decisions and the action which follows are characterised by:

1 Definite pre-planning activities or FORETHOUGHT—can mentally recapitulate a complex line of activities, and prepare in advance for actions and further decisions.
2 The use of elementary principles which have been systematically or scientifically derived.
3 The evaluation of the performance of colleagues or subordinates, whose activities affect the decision taken.
4 The exercise of definite technical skills, i.e. the use of tools or techniques requiring special knacks and training.

INTRICATE DECISIONS BASED ON STUDY OF THE INTERPLAY OF VARIABLES

Solving the problem requires some experimentation with known variables—facts are not readily apparent.

The experience for these decisions is extensive, and needs to be coordinated through additional principles which have been scientifically derived, i.e. some concern with the theory of the occupation. The implication of a decision not readily seen—others who operate independently are involved.

Characteristics of these decisions:

1 The evaluation of systematic searches, conducted by subordinates but which have failed to reveal the cause of events.
2 Experimentation under guidance with some of the variables—or a more extensive and probing search for cause of events.
3 Pre-planning activities involving in part the work of others extending for a period of up to two months, e.g. estimating the needs of a department for next two months—assumptions have to be made on the basis of past records or performance.

4 Some concern with inter-personal relations and awareness of human motivation.

COMPLEX DECISIONS BASED ON REMOTE INFORMATION

Decision requires the coordination of information from a wide variety of related and unrelated sources—novel methods of fact-finding may have to be devised. Decision based on *complex incomplete information* because there are gaps in human knowledge—few people could note all possible inter-relations.

Decision-maker accepts the need to take risks for which he is accountable, e.g. in the manner inferences are drawn, objectives attached, or because there is no clear cut directive or precedent.

DEFINITIVE DECISIONS WITHIN BROAD ORGANISATIONAL OBJECTIVES

1 Formulation of definitive recommendations, and the making of complex decisions—generally NOT subject to review.
2 Definite involvement with the generation of profits and taking significant calculated risks—top level 'guestimating'—cannot escape dealing with uncertainties and imponderables.
3 Managerial competence and professional background to coordinate and integrate activities in an independent area of operation.
4 Decisions taken within the context of broad organisational objectives and specified resources—some scope to generate procedural innovation and to arrive at more realistic definitions of objectives or a clearer perception of business opportunities.
5 Growth and maintenance in value of resources a prime consideration—involved with specific plans to develop and to conserve manpower.

TOP LEVEL ORGANISATIONAL DECISIONS

Decisions involved with the integration of a number of independent areas of control—formulation of strategic plans which resolve conflicting objectives and will optimise the effective use of substantial resources to attain broad organisational objectives (short term and long term). Concern with all activities which would materially influence the survival of the company—or one of its major operating units—in a competitive society. Decisions involve as exhaustive as possible a judgment of highranking specialists and advisers. Decisions go beyond the profit motive—they integrate a personal awareness of business opportunities and community values.

COMMENT

These descriptions and definitions are difficult to distinguish (except, of course, between widely separated 'levels'). They are exceedingly hard to explain to most people, and certainly could not be understood by most members of the non-managerial group. This, in itself, would decrease the method's acceptability. Moreover, these definitions lend themselves to argument—they have a fairly high subjective element. Nevertheless they describe the kinds of decisions set out in the six Decision Bands which, covering wider groupings, are simpler and more easily understood. I shall refer to the usefulness of the Castellion Method for subgrading in *The Manual* on method.

There is a scale of points indicating the relative value of the fourteen decision levels. The scale has been arbitrarily fixed as in most quantitative methods, and although there appears to be recognition of the exponential increase of given points the higher in the scale, this is not explained. The scale is given in Table 8.1, and alongside is placed what is judged to be the equivalent Grades and their subdivisions into a, b, and c.

TABLE 8.1 *Correlation of Decision-making levels and Bands/Grades*

	Points range	Grade	Band
1 Simple decisions involving straightforward comparisons	1–4	0(a)	
2 Simple decisions requiring a little know-how	5–8	0(b)	O
3 Simple decisions based on categorised data	9–12	0(c)	
4 Simple decisions requiring broad estimates which are quickly derived	13–16	1(a)	
5 Simple and varied decisions	17–25	1(b)	A
6 Decisions requiring the coordination of data	26–34	1(c)	
7 Decisions which follow from a reasoned estimate	35–43	3(a)	
8 Decisions requiring practical know-how— understanding of principles	44–52	3(b)	B
9 Decisions involving systematic searches	53–61	3(c)–4	
10 Intricate decisions based on study of the interplay of variables	62–78	4–5(a)	
11 Complex decisions involving some measure of self-reliance	80–96	5(b)	C
12 Complex decisions inferred largely from remote information	98–114	5(c)	
13 Definitive decisions within broad organisational objectives and at the functional level	116–148	7–8	D
14 Top level organisational decisions	152–200	9–10	E

FACTOR 2. PRESSURE OF WORK COEFFICIENT

Figures given are *coefficients used to multiply the score on decision-making.*

	Coefficient
1 FEW DECISIONS—taken at leisure—no great pressure	1·00–1·10
2 FEW DECISIONS—taken at leisure—occasional peaks bring an element of hurry	1·10–1·20
3 FREQUENT DECISIONS—under normal pressure—on some occasions takes immediate decisions	1·20–1·30

4 FREQUENT DECISIONS—under variable pressure—peaks in work load occur from time to time and create time stress 1·30–1·40

5 FREQUENT DECISIONS—under definite pressure—work load allows for occasional breaks in decision-making process   1·40–1·60

6 NUMEROUS DECISIONS—under great pressure—regular deadlines bring definite time stress—decision-making throughout working day, and often beyond it   1·60–1·80

7 URGENT DECISIONS—taken under considerable pressure numerous conflicting deadlines—decision-making extends well beyond working day—frequent weekend work   1·80–2·00

COMMENT

In effect this is recognition of the fact that the more frequent the decision-making the more difficult it is, in line with the argument in Chapter 4. Again, the coefficient is arbitrarily fixed. Moreover, work varies greatly in pace according to pressure. It would be difficult for a grading conference to be anything but subjective in their scoring for this factor.

FACTOR 3. NUMERICAL COMPUTATIONS

Computations carried out, and the interpretations which must be derived from these computations.

		Points
1	ELEMENTARY ARITHMETIC—ADDING, SUBTRACTING, DIVIDING AND MULTIPLYING Additions, and subtractions possibly more complicated: multiplications and divisions remain simple, e.g. comptometrist.	9 10 11 12
2	ARITHMETIC AS APPLIED TO SIMPLE FORMULAE Arithmetic as applied to simple formulae, e.g. percentages, fractions and decimals—should be able to distinguish between different kinds of measures, e.g. weights, fluids, resistance, voltage.	13 14 15 16
3	USE AND INTERPRETATION OF MORE COMPLEX FORMULAE Use and interpretation of more complex formulae—usually repetitive—interpretation of results necessary—direct substitution of symbols in formula, e.g. compound and variable interest rates, annuities, etc.	17 18 19 20
4	USE AND INTERPRETATION OF DIFFERENT COMPLEX FORMULAE/CALCULATIONS Not necessarily repetitive—involving selection of information—interpretation of results becomes quite involved, e.g. computing theoretical cost of new products still to be produced, etc.	21 23 26 28

5 DEVELOPMENT OF SYSTEMS OF COMPUTATION Actively   29
concerned with new systems of computation and the analysis   31
of failures in current systems. Mathematical analysis be-   34
comes more advanced, the interpretation of trends and of   36
data with variable confidence limits.

COMMENT

This scale is a recognition of the fact that up the hierarchy of decision levels the constraints on decision-making are wider, uncertainty and risk increase, and progressively more complex mathematical techniques are necessary to reduce the uncertainty. These techniques are associated with the decision levels, the more complex the technique the higher the level of decision-making.

FACTOR 4. COMPREHENSION ABILITY

Points

1 COMMUNICATION RELATED TO VARIED DOCUMENTS   13
Reports, manuals, regulations, correspondence files. Essen-   14
tially simple, e.g. Comptometrist, Secretary, Overseer.   15
                                                                 16

2 COMMUNICATIONS INVOLVING SPECIFIC BUT BROAD   17
TERMINOLOGY For the understanding of manuals, stand-   18
ing instructions, etc. Precise action and particular attention   19
to detail is necessary as a result of this level of comprehen-   20
sion.

3 COMMUNICATIONS BASED ON KNOWLEDGE OF VARIED   21
TERMINOLOGY Covering a number of fields of activity.   23
Special training and/or experience is necessary to reach   26
the high degree of understanding of varied techniques.   28

4 CRITICAL EVALUATION OF PROFESSIONAL COMMUNI-   29
CATIONS Reads with critical understanding the most   34
advanced publications in his own sphere and also in allied   39
spheres.   44

COMMENT

This factor indicates sources of Information in the decision-making process; the more complex the Information the greater the difficulty in decision-making. The Grouping 1 refers to people in jobs of Bands O and A, 2 refers to Band B, 3 to Band C, Grade 5, and 4 to Grades 6 and 7.

FACTOR 5. VIGILANCE, i.e. 'being on the ball'

Points

1 As exercised in concrete manner over a narrow activity   9
with limited variables. Vigilance here amounts to intense   12
concentration.

		Points
2	As exercised in concrete manner over a complex work area, e.g. driving a motor car, console of an automatic plant.	13 20 28
3	As exercised in the direct control of a group of people or over behaviour which needs to be known in a limited manner, e.g. a person who supervises, a salesman behind a counter, etc.	29 35 40 46 52
4	As exercised over activities which are often controlled indirectly and which involve the application of the intangible, e.g. managerial control involving two layers of supervision, topflight salesman, etc.	53 60 68 75 83
5	As exercised over activities which are controlled indirectly and which require proven professional training to appreciate the intangible, e.g. manager Research and Development, Municipal Engineer concerned with interplay of many departments.	84 92 100 108 115
6	As exercised over patterns of behaviour which are difficult to perceive and understand, e.g. the estate agent in anticipation of property development opportunities, where to go for capital resources and where potential sales exist.	116 123 131 138 146
7	As exercised over material of extreme complexity and abstraction, e.g. an investment analyst must consider every aspect of the National Economy involving most sophisticated variables and must endure uncertainty between cause and effect.	147 156 164 172 180

COMMENT

This factor is obscure in its meaning. Vigilance is not alertness, it means the kind of attention that is given to specific kinds of decision, i.e. '*as* exercised in'. The scale is, therefore, not a scale or degree of alertness but a differentiation in kind. Thus 'as exercised over a complex area, e.g. driving a motor car' (2) is contrasted with 'as exercised in direct control of a group of work people' (3). Yet (2) may require more vigilance and alertness than (3).

These differences in kind relate to the vigilance required ('as exercised') in kinds of decision, and so cannot be thus scaled. However, they can be applied to the job description for jobs in different Bands and Grades, that is, they reinforce the decision-making factor.

FACTOR 6. ERROR: CONSEQUENCE OF ERRORS

'*Consequence of errors*' assesses the *possibility of losses and their extent*. Losses result from vigilance not being properly exercised in the job, from taking wrong decisions, and involve human and material resources used in a job.

		Points
1	Errors for which there are backstop provisions. The cost is usually wasted time and labour.	9
		15
		21
2	Errors which are appreciable but their consequence is restricted to a limited sphere of human or material assets.	22
		27
		32
3	Errors which are appreciable and costly but still limited to a smallish sector. They may be cumulative in effect, consisting of poor supervision, ineffective administration procedures and involve several people and/or substantial material.	33
		36
		40
4	Errors resulting in substantial reduction in profit expectation, e.g. faulty staff appointments, bad investment, wrong market strategy affecting a branch as a whole and which become apparent only after a year.	41
		48
		56
		64
		72
5	Errors seriously affecting the firm and its capacity for survival, e.g. faulty long-term decisions; not generating resources for expansion and diversification; making wrong top level decisions as well as failing to make a decision.	73
		84
		96
		108
		120

COMMENT

This factor is closely related to the factor 'responsibility' as used in most Point Methods. But here money values are not given, the effects of error are broadly stated. However, the word 'error' refers to decision, being a poor decision. This is supported by the phrase 'losses result from vigilance not being properly exercised in the job, from taking wrong decisions'. Like vigilance this is a factor reinforcing the decision-making factor; and this is very clear. Degree 1 refers to decisions in Bands O and A; degree 2 refers to Band B; degree 3 to Band C; degree 4 to a complex of Bands D and E (a complex that frequently occurs in small firms); and degree 5 to Band E.

FACTOR 7. EDUCATION

1	Standards 8 and 9	13–16
2	Matriculation	17–20
3	Post-matriculation Certification or Diploma (scaled in local or regional values)	22–28
4	A first, or pass university degree (scaled in regional values)	30–40
5	An Honours degree (four years)	42–52
6	A Master's degree	54–64
7	A Doctorate	66–70

COMMENT

It may well be that a university degree is necessary for performance of some specialised jobs, but not for all of the higher echelon jobs in a firm—many firms are efficiently staffed by non-graduates. This factor is related to the time required to learn a job—required experience is shortened if certain basic education is already in being (Chapter 11). In other words this factor is an indication of relative difficulty of particular jobs *within the same grade*, and can, therefore, be used for subgrading. It must always be remembered that a matriculation standard person can make integrative decisions of the highest level. These points are essentially rewards for past performance not present.

FACTOR 8. EXPERIENCE

That minimum period of time needed to acquire those mental and manual skills necessary to *perform the work satisfactorily.*

It is that time normally required for an individual with the educational level previously specified to acquire necessary *practical experience which would enable him to assume responsibility for the work assigned*, i.e. to apply to practical situations the theoretical knowledge acquired in a formal course of studies.

The measurement should include that experience attained through the actual performance of the work, plus necessary experience on directly related work. The following *values are FACTORS* for education scores.

Over 15 years	× 5·0
Over 10 years	× 4·5
Over 6 years	× 3·5
Over 5 years	× 2·4
Over 4 years	× 2·0
Over 3 years	× 1·8
Over 2 years	× 1·4
Over 1 year	× 1·2
Less than 1 year	× 1·1

COMMENT

The comments on the factor Education are to be borne in mind here. This coefficient is a furthering of the reward for past performance and does not indicate relative difficulty of the job. If there had been an allocation of points (instead of a multiplication of Education) then it would have been a straightforward criterion of relative difficulty since time to learn is correlated with difficulty of what is learned. For instance 'over 15 years' indicates how long it takes a person to 'go through the mill' of learning progressively more difficult decisions in reaching Band D.

Summarising—these comments on each factor suggest that the 'major grouping', the decision-making factor, is basic to most of them. They become, therefore, reinforcement of that factor which, in practice, has been found, by itself, to give results that range from 93 to 97 per cent correlation with results from use of the total set of factors. The significance of this will be referred to under the general critique in Chapter 11.

Chapter nine   **The Time-span Method**

This Method is uniquely associated with the name of Professor Elliot Jaques who first enunciated his ideas in 1956 in his book *Measurement of responsibility* [23]. Jaques, apparently, first observed the time component inherent in the difference in method of payment expressed as hourly paid, weekly and monthly paid, and annual salary; and, similarly, that the length of time a person gives or is given notice seems to be correlated with the form of payment. From these initial stimuli his investigations led to the observation that the time which elapses before a person's work is examined has a linear correlation with reward. This crude statement requires an analysis of the accurate definitions put forward by Jaques mainly in his second book on the subject *Equitable Payment* [24].

Work "is the application of knowledge and the exercise of discretion within the limits prescribed by the immediate manager and by higher policies, in order to carry out the activities allocated by the immediate manager, the whole carried out within an employment contract for a wage or salary" [24, p. 71]. In the terminology outlined in Part I here, the exercise of discretion must mean the decision-making process within the constraints imposed by the manager's coordinative decision, that is, a person's function or job. For fulfilling this function, which he obliges himself to fulfil, the person is rewarded. The undertaking of the obligation and the reward constitute the essence of the social contract.

"There are always to be found two different aspects to the responsibilities which a manager sets out to be discharged. He sets them out partly in prescribed terms; that is to say, in such a manner that his subordinate will be in no doubt whatever when he has completed his task, and completed as instructed" [24, p. 71]. The word 'responsibilities' is thus used in the sense of that for which a person is responsible, that which he has obliged himself to do, his function. "And he sets them out partly in discretionary terms; that is to say, in such a manner that his subordinate will have to use his own discretion in deciding when he has pursued the particular activities to the point where the result is likely to satisfy the manager". "In the case of the discretionary content of the responsibility" (again meaning function) "no one can know definitely if the work has been done as set out by the manager until that manager—or someone else officially on his behalf—has reviewed the results of the work and accepted it as satisfactory or rejected it as sub-standard." The 'discretionary content' is, therefore, the procedure decided upon in fulfilling the function—for, unless a person has discretion, freedom to choose procedure, he cannot be held responsible.

Jaques [24, p. 77] distinguishes discretion and decision this way. "The use of discretion is a *process* internal to the person. It cannot be seen from outside. It has to do with thought, judgment, sense, feel, discrimination, comparing, wondering, foreseeing and other contents of mental work—both conscious and unconscious. Decision, by contrast, is concerned with action". Jaques uses "the term decision only in the full executive sense of action taken . . . not . . . in the loose sense of someone 'deciding' to do something. An executive decision exists only when a manager or his subordinate has committed himself—issued an instruction, or otherwise actually carried out some observable work. Intentions do not constitute a decision. They are part of the *process of discretion leading up to the taking of decisions.* No decision in the executive sense occurs until the member has *acted on his own discretion.* Good discretion is thus definable as discretion which leads to good decisions; sub-standard discretion leads to sub-standard decision." (My italics.)

He is thus describing the decision-process. Discretion is that part of the process leading from Information through the thinking Conclusion to the commitment to action, the Decision, followed by the Execution which Jaques calls the decision. Although he becomes somewhat confused when he remarks "the discretion of which we are speaking is discretion in action" [24, p. 82].

The word 'responsibility' is also confusing. "What is it that it (the enterprise) pays a wage or salary for—we get a two-fold answer. First, it employs that person's capacity to carry out the prescribed responsibilities and to conform to them". That is, responsibilities refer to the function as in three paragraphs above. "Second, it employs his ability to exercise sufficient discretion on his own account to cope with uncertainties, the vicissitudes, the unknown, in the job." "It is the second of these responsibilities—the exercise of discretion—which is mainly connected with the sensation of the amount of responsibility in a job. We appear to derive our sensation of level of work or responsibility from the discretion we are called upon to exercise, and not from the regulated or prescribed action" [24, pp. 80–81]. That is, responsibility now refers to a sensation, for, as Jaques himself says, the prescribed responsibilities are overt, external and can be seen. A sensation cannot. "By responsibilities I wish to refer, therefore, simply to the particular activities to be carried out in the job, with the results to be achieved stated in concrete terms of the specific things to be done". "How does each one contribute? Clearly he contributes by doing something, by carrying out certain activities. Is that, then, all that he is responsible for? But surely, yes. Work refers to activities" [24, p. 62].

There can be no question that Jaques is saying a person is responsible for his contribution, his function, and he has choice in procedure, discretion in decision-making, in fulfilling his function. The activities are the decision-making and the execution of the decisions.

He puts it clearly in this way [23, pp. 73–74]. Of three unrecognised principles—"First, *status and payment were accorded for the level of work* that a person was expected to do and succeeded in doing, and not for his skill, experience, training, or qualifications". (Surely, a plain, simple, refutal of the current job evaluation principles.) "Second, *the level of work allocated to a person could be defined solely in terms of the decisions* that he was called upon to take and act upon in his job, and except in these terms was not related to the quality of the results achieved nor to those aspects of method that were prescribed". (Again surely this is a statement simply that decisions define level of work and so status and payment.) "Third, what they experienced as level of work was the space of time during which a member was authorised to make his own decisions without opportunity of reference to his managers for judgment of their quality or a decision to change or to re-affirm his terms of reference". The last refers to 'time-span of discretion', the 'measure' of level of work and so decisions, status and payment. It is this clear-cut statement of the relation of time-span of discretion to decision-making and executing which makes analysis of this Method important.

The most recent definition of time-span [25, p. 17] is "the longest period which can elapse in a role before the manager can be sure that his subordinate has not been exercising marginally sub-standard discretion continuously in balancing the pace and quality of his work". Marginally sub-standard discretion is that "which leads to results which are just outside the standards of time or of quality set, i.e. the work is done just too slowly, or is just not quite good enough in quality". Since these standards are 'set' they are prescribed, i.e. function, and so marginally sub-standard discretion means poor decision-making in procedure, but how poor is not objectively stated.

The technique is difficult to describe but Jaques has reduced it to its simplest in his third book *Time-span handbook* [25]. "It should be added that the technique is not an especially easy one to learn. The difficulty lies in the great trouble experienced in getting away from looking at the level of work in terms of the skills and experience required in a person to do the job, and dealing with level of work in terms simply of activities and managerial review. This change in outlook is harder to accomplish than might at first be realised" [24, p. 118].

The first information sought about a job is whether it is single task or multiple task role. A role "refers to a position in an executive system—the position to which a person is appointed" [24, p. 99]. A task is "a discrete unit of work with target completion time and quality standards either given by a manager to a subordinate explicitly or implicitly, or generated by a general responsibility". "A task has the character of an instruction to do something specific, to reach a stated objective: i.e. to 'do this' " [25, p. 13]. A task is therefore prescribed and so part of function.

A single-task role is "a role into which nothing but continuous tasks are allocated, and the order in which the tasks are to be done is prescribed" [25, p. 12]. The occupant has only one task to do at a time. A multiple-task role "normally contains a number of intermittent-tasks (with possibly some continuous tasks as well) with differing target completion times, so that the occupant of the role must organise and progress a programme of tasks" [25, p. 10]. He must decide task priorities.

The time span of a single-task job is the time from commencement to review of the longest task or task sequence, that is tasks or task sequences which give the longest periods without being checked on, during which the manager relies on the member to make proper decisions to achieve the task objectives. The time span of a multiple-task job is obtained from the target completion time of the longest extended task, which is that task "whose target completion time is later than all previous tasks".

Originally Jaques required an analysis of the times from completion to review of all the tasks in a job, which meant an intensive time-consuming search. In *Time-span Handbook* he has streamlined the technique—just as all researchers in this field do as a result of experience. He says [25, p. 3] that the full description and specification of a job is no longer necessary, the analyst goes straight to the longest time-span task. This is why the word 'target' now enters into the somewhat difficult vocabulary of time-span technique. This target time is that set by the manager. "It considerably shortens the amount of time required for measuring, since it eliminates the need to investigate the actual review points. It does not significantly change the measurements obtained by means of the previous instrumentation" [25, p. 44]. If the target's completion time is altered by the manager after the task has begun it should be treated as a new task. This looks simplicity itself if modern *Management by objectives* techniques are employed, i.e. techniques of clear-cut target-setting for, with and by subordinates.

The next stage is to corroborate the manager's information with the subordinate. Jaques apparently prefers to rely more upon the manager's opinion since it is he who usually sets the target time, that is assigns the function, leaving the procedural decisions (discretion) to the subordinate.

Having thus established the longest time span this is compared with the payment levels in a Chart of Equitable Payment Levels. This is the *earnings* (not basic pay) which Jaques (and presumably his colleagues in this field) establish as the 'fair payment' for jobs of different maximum time-span. For Jaques holds that this equitable work-payment scale "represents that distribution of earnings in employment work which would give relatively the same experience of satisfaction throughout the whole scale of levels of work, and the individual capacities corresponding to those levels of work, under the conditions of the British economy at the present time" [24, p. 166]. He believes that there is a distribution of individual capacities in a population so that people can make only differential contributions to achievement of the whole, hence they are rewarded differentially. This individual capacity is the capacity for exercising discretion (which is overtly seen as a capacity for discriminating expenditure) directly correlated with capacity for production work as measured in time-span [24, p. 165]. People have "intuitive norms of fair payment for any given level of work" and these are, according to Jaques, universal. He says [25, p. 116] that the differential between any two levels of felt-fair payment for two given time-spans is the same whatever the country. "Thus, if for example, X is found to be the equitable payment level for one-year time-span, then $2X$ will be found to be the equitable payment level for two-year time-span, $\frac{3}{4}X$ for six-month time-span etc., as obtains from the United Kingdom equitable work-payment scale." He reproduces this scale for 1964 in *Time-span handbook.*

This scale of what is felt-fair earnings—which are not affected by hours worked and include fringe benefits such as use of car, assistance with purchase of house, provision of canteen meals, etc. [24, p. 125] is obtained only by establishing with employees what Jaques calls a social-analytic relationship which gives access to private aspects of a person's feelings, judgments, attitudes. This relationship is confidential so there is no way of checking accuracy of findings.

After the time-span and equivalent earnings have been arrived at the manager's superior is consulted to corroborate the limitations within which the manager can prescribe the function of the subordinate, so authorising the time-span measurement as valid and the corresponding earnings level.

COMMENT

A constant theme of proponents of the Time-Span Method is its objectivity, even to the extent of establishing a fixed Equitable Payment Scale, nationally and internationally. Yet the Method shows many of the aspects of *subjectivity* encountered in the quantitative and non-quantitative methods of job evaluation. Take for example the definition of 'marginally sub-standard discretion'—work done 'just too slowly' or 'just not quite good enough', 'just outside the standards of time or of quality set'. What is precisely, objectively, defined by 'just too', 'just outside', 'just not quite' is difficult to understand. Again, the decisions of the manager who is interviewed are the "product of his subjective judgment and standards" [25, p. 66], and Jaques admits the manager may give a different target or review time on another occasion or to another analyst. If he does change his target times "time-span measurement allows you to measure the oscillations in level of work created by a manager who is constantly changing his instructions" [25, p. 67]; but this does not provide the time-span for the earnings determination.

The interview with the manager may also show considerable subjectivity. The technique of "successive approximation" helps the manager to "structure his intuitive experience" [25, p. 29] for he cannot always be expected to give his time targets. "They are often set as a matter of intuitive understanding between the manager and his subordinate" [25, p. 33]. An example of 'successive approximation' is best quoted [24, pp. 92-3]. "Take, for example, output per week from a particular section. The manager says he expects, say, an output of five hundred articles. He does not know offhand what he would consider to be marginally sub-standard. Fifty per week? Impossibly low. Five thousand? Impossibly high. One thousand? Exceptionally good. One hundred? Not at all good enough. Three hundred? Not good enough. Five hundred? Not bad. Five hundred two weeks running? Would perhaps worry me. Three weeks running? I would have to look into it. Six hundred? Quite good. Six hundred for week after week?

8

Excellent. Detailed explanation would probably reveal that the margins of the limits are between five and six hundred per week. Steady performance of less than five hundred per week would cause concern. Steady performance above six hundred might cause the manager to revise his standards." Apart from the fact that such a manager ought to be sent on a course in elementary techniques of management, the percentage error in fixing the marginal sub-standard could range up to 10 per cent. A better manager would have knowledge of changes that are occurring day by day and would not wait for weeks to pass before reviewing. Would, then, this department be paid less because he is a better manager and gets higher production from his department?

The same kind of anomaly appears in the allowable errors in application of the Method. Jaques [24, pp. 132–3] finds that "individuals whose actual payment bracket remains within ±3 per cent of equity, tend to express themselves as feeling that their role is being reasonably paid relative to others", but if the payment bracket falls 5 per cent below equity he feels he is being treated to some degree unfairly, at 10 per cent below he feels he is definitely being treated unfairly, and below this he begins to think about another job. At 5 per cent above equity he feels he is getting more than a fair deal, and at 10 per cent above "compulsive elements begin to enter into his attitude", feelings of anxiety and/or guilt. And these phenomena appear at all levels in the firm.

But Jaques notes [25, pp. 30–1] variations in accuracy of time-span measurement. "Tasks of time-spans of 5 years and over are commonly assigned to be taken to the nearest year; time-spans of 2 years to 5 years, to the nearest half-year; times of six months to a year, to the nearest month; 1 to 6 months to the nearest week; 1 to 4 weeks, to the nearest day; under a week, to the nearest hour, or half-day; and under 1 hour, to the nearest 5 to 10 minutes." This could produce errors of 10–15 per cent. Far from producing a sense of equity such errors might produce feelings of anxiety, guilt or aggression.

Jaques rightly points out the paralysing kind of industrial stress that may flare up over differentials, over the rate for the job. "Everyone knows that it is possible, in a rough and ready way, to compare jobs—to recognise that this one is a more important or a bigger job than that one, or that this category of job is growing in skill and responsibility . . . But intuitive judgment of this type does not prove very helpful in a wage-negotiation situation . . . Intuitive judgments are too coarse for such a purpose. And they are not only too coarse. The making of intuitive comparisons between jobs as a means of settling rates of pay suffers from other very great defects as well: people do not look at jobs in the same way; nor are they equally familiar with different jobs; nor, since jobs change, do they necessarily know a job today because they have done so at some time in the past; nor are they necessarily even talking about the same job, since the same job title can often cover a multitude of different kinds of work". "Much of job evaluation", Jaques properly remarks, "is based on such judgment . . . Judgment of this intuitive kind, while possibly having a limited use under local conditions, is of no use at all in negotiations affecting numbers of people in widely distributed establishments . . . Intuitive judgment is difficult, if not impossible, to frame in words. So long as judgment about work remains intuitive, negotiation in terms of principle remains impossible." These remarks could equally be applied to the idea of felt-fair pay discovered by Jaques in a "social-analytic relationship". "The results suggest the existence of an unrecognised system of norms of fair payment for any given level of work, unconscious knowledge of these norms being shared among the population engaged in employment-work" [24, p. 124]. It was because of these "intuitive norms" that Jaques had recourse to the concept of equity in describing the scale of felt-fair differential payments.

"The *usefulness* of time-span measurement derives not from the instrument itself but from two facts: the fact that time-span measurements of jobs appear to correlate closely with such important matters as the intuitive sense of individuals about fair differential payment for work and for the level or intensity of responsibility carried in a job; and the fact that they give a systematic and comprehensive picture of the time characteristics in organisation of executive work" [23, p. 64]. In his first and second books Jaques pointed out the value of a thorough knowledge of job content in tasks and completion times from which a better organisational view of the firm could be obtained. In his latest work, *Time-span handbook*, only the longest and extended tasks are sought for and then target times, and job descriptions and specifications are no longer considered necessary. The organisational value of the Method has been eroded. Moreover, it seems that the Method is limited to use only in managerial grades even though Jaques has shown how to apply it to manual and clerical workers, and has listed appropriate time-spans and their correlated payments.

It appears that the *acceptability* of the Method has been questioned. The Method is claimed to be factual and objective [24, p. 13] and on the basis of this and the intuitive norms of felt-fair payment, the payment for a job is fixed, there is no need for negotiation. No trade union would ever accept a method that eliminates negotiation or bargaining. Jaques openly discloses that in the Glacier Metal Company, where he carried out his original investigations, the "Works Council has not so far accepted, even on an exploratory basis, the notion of the time-span yardstick and the associated equitable work-payment scale" [24, p. 141]. The Works Committee have opted out of any participation in the use of the Method. "This experience in the Glacier Metal Company . . . represents in microcosm the more general industrial situation. The best-willed attempts to achieve equity run foul of existing anxieties and suspicions, and the resistance against giving up bargaining."

It may well be, of course, that among the manual workers there is an intuitive sense about the possible inequities that could arise from application of the Method. For example, a skilled tradesman working on production, having the same apprenticeship and working on a similar machine as those of another tradesman, but with more frequent reviews would, according to the Method, be paid less. It is doubtful if he would stand for this. Even now, as noted in a previous chapter (Robinson), skilled men earning less than semi-skilled working on piece rates (and the Method refers to earnings whatever the hours worked, not to basic rates) demand lieu bonuses to bring them up at least to parity. And surely, if he is being employed properly, the skilled man has a longer time-span of discretion.

And one last point on acceptability—the fact that the manager is regarded as the source of information, the subordinate only seen to be corroborative, is liable to add to the suspicion of a Method that is not easily understood. It is "a method of measuring employment work in terms of what the manager in charge of the work is authorised and expected to do, rather than by observing and measuring the activity of the employed person at work—although such direct observation may often be helpful in discovering the content of the work being allocated" [24, p. 64]. "The technique is not an easy one to learn. The difficulty lies in the great trouble experienced in getting away from looking at level of work in terms of the skills and experience required in a person to do the job" [24, p. 118]. The manual or clerical worker is likely to have even more difficulty than analysts who, even among themselves, frequently disagree [64, p. 136 et seq.].

There are a few anomalous concepts about the relation of time-span and payment which Professor Jaques will, no doubt, resolve as he continues his research. "Time-span is neutral with regard to the relative importance of any particular task in a role" [25, p. 64] and, during the Method, "no reference whatever (is made) to the discovery of what may be felt to be the most important tasks" [25, p. 74]. It is usually assumed, if a task is said to be more important, that it implies it is of more value or worth to the firm, and payment is made accordingly—"Payment is the practical and concrete means of expressing the evaluation and recognition of the relative value of a man's work—and in precise quantitative terms" [24, p. 153]—which suggests that time-span does not measure importance and so relative worth. On the other hand it may well be—and the chances are it is so—that the longest extended task is the most important. In which case the correlation of time-span and payment becomes valid.

Unfortunately the shop-floor people may not see payment in the same way. The payment Jaques refers to is total earnings, and time-span is not affected by hours worked. Since overtime, therefore, increases earnings but does not change time-span, there must arise an anomalous situation in accounting for the difference in payment to the member who works long hours and to the other who does not, yet is doing the same kind of work. The first is doing a job of more value or worth to the firm, greater production, so he is paid more; yet their jobs cannot be distinguished by time-span. Nor would one less 'hard-working' man 'feel' the extra payment to his long-overtime colleague as unfair. Give them the same payment because their time-span is the same and there would be a problem.

To my mind, admittedly biased by my own 'decision-making approach', Professor Jaques' remarkable sensitivity to the feelings of members of his firm is most important in the application of time-span to his concept of *ranks*. His first statement [23, p. 47] showed that his 'interviewees' tended to group jobs of different time-spans into categories, which he then called ranks. "Thus, for example, of those positions at, say, three-week, five-week, and six-month time-span levels, the five-week and six-month time-span positions were felt by the members as having an affinity in status. The three-week level position was experienced by all three members as being in a junior category, although mathematically the three-week and five-week positions were closer. In this fashion, groupings were found for jobs of time-span up to one hour, between one hour and one day; one day and one week; one week and one month; one month and one year; one year and two years, two years and five years; and over five years.

The boundaries between the categories at the one-month level and above were experienced as firmer boundaries than those below the one-month level. The main reason for this appeared to be that no positions at lower than one-month level of work were found to carry full managerial authority and responsibility—that is to say, authority over subordinates in the sense of selecting them, assessing their work, dealing with their salary increases, and in all respects being managerially in charge of them". The shortest possible executive line between managing director and shop-floor would be as shown in Table 9.1.

Increase in time-span within a rank was felt as increase in work but increase across a rank boundary from the top of one to the bottom of the next was felt to be promotion. "Thus, movement over the one-month boundary meant movement into the managerial area. Similarly movement across each of the succeeding boundaries was experienced as movement into a higher managerial region" [23, p. 48].

Since that first book Jaques was able to do more research on time-span of manual workers and he has been able to recognise nine brackets (sub-ranks) of 15 minutes, 1 hour, 2 hours, 1 day, 2 days, 3 days, 1 week, 2 weeks, and 1 month in Rank 1; and he has also found manual jobs "whose time-span bracket is up to three months. There may well be hourly-rated manual

TABLE 9.1   *First rank Time-span correlation*

Rank	Time-span
1	Less than 1-month
2	1-month to 1-year
3	1-year to 2-year
4	2-year to 5-year
5	Over 5-year

TABLE 9.2   *Second rank Time-span correlation*

Rank	Time-span
1	11 sub-ranks up to 2 months
2	3 to 9 months
3	1 year to 21 months
4	2 to 4 years
5	5 to $7\frac{1}{2}$ years
6	10 to 15 years
7	20 years and upwards

(Ranks 6 and 7 refer to top positions only in very large corporations.)

roles carrying time-spans longer than this" [24, p. 103], which contrasts
with his earlier finding that movement across the one-month boundary
meant moving into the managerial area. The new ranking [25, p. 107] is as
shown in Table 9.2.

In 1965 Jaques [26] reported that he could distinguish these Ranks
according to the "level of abstraction a person can manage", the higher the
level the longer the tasks or projects he will be able to plan and progress.
These levels he names and describes as follows.

RANK 1   PERCEPTUAL-CONCRETE

The object of the task must be physically present, there must be immediate
personal contact, otherwise the individual is unable to work. The objective
of the task must be set in terms of "work upon this piece of metal" or "upon
these sheets of paper".

RANK 2   IMAGINAL-CONCRETE

The actual physical object need not be present, for the person can work
with it in mind. So he can manage the doing of work, the execution of decisions by those in Rank 1, by planning, directing, allocating, programming,
progressing it and training for it.

RANK 3   CONCEPTUAL-CONCRETE

Here the person requires to deal with the future, to have a capacity for
prediction to the extent that he can plan the "forward load of tasks and the
changes needed to be put in train to meet it". He can allocate categories of
task for this purpose but he is still concerned with these tasks and with the
activities of Ranks 1 and 2 in dealing with the physical objects. He is like a
"production unit manager" close enough to the actual production (execution) to see the effect of his decisions.

RANK 4   ABSTRACT-MODELLING

Jaques admits he is not yet able to formulate this clearly. "Its essence lies
in the capacity not only to use abstraction (we all do) but to detach oneself
from reliance upon the presence—whether perceptual, imaginal or conceptual—of the actual object while yet maintaining a sufficient intuitive contact
with the concrete world for one's work with the abstractions to be translated
into concrete things which will give practical results" [26, p. 106]. Such
people are in charge of development, manufacture and sales functions.

RANK 5   THEORY CONSTRUCTION

Again Jaques is not quite sure about a definition, but he says, "Individuals
operating at this level need only one-time contact with the concrete. A good
theory is one which applies over a wide range of concrete cases in such a

manner that, given the theory and one detailed example of its application, it becomes possible to understand what will happen in other cases similar to the example and covered by the theory". In the next paragraph he calls these 'theories' "intuitively held generalisation . . . having the characteristic of an intuitively constructed theory". People in this Rank control Rank 4 managers in charge of the three major functions and are concerned with the "full profit and loss account".

Ranks 6 and 7 are concerned with setting financial, market and product policies in terms of progressively wider markets. They are not defined by Jaques. They are, in fact, Rank 5 people handling problems with more variables but in the same way. At this point I draw attention to Table 8.1 in Chapter 8, on the Castellion Method. Dr Cortis tells me that he has applied the Time-span Method and finds a rough correlation of the kind below in Table 9.3 (to which I add the Decision Band). This correlation is striking

TABLE 9.3   *Comparison of Castellion decision level, Time-span ranking and Decision Band*

| Castellion decision level | Time-span | | Decision band |
	Rank	Time-span	
1–10 (i.e. 10 levels)	1	(11 sub-ranks but no consistent time-span)	Bands O, A and B
11	2	Up to 6-months	5b ⎫
12	3	1 year to 15-months	5c ⎬ Band C
13	4	Up to 3 years	Band D
14	5	Up to 10 years	Band E

—the difference in actual time-spans between Jaques' Ranks and those of Cortis are of no real moment compared with the sequence. The ranking by time-span must be a ranking of decision-making. A comparison of Jaques' list of appropriate 'levels of abstraction' shows that, apart from the definition of Perceptual-concrete (which really means capacity to make decisions in handling 'things'), the definitions could be clarified by attaching Cortis' definitions. Again there appears the little problem of the 2- to 3-month time-span. It refers to that hoary old bogey of 'manager' definition—is the foreman or supervisor (of Grade 4) a manager? He does not make the predictive decision of the Middle Manager (Rank 2) yet he is managing. But this matters little in face of the general correlation. It also explains the sense of promotion on moving across the rank boundaries. Men always feel movement into foremanship, then to middle management, then to senior management and so to the board, top management, as promotional steps.

Chapter ten   The Guide-chart Profile Method

This Method (a form of the Point) was developed by E. N. Hay and Associates, published in a series of papers from 1951 to 1954 [17], and now practised by that firm, and others in collaboration. The Method appears to be applied mainly to managerial jobs, and is here given prominence in the modern form (as applied by Hay-MSL, Limited, of London) because of the importance of its basic premisses.

Mr W. F. Younger of Hay-MSL very kindly sent me some notes. He tells me that the Method "has been applied to managerial, technical, financial, government, armed forces, professional and medical jobs, primarily at salaried levels, but also covering some shop floor situations. Jobs in which over 300,000 people are employed have now been covered in the UK and the system is used widely for international comparison in America, Europe, Australia and Africa".

"The system is concerned essentially with analysing and measuring the importance of jobs *relative* to one another, and the relative importance of jobs is determined primarily by the purpose of the company or institution within which they operate, i.e. structure is a function of purpose, and Guide Charts are built to represent the structure of the institution in which jobs are being measured."

"Answerability for the consequences of decisions, the degree of freedom to take decisions and bring them to fruition, the degree to which there is prime accountability, as compared with shared or contributory accountability in a job are certainly elements which are measured in the Guide Charts."

"But also of significance is the profile of a job i.e. the degree to which it is advisory as distinct from decision making, the degree to which it is concerned with analysis of problems as distinct from making decisions about alternative courses of action."

These last two paragraphs indicate that the Method is concerned essentially with decision-making and responsibility, and with sapiential authority and the relation advisability.

"The numbering symbols are geometric because we are concerned with *relative* differences between jobs at various levels;" but Dr Hay has nowhere expounded a theoretical basis for the use of the geometric progression.

"Hay Guide Charts also define and provide a measurement basis for management breadth which is the co-ordinating function of management, whether over diverse functions, or different periods of time, or over the elements of planning, organising, communicating, evaluating and development which are common to all management roles. Distinction is made between these requirements, and technical or professional 'depth' requirements."

"In essence the Hay Guide-chart Profile method, is concerned with providing a common language to describe the relationships which exist between different roles in any organisation. This common language allows people who are knowledgeable about the roles under consideration to come to a consensus judgment of the relative significance of the different roles in that particular environment."

There are three factors, Know-how, Problem-solving and Accountability, which determine the value of different jobs. For the first and last factors points, in geometric progression, are arbitrarily allocated—"developed for individual organisations on a copyright basis and the points span varies according to the company". Reasons for such variations are not stated.

1. KNOW-HOW

This is the total of every kind of skill *required for average acceptable job performance*. It is knowledge and experience in professional, managerial and human relations activities necessary to fulfil the job. [In the following notes the near-equivalent in Decision Band and Grade for which such skill is required is given for purposes of comment.]

Know-how is "measured in depth" by eight degrees of:

SKILL–EDUCATION–TRAINING

	Jobs requiring:	*Decision*
A	Education to post-primary level.	Grade 0
B	Practised in standard work routines and/or use of simple equipment and machines.	
C	Procedural or systematic efficiency and use of specialised equipment.	Band A
D	Specialised skill gained by on-the-job experience or through part professional qualification.	Band B
E	Understanding of theoretical principles normally gained through professional qualification or through a detailed grasp of involved practices and procedures.	Grade 5

Jobs requiring: *Decision*

F   Seasoned proficiency in a highly specialised   Grade 6
     field, gained through experience built on
     theories or a broad and deep understanding of
     complex practices.

G   Mastery of principles, practices and theories   Grade 7
     gained through wide experience and/or special
     development.

H   Unique command of principles, theories and   Grade 8
     practices.

Know-how is 'measured in breadth' by five degrees of:

BREADTH OF MANAGEMENT KNOW-HOW

                                                            Decision

I   Non or minimal—performance or supervision   Bands O
     of jobs which have closely specified objectives.   and A

II   Homogeneous—integration of operations which   Band B
     are homogeneous in nature and objective, and
     coordination with associated functions.

III Heterogeneous—integration or coordination of   Band C
     diverse functions or sub-functions in a company;
     or inter-company coordination of a tactical
     function.

IV   Broad—integration of the major functions in an   Band D
     operating company; or group-wide coordination
     of a strategic function affecting policy formation.

V   Total—the management of strategic functions   Band E
     and policy formation.

Each degree of skill is sub-divided into three (a total of 24 levels); and
each degree of breadth of management know-how is also subdivided into
three according to required *Human relations skills*:

   1 Basic—ordinary courtesy and effectiveness in dealing with others.
   2 Important—understanding and influencing people, important but not
     over-riding considerations.
   3 Over-riding—skills in developing and motivating people are over-
     riding considerations.

A matrix of the 24 × 12 sub-degrees is drawn (Table 10.1) and points
assigned as indicated above, the range extending from 50 to as much as
1,840 points, this last representing 'depth of H', 'breadth of V' and the
need for over-riding human relations skills.

COMMENT

The 'depth' degrees are descriptive of 'jobs requiring' particular skills which,

TABLE 10.1 *Matrix of depth and breadth of management know-how*

Human relations	I None or minimal			II Homogeneous			III Heterogeneous			IV Broad			V
	1	2	3	1	2	3	1	2	3	1	2	3	Total
A Primary	50	57	66										
	57												
	66												
B Elementary vocational													
C Vocational													
D Advanced vocational													
E Basic professional, etc.													
F Seasoned professional, etc.													
G Professional mastery													
H Unique authority													

Breadth is shown across the top; *Depth* is shown down the left side.

as they are distinguished from each other, are indicative of the skills required to make the decisions of the various kinds of Band and Grade which I have listed alongside. Similarly the degrees of 'breadth of management know-how' are descriptive of the coordinative decisions required of each Decision Band. So, in effect, the 'depth' and 'breadth' are dimensions of the same kind. That is, they must be closely correlated—'increase' in one must be accompanied by increase in the other.

Hence the know-how for 'breadth' degree I, i.e. 'depth' degree of A or B, is not applicable to a decision of breadth degree IV or V. If it were then we could expect a 15-year-old schoolboy to be able to act as a general manager or a director. Conversely, to assign points for a combination of G 'depth' with a decision of 'breadth' I (because that decision *requires* G 'depth' for 'average acceptable performance') is not sense. It is a certainty that 'determinative mastery of principles, practices and theory' is not required for average acceptable performance of unskilled and semi-skilled work.

In other words these two dimensions should not be integrated in one matrix. They can be integrated as one dimension *or* they can be kept separate as two and, provided they have the same number of appropriate and equal degree intervals, the points assigned can be totalled since they are complementary.

And it is surprising that Dr Hay (who is an acknowledged authority in this field) should create so many as eight degrees with indistinct and overlapping definitions when he himself [16] argues that Weber's Law applies. "In any given kind of perception, equal relative (not absolute) differences are equally perceptible", and he finds that "just noticeable" equal differences of 15 per cent are the minimum in this field (quoted in [3, p. 270]). Nor, as I have already pointed out, does he give a theoretical explanation for the geometric progression of assigned points to such equal differences; and, lastly, to take these points to four significant figures is unjustified under any theoretical scheme of comparative quantification of such abstractions.

2. PROBLEM-SOLVING

This is the intensity of the mental process that employs Know-how in order to resolve a problem. It is, therefore, *treated as a percentage utilisation of Know-how*.

Problem-solving is 'measured' in the two dimensions of the 'environment' where the thinking is carried out and of the 'challenge' to the thinking. The environment is essentially a statement of the limits or constraints within which decisions are made on resolving problems, and the challenge is essentially a statement of the kind of job, thus:

THINKING ENVIRONMENT (8 DEGREES)

	Thinking within:	*Decision*
A	Detailed rules and/or rigid supervision.	Band O
B	Standard instructions and/or continuous close supervision.	
C	Well-defined procedures, somewhat diversified and/or supervised.	Band A
D	Substantially diversified established company procedures, and general supervision.	Band B
E	Clearly defined company policies, principles and specific objectives under readily available direction.	Band C
F	Broad policies and objectives, under general direction.	Band D
G	General policies, principles and goals under guidance.	Band E
H	Business philosophy and/or principles controlling human affairs.	

THINKING CHALLENGE (5 DEGREES)

		Decision
I	Repetitive—identical situations requiring solution by simple choice of things learned.	Bands O and A
II	Patterned—similar situations requiring solution by discriminating choice of things learned.	Band B
III	Variable—differing situations requiring searching, finding and selecting solutions within the area of things learned.	Bands B and C
IV	Adaptive—situations requiring analytical, interpretive and/or constructive thinking. Judgment is required.	Bands C and D
V	Creative—novel or non-recurring pathfinding situations requiring the development of new concepts and imaginative approaches.	Bands D and E

Each degree is divided into two sub-degrees and the matrix (16 × 10), as with Know-how, is constructed ranging from 10 to 100 per cent of Know-how.

COMMENT

The same kind of comment as for Know-how can be applied to Problem-solving. The degrees of 'thinking environment' are descriptions of different ways of making decisions, 'thinking' according to the progressive weakening or spreading of the constraints within which the decisions are made. The 'thinking challenge' degrees describe 'situations', that is jobs requiring solutions, that is making decisions, again correlatable with Decision Bands. That Know-how and Problem-solving are inextricably linked up is recognised by the latter being treated as a percentage of the former.

Again one could hardly conceive of 25 per cent of 'mastery of principles, practices and theories' (G, Know-how) being necessary to solve problems by simple choice of things learned (I, Repetitive). Nor could 33 per cent of post-primary education (A, Know-how) solve problems 'requiring the development of new concepts and imaginative approaches' (V, Creative). These two dimensions shall not form a matrix, they are correlatable in a unidirectional fashion.

3. ACCOUNTABILITY

This is 'the answerability for action and for the consequences of that action'. Since accountability and answerability are synonymous this must be interpreted as meaning *'responsibility'* when that word is used, loosely as I have already pointed out, for a job or function for which a person is responsible and which he has obliged himself to fulfil.

There are two 'dimensions', Freedom to Act and Magnitude, of which the first is divided into eight degrees or kinds of job (each with three sub-degrees) and the second into four degrees with four sub-degrees each.

FREEDOM TO ACT

	These jobs are subject to:	*Decision*
A	Prescribed—direct and detailed instructions, and close supervision.	Band O
B	Controlled—established work routines and close supervision.	
C	Standardised—standardised practices and procedures, general work instructions and supervision of progress and results.	Band A
D	Generally regulated—practices and procedures which have clear precedents.	Band B
E	Directed—broad practice and procedures covered by functional precedents and policies and managerial direction.	Band C
F	Oriented direction—functional policies and goals, and general managerial direction.	Grade 7
G	Senior guidance—inherently and primarily to direct top management guidance.	Grade 8
H	Ownership guidance—only to ownership review and public recreation.	Band E

The 'dimension' *Magnitude* of Accountability is divided into four degrees *Very Small, Small, Medium* and *Large* to each of which is assigned a number of dollars representing a money value of that which is at risk or is affected by the decisions made in the jobs under Freedom to Act.

Each of these Magnitudes is divided into four sub-degrees according to the way in which the decision-maker plays a part in the doing of his job. In other words an expression of shared responsibility, thus:

1 REMOTE—giving information on other incidental services for use by others involved in the action.
2 CONTRIBUTORY—interpretory, advisory or facilitating services to those involved in the action.
3 SHARED—participating with others (except superiors and subordinates) in taking action.
4 PRIME—wholly responsible, with little or no shared responsibility.

Again these two dimensions are constituted as a matrix (24 × 16) and points assigned accordingly.

COMMENT

First a comparison must be made of the degrees of Freedom to Act and Thinking Environment of the factor Problem-solving. For example, there seems to be little difference between the A's; "thinking within detailed rules, instructions and/or rigid supervision" and "subject to direct and detailed instructions, close supervision"; or between, say the F's; "thinking within broad policies and objectives, under general direction" and "subject to functional policies and goals, general managerial direction". In fact Thinking Environment and Freedom to Act are the same.

Again there are the anomalies stemming from the complementarities of the two dimensions. I cannot conceive of the managing director of a firm (H, Freedom to Act) being responsible for only, say, $10,000 per annum (Very Small Magnitude). Nor can I imagine a person in a job under "close supervision with direct and detailed instructions" being held responsible for, say, $15 million (Large Magnitude). Indeed, the very words "detailed instructions" and "close supervision" rule out responsibility other than for the minimum of decisions on element or operation. So again the two dimensions should not form a matrix and are also correlated in a unidirectional fashion.

The use of the word accountability, here synonymous with responsibility meaning job, is indicative. Responsibility is dependent upon freedom to act, or as Professor Jaques says, discretion in action to achieve a prescribed function. This freedom to act lies in the decision-making, and the constraints determine the kind of decision. Therefore, Accountability and Problem-solving are indicative of practically the same entity—the kind of decision. Since the making of a decision depends on Know-how (and Problem-solving is expressed as a percentage of Know-how) it follows that Know-how, as already indicated, is also concerned with kinds of decision. In other words all these factors are 'measures' of the same thing.

The *Guide-chart Profile* is expressed as shown in this example:

Know-how	G III	3	608
Problem-solving	G IV	57%	350
Accountability	F IV	3	350
			1308

This point sum is compared with a copyrighted distribution of salaries-according-to-points which provides a chart of high-paying, medium-paying and low-paying firms and the evaluating committee makes its choice as to how it will conform to the market range so expressed.

It is interesting that Dr Hay has found a near linear correlation between his point distribution and existing salaries. He gives no explanation for this. Presumably, if the distribution of points assigned to degrees were not geometric but linear, the salary curve (pay-points) would not be linear but more nearly exponential, rising faster the higher the degree of Know-how/Problem-solving/Accountability.

As I have already said, this method is important because of its basic premises which, reduced to their simplest, imply that kind of decision is a fundamental criterion for differentiating jobs.

Chapter eleven   **A Logic for Job Evaluation**

The foregoing descriptions and analyses of methods of job evaluation suggest that there are three main categories of requirements of any method that will satisfy most if not all of the objectives of job evaluation. These requirements are acceptability, operational principles, and a theoretical basis or theoretical principles. I put them in that order because the first is the most important—and acceptability may not depend on the logic of principles, far less on theory; it depends mainly on some fundamental value systems that are the basis of human and, therefore, of industrial relations.

ACCEPTABILITY

1 The method must have *simplicity*, it *must be readily understood* by the great majority of members of the firm. (One of the drawbacks of the Factor-comparison and Time-span Methods is their complexity.) Men are loathe to rely on something they do not understand which purports to establish, through pay, the importance of their jobs and so their status in the firm. The fact that managers can understand a method is no reason for assuming that unskilled members on the shop-floor can do the same.

2 Because there will always be a subjective element it becomes essential to *involve members by participation in* application of a method. A man does not like, far less accept, that others make subjective judgments about his work which he knows better than they do. He must know better—he does it. May be a manager knows better about target times than his subordinate, as Jaques insists, but cannot know better what the subordinate actually does; and in subjective matters, for example the element 'conditions'—and their effect upon him—he is the one who can best appreciate working under them. This does not mean that he is better at comparing his conditions with those of another member but, in the process of evaluation of conditions, he brings

to that process his knowledge or experience, his sapiential authority. One who is given the right to be heard on matters affecting him is more likely by far to be positively orientated, he has participated. He is the first *source for analysis of his job*, he is not a corroborative stand-by.

It is unlikely that all members of a work force are capable of taking part in the actual grading or rating process succeeding analysis. It is probable that the unskilled and perhaps many of the semi-skilled cannot understand even simplified hypotheses or theories underlying a method, but most people can appreciate operational principles—and doing so, are more likely to accept them, the matter of understandability. However, if *trade unionists or elected agents* (acting for managers) *participate* in the grading and assessment members will know that their interests are kept in mind. Acceptability of a method will be increased if everyone knows that their elected agents are involved, that the findings of job evaluation are not imposed upon them arbitrarily.

Acceptability is also enhanced *the greater the number of jobs* to which the method is applied. This aspect of 'justice' is referred to below.

3 There must be compatibility with a *sense of justice and of fairness; justice through sense of equality, that the jobs of all members of the firm are graded and assessed in the same way; fairness through the sense of equity, that differentials are appropriate to the value to the firm of the work done.*

If a method can be applied only to clusters, or to classes of jobs, if there are different methods for clerical, shop-floor and managerial staffs, then there can be no sense of justice. If the jobs of the clerk, the machinist and the works manager are all analysed and graded in the same way, if the jobs are assessed in the same way and *simultaneously*, then the sense of justice is enhanced, and with it the sense of team, of being colleagues, not 'others', 'them', or 'bosses'. A method should apply to as big a cross-section, horizontal and vertical, of the organisational structure as possible; the Time-span Method and the Castellion are the only existing methods which do this.

If a method gives a greater sense of equity it will be much more acceptable. The mere fact that apparently any method is 'better than none' is indicative, and undoubtedly Jaques is right about the existence of the sense of equity in a firm where jobs can be compared. For this reason job titles may be misleading and a method should be able to provide easily understood supportive titles that indicate differentials, either grades, or numbers of points, or ranks.

4 One of the advantages of leaving conditions and market factors out of the job content is that their removal *reduces the subjectivity* of a method. But, by that same token, it not only increases objectivity of what remains but it leaves these two factors, conditions and the labour market, especially the first, as matters for negotiation particularly at shop-floor level. In other words negotiations on these two factors should be regarded as marginal, additional to the main job evaluation method which should be as objective as possible. But it cannot be entirely objective as, for example, the Time-span Method is claimed to be.

Just as some methods require key jobs as anchors for their scaling and

9

weighting of factors so there must be some *objectively defined* key points or nodes on the scale or ranking of jobs. Between these nodes subjective judgments become possible and hence the possibility of discussions, argument and agreement.

5 The method must produce a guide line for change to a pay structure that is *not too far from the existing structure*. If the method ends by requiring drastic alterations then, however logical these may be, there will be resistance to such a change. Undoubtedly there are cases of gross inequities in some pay structures and the method must not only expose them but, by its very nature, show how they can be reduced, say by job structuring based on the method, or step-by-step alteration of the pay curve while retaining the logic of the method. It is difficult to alter a pay structure based on the Point Method without manipulating factor degrees and their weighting and so the logic.

6 A method must permit of assessments leading to a pay curve for which *the firm has the ability to pay*, it must not cost too much. In a way this is closely related to (4) above; the result must not be too far removed from the existing structure. (The Factor-comparison Method is the best of those described to ensure this.) The board of directors will not accept a result that is economically impossible or difficult to implement. Similarly, the board would be more likely to accept a method that:

(i) absorbs the cost of bringing up lower paid jobs to equity in the general cost of up-grading the pay curve, and that
(ii) provides a relatively easy method of calculating the general cost of adjusting the pay curve and so of the payroll.

7 A method should be *time-saving*. Most existing methods require an inordinate time in 'committee work' by reason of their subjectivity and the need to reach agreement. A directorate would prefer a method that reduces this 'waste'.

8 Because of advancing technology and rapid changes in the markets, job content alters frequently, and key jobs are hard to find. One example of this change is emergence of jobs on the shop floor and office with wide varieties of 'skill mix', skilled, semi-skilled, unskilled; and in the managerial quarters the appearance of new 'breeds of boffins' with obscure jargons and mystiques. This is one reason why there is a tendency to reduce the number of grades and, with this, the tendency to reduce the details of job specifications so as to allow internal mobility of all staff. By reducing the number of grades there are wider upper and lower limits of each grade of pay within which there can be change without altering the grade and so status. A method is more acceptable if it permits of quick reaction to such changes, *adjustability*. This is best achieved by reducing subjectivity as much as possible—objectively determined criteria are usually faster in acceptance.

9 A method should be such that it cannot be easily manipulated, and so *reduce leap-frogging*. Managers seek a method that gives them control of wage-drift. The non-quantitative methods and also, particularly, the Point Method lend themselves to 'adjustments'. It is not unknown for changes to be made to a points score to increase it and so the pay, in order to keep the job incumbent at his post or even in the firm. "In several instances it was said that managers either 'looked the other way' where production or other bonus fixing was concerned, or 'fixed job times in order to be able to pay workers the wage they believed was necessary to keep production figures up'. Such statements reveal two kinds of confusion: first the fact that jobs and rates had evolved separately and in such a way that any apparent rational relationship between the two things had been lost; second, the distinct purposes for which the different components in individual pay existed had been obscured. Deliberately or otherwise, the separate components in pay had been so manipulated that their real purpose became very different from their ostensible ones" [47, p. 12]. As times goes on the pay curve becomes irregular and whole-scale smoothing has to be made.

10 The factor of *working conditions cannot be objectively scaled*; and this is one which members on the shop floor regard as of considerable importance in comparing their jobs, and so pay, with those of office members and others working in better surroundings. More important is that working conditions can change; indeed, if, in the quantitative methods, this factor is given a heavy weighting of points, the employing managers will tend to improve the situation in order to reduce the pay. And if the conditions factor is built into the pay there will be difficulty in persuading acceptance of a reduction in the points assigned, which tend to remain as a permanent part, even though the conditions are bettered.

11 Similarly the *labour market, national and local, can alter*. There may be shortages or excess of particular kinds of labour, managerial as well as manual; and, secondly, members are affected in their attitudes to differentials by comparability, especially in the local market. Payment for market conditions, over and above the job evaluated pay (a 'contingency payment' as I prefer to call it) should also be kept separate and not built into the structure. Labour markets alter—an employee should not continue receiving contingency payments when the need for them disappears. For example, there has been of late a shortage of computer programmers who have been receiving pay well above that of members with greater skills and more important jobs. It will not be long before the supply of programmers will increase fairly rapidly and the contingency payment will decrease.

12 A method should, if possible, permit of *ease in the introduction of incentives*. It has already been pointed out that the Time-span Method relates time-span to earnings without regard for hours worked; and, therefore, since time-span does not alter, a man's time-span-determined pay cannot be altered even if he works longer hours. Again, an incentive is given for extra effort, so if a man's job is evaluated on the basis of, say, the NEMA factors of the Point Method, his extra effort is not due to an increase in the skill (measured as

years of apprenticeship) which he brings to the job, nor is there a change in conditions of work. Only the two factors effort and, perhaps, responsibility are changed. Hence the relation of points to payment must alter, incentives become a matter of negotiation on a new basis not the existing. Concurrently with this is the general movement away from piece-rated jobs to time-rated, yet the need for incentives for the latter.

Of all these items that affect acceptability probably the most effective are simplicity (1), participation (2), and sense of justice and fairness (3). In my experience there is *always* a question that is asked, "Will this mean that my pay will be reduced?", so to these three must be added the ability to pay (6) because the application of a method will always involve the raising of some pays—lowering of any will be resisted.

OPERATIONAL PRINCIPLES GOVERNING A JOB EVALUATION METHOD

"Empiricism is valuable and even essential up to a point. In a complex and changing field like that of wage determination it is all to the good that practitioners should be ready to feel their way, to experiment, and to discover and concentrate on what actually works. But to enter into a maze as complex as this without guidance of any basic principles at all is to reduce oneself rapidly to the state which David Riesman has labelled 'other direction' " [13, p. 107].

1 Frequently the exponents of this or that job evaluation method state that they are measuring *job content*. This is doubtful, and some clarification is necessary. Function, hence role, has no meaning (it does not exist) unless it is one of a structure of functions necessary to achieve the purpose of a group, however vague that purpose may be. There is no middle management function unless there are other management functions and functions to be managed, a team in battle for commercial survival. If a man performs no function of significance to a group he cannot be a member of that group; he would be ejected. A hobo is an 'outcast' because he performs no function of purposive significance.

If the word 'work' is taken to be synonymous with 'job', which it is so frequently in ordinary parlance, then *work* may be said to refer to what a man does when what he does has functional significance, his contribution to group activity. *Work* is what he produces and what he performs in producing. One might distinguish work from labour when the latter describes what a man does when what he does has no functional significance. (There is here something of the difference between the Latin 'opus' and 'labor'.) A man working fills a role. He and his role are identified and in this he becomes of meaning in society. So his work has meaning. He identifies himself with his role. "I am a turner. Turning is me". "I am a teacher. Teaching is me". "I am of meaning to others because I am a teacher, contributing the function teaching towards the survival of my fellows." This is what is implied when we talk of meaningfulness or meaning of work. A corollary is that, unless there is a structure of functions, work is not meaningful. Dostoievski said something to the effect that "Give my work the character of nothing and I am nothing".

If there is only labour, then purpose behind the labouring is not group purpose but individual. A hobo at my kitchen door chops wood. He labours for money, but does not work. If the local handyman chops wood he works, for it is a social function he is fulfilling; he is the local chopper of wood. The hobo can have no sense of contribution but the local handyman has. Moreover, because in his role (working) he plays a part, he *is* a part, therefore he *belongs*. To engender the sense of *belongingness* role, hence structure, is essential.

The more important a job, i.e. the greater contribution it makes in helping a firm survive and grow, the greater the *status* of the job, the greater the worth or value it has for the firm; and, therefore, at second hand the greater the status of the man fulfilling the function, holding the position. (As I propose to argue later the greater the worth of the function to the firm the greater the reward.) If a man fulfills his function by performing well, i.e. if the procedure he chooses to adopt is a bettering of the way to fulfil the function, he is accorded *prestige*; and this is accorded at first hand, not because of the worth of the job but because of the worth of the choice of procedure the man has made. *In job evaluation we are measuring the worth of the job and not the man; in performance appraisal we are measuring the worth of the man.*

The man says (or feels) "My job is important so I am important, I am doing something worthwhile; I do it well, so people respect me for it, I am somebody." "Such", says Bartlett [2], "is the secret of a thoroughly sound man and of a cohesive and powerful group". The man has expression of service (status) drive in work, and through that, satisfaction of his prestige drive—the two are compatible. He is a happy man [50, p. 96 *et seq.*]. A group of such men has team spirit and work as a team; it is cohesive and powerful. The sound man 'knows where he stands' in the meaningfulness of his work. It is a form of security, for the meaningfulness stems from the function as being part of a structure of functions and, filling the role in structure, the man belongs. Belongingness gives security.

If the national purpose is unclear, as it seems to be in the USA and UK at the time of writing, the meaning (in national terms) of a man's work is unclear as well, and hence his sense of security. This lack of clarity shows itself in several ways. Since security in the work sphere is reduced, a man will seek it in some other ways allied to work. He might, for instance, seek it in membership of a trade union, merely belonging, not necessarily active and so 'apathy of the rank and file' in union matters, unless some emergency threatens still more what sense of security is left to him. Failing in this direction in his search for security he may join 'organisations' outside his work, through conformity-seeking belongingness. Frustration of his service drive leads to aggression outwards, perhaps against employers and even his trade union (looking instead for security in his work-place groups); it is an irrational form of aggression since he feels it but does not understand it. Wildcat strikes are probably in part expressive of this aggression.

In the absence of a belief system and security, confusion of the national job-status system ensues. The demand for a national wages structure implies a need for a national work-status system, i.e. meaningfulness of work. In the absence of a national wages structure local structures are negotiated at factory level—belongingness is sought at the level of the firm where a local purpose can be found, and a local belief system regarding the status of occupations. This is the fundamental value of job evaluation in the firm, the expression of belongingness, meaningfulness, and status through the practice of justice and fairness.

2 *Job content* is what is evaluated, not the man and what he brings to the job, but what he does and what is the result. (To repeat, the man is evaluated in performance appraisal.) Given this principle the factors used in the various methods can be analysed in terms of their measure of job content.

The Ranking and Classification Methods do not give a measure of job content (the Institution of Office Management Method is explicitly based on the calibre of the person necessary for the job) they are all subjective guesses, intuition, feels, about relative importance or difficulty of jobs without definition of importance and difficulty.

The Quantitative Methods are more objective in that they rely on criteria which are related to job content but are not part of job content as defined above. Skill is 'required', effort is 'required', 'responsibility' is undertaken. (Conditions can be placed aside, as usually they are recognised as not part of the job content but of the environment of the job. They must be recognised, for working in poor conditions should be rewarded. Conditions are extraneous.) To take these three factors:

Skill is recognised as the major factor in the quantitative methods, alone it might give more than 90 per cent agreement with the results of application of all the factors. In the Guide-Chart Profile Method points for Know-how and Problem-solving, which are much the same thing, constitute two thirds of the total. But skill (education and experience) are what is brought to the job by the man. What is rewarded is the utilisation of that skill not the skill itself, or, what is of value is the product of the use of skills not the skills themselves. Both education and experience, as components of skill, can be ranked in terms of time. It is recognised, for instance, that a length of education of a particular kind may be necessary for a particular person to be able to read design drawings and decide what process and tools are necessary to make the product; and some months or years of experience may be necessary to train a person to develop the sensori-motor coordination required to use the processes and tools. These times are those believed necessary for the 'average' person, that peculiar and non-existent personage; and, with the advent of modern methods of education and training these periods of time can be shortened. Unfortunately there remain fairly fixed concepts of and stipulations about lengths of apprenticeships and the values attached to examination-passing and the like. What the 'degrees' of skill tell us is that jobs are relatively more difficult because they need relatively greater skills.

But difficulty in what? A turning job and a fitting job both 'require' five-year apprenticeships and, because of that, they are assigned the same degree of required skill. The end-products are different, what is common to them and is equated by the five-year degree of skill, is the kind of decision that is made. An invoice clerking job requires six months training, the senior invoice clerk's job may require a certificate of secretarial practice. The second job is more difficult because it involves making decisions of Band B, and the first of Band A, not because a difference in training is required.

Responsibility is usually expressed in terms of being 'responsible for' something or other, and degree points arbitrarily assigned. As Jaques long ago pointed out a night watchman is not responsible for all the materials inside the locked warehouses, he is responsible only for locking them up and keeping a look out to see that they are not opened or that the presence of suspicious characters is questioned. He is responsible for the doing, i.e. locking doors, etc. He makes decisions about locking doors (choosing his own procedure) and he is responsible for the results of these decisions, e.g. if he fulfills his function the doors are locked, if he does not the doors are not locked; and in the latter case if materials are stolen he is responsible only for failing to lock the doors, not for the loss of very valuable stores. His decision is of Band O. On the other hand the skilled turner is 'responsible' for a particular piece being turned. It does not matter how little the value of the piece may be, what he is responsible for is turning it. If he makes too big a cut he is responsible for that result, he is not responsible for the value. His decision is Band B, for which reason he is paid more than the night watchman. To 'measure' Responsibility properly is to find out what kind of decision is made for the result of which the job incumbent is responsible.

Effort is measured as 'required' physical and mental effort. Before analysing what this means it is worth returning to the factor 'conditions'. As I have already said this factor can only be subjectively evaluated and deserves negotiation separate from evaluation of job content. Conditions refer to the external environment within which work is done; conditions are not part of the work, not part of job content. A blast-furnace bricklayer has the job of furnace-lining; the job remains the same whether the furnace is cold or hot—but he surely ought to be rewarded *extra* when he works in the heat. The point is that the job remains the same.

Under 'physical effort' some methods list a sub-division by weights to be lifted, and points are accordingly assigned; for example lifting heavy moulds in a foundry. One of the tasks (or process or operation, as part of a task) is moving a mould. Whether the mould is heavy or light the task remains the same, the decision on moving the mould is the same. Undoubtedly heavier weights require the muscular strength the moulder brings to his job like the skill he brings to his job, but the decision, the non-overt element of work, is internal. A weight is part of the environment, of conditions, external to the job.

It could be argued that lifting heavy weights is more difficult than lifting light, and job evaluation measures relative difficulty. This may be so because more Defined decisions, Band O, may have to be made, but we cannot be certain of this—much depends on what movements have to be made, requiring the use of Work Study. (See the Allpat Method, Appendix 2, in *The Manual*). And the words are 'relative difficulty'. For a muscular person, moving a weight will be less difficult than for a slightly built person. Do we then pay for muscularity? Or do we pay for the recognised value of moving the weight? The value of the movement remains the same, so we pay for muscularity. In other words we are paying in terms of the labour market value of muscularity and not of the work—and this, too, (the labour market effect) must remain negotiable, and not be included in job content. And on this same point, since the decisions involved are confined to Band O, then 'weight lifting' cannot be a factor common to all jobs, it is of no comparative significance above Band A, and so should be eliminated from a method which attempts to be just.

The same kinds of argument may be used for other aspects of the factor 'physical effort'. Monotony is an example. One reason (but not the only one) why unskilled jobs on a continuous production line with constant repetition of the same movements are paid so highly is that people would not remain in these jobs because of the monotony and the constant pace of the machine. The market for people prepared to do this work varies, but the work, the job content does not. This unskilled work can be compared with other unskilled, or contrasted with semi-skilled or skilled, only in terms of job content, not in terms of the labour market.

On the other hand the factor 'pressure of work' *may* be a part of job content. If 'pressure' means relatively greater frequency in having to make decisions, or in being frequently involved in some aspect of the decision-making process, then number of decisions of a particular kind per unit time is a quantification of content which can be compared with other similar quantifications. The argument is simple and logical. Assuming one product requires x number of decisions, then, if more than one product is completed in the same time, there will be $x + nx$ decisions, i.e. the job content has been increased. The skill involved has not increased, the environment has not altered, physical effort has not altered, mental effort has but defined in terms of job content, not in terms of 'close attention', 'visual concentration' and such subjective phrases.

I return to the crude analogy I have already used in commenting upon the quantitative methods, where I suggest that summation of points for weighted factors and degree factors is like adding numbers of different kinds of fruit, and using only the number sum as a basis of comparison. The irrationality of the procedure is apparent but one could ask the question, as I suggested, is there one common denominator for them all? (Such as calories or vitamins for the fruit.) There is, and this emerges in the three Methods which I have described in greater detail, the Castellion, the Time-span and the Guide-chart Profile. All have one thing in common, and converge on that one thing, especially the last Method; they are concerned with decision-making as the basic criterion of job comparability. The Time-span Method is essentially a one-factor method, that factor being a time-span distinction of kinds of decision. The factor Decision-making in the Castellion Method itself could give the same result in up to 97 per cent of job comparisons as could the use of all the others. The Guide-chart Profile is a method wholly concerned with Problem-solving, the decisions made, Accountability measured as depending on results to be expected from these decisions, and

Know-how the distinction of decisions made in terms of kinds of thinking capacities required.

The inevitable conclusion is that if we devise a method that concentrates on distinguishing jobs by the single factor kinds of decision (as people seem to do naturally anyway—Chapter 3) then we shall have the advantages of these other methods and not their disadvantages and anomalies. Moreover, by divorcing the external environment, conditions and labour market, from job content, the method will be much less subjective and, moreover, make it more acceptable to those whose work and evaluation of it is affected by such environmental factors.

The basis of such a method must, therefore, depend upon *Work Analysis* which I define as the analysis of work in terms of the kinds and quantity of the decisions made. Defining 'kind' precisely, and 'quantifying', the objectivity of work analysis is more likely to be greater than that for the job analysis and grading used in any existing methods of job evaluation. Given this definition of Work Analysis some further conclusions are possible.

3 Since Training and Development of members of a firm are for the express purpose of helping them to carry out their work better, then Work Analysis and grading must be the basis upon which the firm's Training and Education programme is organised. Logically there can be neither of these without a knowledge of what members are being trained and educated for, and that is for their work. Even though the training may be in specialised subjects the ultimate aim is better decision-making in these specialised subjects, hence the training in any subject whatever must be organised in terms of kinds of decision-making in that subject.

4 *Performance appraisal* (merit rating). Performance is what the incumbent of a job does, chooses to do in fulfilling his function, and this is appraised against a standard of production per unit time, or against a standard of quality of production. It cannot be based on acquisition of skills (passing examinations or attending courses), it is impossible to rate performance on time span (which 'measures' the decision-making of the job and not what a particular incumbent does), it is not possible to compare in justice and fairness, performance on, say, assembly, with maintenance, with invoicing, with selling, with researching, etcetera, unless the common denominator for all kinds of work, decision-making, is used. It follows that Work Analysis is the basis of appraisal.

5 *Promotion* is movement across ranks (Jaques) or across Decision Bands or Grades. Since promotion normally is based or should be based on performance appraisal, (sometimes it is based on nepotism or bureaucratic politicking), and since appraisal must be based on Work Analysis, it follows that promotion must be based on Work Analysis too, but not only because of appraisal itself, but because Work Analysis establishes differences of Band or Grade of jobs. Performance reward that is not promotion is usually in the form of increment in pay within the range of pay of a Grade or Band.

6 *Incentives* are promised rewards for the bettering of some aspects of work, production, quality, consistency, time-keeping and the like. Rewards must be fair and just (if we assume that better human and industrial relations are valued as desirable); therefore incentives must be based upon Work Analysis as providing criteria for fairness and justice in work.

7 Since the firm's structural organisation is 'division of labour', a relating of positions (roles, jobs, whatever they may be called) it follows that organisation must, logically speaking, stem from knowledge of work to be done and being done—one cannot organise to the optimum unless what is being organised is known. Therefore Work Analysis and grading should provide the basis for all aspects of *organisational structure*. It would be non-logical to have one basis for the evaluation of worth of jobs, their status, and another for organisation which ends in the system of relations (structure and position) from which the concept of status derives.

THEORETICAL PRINCIPLES

Some theoretical principles governing decision-making have been summarised in Chapters 2 to 4. Since job evaluation is mainly concerned with reward and, in particular, with differential reward in a firm, a theory to explain why there are differentials in the first place, and why these differentials appear to form a pay structure of the same gross form in every enterprise, is needed. In the following chapter I summarise the abortive attempts of the economists to produce a theoretical explanation; and the behavioural scientists have done little better, although Jaques has put forward an hypothesis which has not yet been tested. (I shall refer to this hypothesis in detail later.)

A failing common to all the described methods of job evaluation is the lack of theory at the job assessment stage. If the y-axis be taken to represent pay and the x-axis the numbers of points or grades, there is no logical reason for believing that the intervals between successive numerals along the x-axis are equal. Secondly, some believe that the pay curve is linear, that there is a linear relationship between pay and points; others, however, believe the relationship is geometric, the curve steepens progressively, and is log-normal at that. These are beliefs, neither theories nor logical principles that have been proved.

In the absence of theory a great number of forces have been assumed as being determinative of differentials. Belcher [3, p. 75] lists over 80 of them. Here it seems appropriate to suggest that Occam's razor could well be applied, that we should seek for the simplest theoretical explanation that can cover the maximum number of situations. (To put it in managerial jargon we should apply the 80:20 principle.)

Theory can be explanatory, that is *a posteriori*, explaining given data; but if it is truly theoretical it should have predictive, *a priori* value. As Belcher puts it [3, p. 34] "It may be useful to remind the reader that theories are tentative explanations of behaviour. They must often cut through the underbrush and seek out salient causal relationships. This may involve some abstraction from the real world as observed in everyday life. Assumptions are necessary in stating any generalised rule of behaviour. The relevant question about assumptions of a theory is not whether they are descriptively realistic but whether they are sufficiently good approximations for purposes of understanding." But we must go further than that. The crux of the matter says Robinson [61, p. 25] is this, "If the explanation is a good one does it lead to any guide or set out guide lines as to how companies, employers of labour, can improve industrial relations and increase their manpower utilisation". This is pragmatism allied to theory and the purpose of the theoretical arguments that follow is that they should be thus helpful to all employees, managers and men alike—they are all workers!

Part 3   THEORY AND PROOF

It is a matter of observation that, in any human society, people are rewarded differently for different work; and in our modern industrial society we believe that bigger pay is given for more important or more difficult work without defining what these mean, and certainly never questioning why there should be such differential payments. The economists have long thought to explain these payments in terms of the classical supply–demand theory; and, finding this was not good enough, came to believe the labour of a man is bought only when an employer believes the extra production will yield profit—the marginal productivity theory. But this theory requires a 'perfect' system which does not exist. So the theory was adjusted—a man will sell his labour if the 'net advantages' are on the positive side, meaning that there are intangibles, which cannot be expressed in money, which keep a man in a job or motivate him to seek a job. Men are willing to accept less money for the same job if other advantages are there. Which tells us nothing. One economist believes there is a natural distribution of capacities, that jobs are structured because of these capacities, and they are paid accordingly. The capacities are not defined. There is no satisfactory economic theory to fit the facts.

Importance and/or difficulty are associated in people's minds with decision-making, the 'higher' the kind of decision the greater the reward. This differential importance is subconsciously recognised as being related to survival and growth, for these higher decisions are of more value for survival. Each grade of decision is related to that below by the relation 'responsibility'; and, assuming that this relation constitutes one 'unit', there is a regular (geometric) accumulation of units from grade to grade 'upwards' in the hierarchy. If one unit of money is the reward for each 'unit of responsibility' the relation of pay to Grade of decision, the pay curve, becomes exponential, i.e. pay shows a constant percentage increase from Grade to Grade.

Since the percentage will depend on such factors as size of payroll and policy for its distribution, the slope of the curve will vary for each firm; and, since each pay in the existing pay structure, from top to bottom of the hierarchy, is guessed, negotiated or job evaluated, the pay curve will only approximate to the theoretical. It does, and the significance of the correlation is remarkably high. It appears that people deciding about pay have a subconscious 'feeling' about what constitutes 'fair pay' (as Professor Jaques has already found). The explanatory content of the theory is proved. Since the pay curve is exponential it becomes possible by simple mathematical method to predict the pay of any Grade given the slope of the curve and any one pay accepted as fair. Dr T. M. Husband has used the theory to predict pay of middle and senior managers, given the data of sales turnover, industry and region in the UK, and also finds the predictive value of the theory is high.

Chapter twelve   **Differential rewards**

Differential rewards for manual employees are known to have existed in Ancient Greece [45]. An unskilled labourer was paid 1½ drachma per day, a sawyer of wood (which we may take to be the equivalent of a semi-skilled person) was paid 2 per day and skilled men, such as carpenters and brick-layers, 2½. The ratios 1:1·3:1·25 and unskilled to skilled, 1:1·7, are not far removed from the ratios of unskilled to skilled in mediaeval and later times

TABLE 12.1   *Ratios of unskilled to skilled rewards*

	Unskilled	Skilled	Ratio
4th Century BC	Dr. 1·5 p.d.	Dr. 2·5 p.d.	1:1·7
13th Century AD	£ 2·5 p.a.	£ 5·0 p.a.	1:2
16th Century AD	Sh. 2·0 p.d.	Sh. 4·0 p.d.	1:2
17th Century AD	£ 10·4 p.a.	£ 15·6 p.a.	1:1·5
18th Century AD	Sh. 5·75 p.d.	Sh. 13·0 p.d.	1:2·2

[43, 62]. Since that time the ratio has fallen in the USA from 1:2 to about 1:1·5 and in the UK to just under that [30].

Adam Smith was the first economist, naturally, to try to explain occupational differentials, and his general proposition has been accepted by economists ever since, although most economists writing on this subject seem to have forgotten that Adam Smith did mention that a wage is given for hardship, difficulty in learning a job, stability of employment, responsibility of the job and the chance for success or failure in the work.

The general proposition is that differential occupational wages depend on the demand–supply system. This is clearly stated by Hicks in his book *The theory of wages* where he begins:

"The theory of determination of wages in a free market is simply a special case of the general theory of value. Wages are the price of labour, and thus, in the absence of control, they are determined, like all prices, by supply and demand".

The demand for labour will, of course, depend upon the demand for the firm's product and upon the productivity of the labour. So an employer, the economists believe, will calculate how much productivity he will get from those he proposes to employ and place this against the cost of employing them, that is, their wages. In other words, if the employer thinks he will get more than the wage he offers to the prospective employee, it will be worthwhile to take him on. This is a very simplified statement of the *Marginal Productivity Theory* whose detailed ramifications need not be explored here.

First, this theory, put forward by Clark [9], assumes perfect markets, perfect information, perfect mobility of labour, constant population and similar factors, including labour reduced to units of unskilled labour, that is, the system of perfect competition—and this static society does not exist. Secondly, it assumes that the employer can estimate the 'marginal productivity' of an additional man. In actual practice he does not and cannot unless he has a most complicated and expensive system of costing and a survey of the local labour market, for 'going wages'. What he does do is hire people if he thinks it worthwhile to do so and even then the theory assumes that the employer is concerned only with maximising profits. He is not. He is concerned with the good name of his business, the good of his employees, the status of his firm, and the like. Nor are his business decisions predicated on present prices, they are estimates of the future. Thirdly, the theory is based on a concept of homogeneous units of labour and they do not exist—there are different occupations and different levels of skill. (The marginal productivity theory would require a demand curve for each and every one to produce a wage structure.) And there is no true mobility of labour; men do not readily move from job to job because, for three examples, their existing skills may not be adequate elsewhere and they have to learn new ones, some cannot learn, and they cannot move on short notice. Nor do they know for sure where there is another firm paying more for their skills—that information is scanty and rumour-laden. Besides, there is evidence [70] that money is low on the list of motives for mobility, and that it is less important as a motive for moving into higher paid jobs than it is for getting out of low paid jobs.

The supply of labour is also an obscure concept because it cannot be calculated just in numbers; it must involve other factors which are non-quantifiable, the emotional factors, social, sociological, psychological, ethical and geographical. A person surely takes into consideration more than money when deciding to take on or leave a job. This produced a problem for the economists who solved it in a typically facile way without giving up their basic proposition. This is the concept of *net advantages* most succinctly put by Marshall.

"Every occupation involves other disadvantages besides the fatigue of the work required in it, and every occupation offers other advantages besides the receipt of money wages. The true reward which an occupation offers to labour has to be calculated by deducting the money value of all its disadvantages from that of all its advantages; and we may describe this true reward as the net advantages of the occupation."

Some economists followed this up, Machlup in particular [39] whom Chamberlain and Kuhn [8, pp. 319–320] explain as saying "The marginal product is not an objective value but is something which exists only in the employer's mind. The marginal value product of any factor is whatever the businessman thinks it is. There is no possibility of an error of judgment for theoretical purposes then. One cannot say that a businessman has incorrectly estimated the marginal product because, whatever he believes the marginal product to be *is* the marginal product, for purposes of explaining his behaviour. In deciding whether to hire or fire, to substitute capital for labour, or to give a wage increase or make a wage cut, the businessman will be concerned with the given wage relative to what he thinks the marginal product is. To a particular employer, the marginal product may include not only the actual net addition to revenue resulting from the employment of an extra unit of labour but also those additions he subjectively values. To the marginal value product he may add such things as the effect of the wage rate on the workers' morale, the impact of a wage increase on a union organising drive, and consumer reaction to his labour policy. The appraisal of marginal product thus varies from employer to employer; only if one can reduce the subjective appraisals to common pecuniary values is a comparison possible between the marginal product in one line of employment and that in another". "Machlup's statement (of the Marginal Productivity Theory) boils down to the proposition that any individual businessman will pay a wage rate and hire any given number of men at a rate only if he *believes* that the last man hired, like those who precede him, will add something to the total revenue".

This does not help a bit. One cannot "make any statements stemming from a theoretical basis about the actual behaviour of groups of individuals in specific circumstances or the way in which they will react to changes in circumstances. This theoretical purity is of relatively little assistance to those attempting to operate in a real labour market", says an economist [61, pp. 262–3]. The theory cannot be validated because so many of these disadvantages/advantages cannot have a money value put upon them. The theory merely says "it's not just money that matters, it's whether I like the job or not". And it does not hold unless there is freedom to move and there is choice of jobs, but only within his own occupational group and not in other non-competing groups. So it could be postulated on this theory that unskilled sewermen are likely to be getting higher wages than unskilled sweepers, but not as high as unskilled automobile workers or as high as skilled tradesmen, which are non-competing groups. But it does not explain why there are non-competing groups such as managerial, skilled and unskilled, far less why they should be paid differently.

"A once respected theory is thus covered with the shame that it can no longer be proved descriptively valid, nor is it susceptible even to meaningful application as a norm", said Chamberlain and Kuhn [8, p. 320]. In fact it was not a theory ever; it was, at most, a weak, armchair hypothesis.

There are a great number of factors such as geographical, sexual, educational, and so on, which do not permit of a uniform labour supply. The result is a diversification of labour markets with different characteristics [3, p. 53].

Some sociologists have stepped in here and refer to such different markets as the bureaucratic labour market (wages are proportionate to status, not status to wages), the industrial labour market (mainly of semi-skilled labour in demand by employers with the 'going rate' of wage settled by collective bargaining), and the craft labour market (identification with the craft and not with the employer—in prosperity the highest pay consistent with full employment, in depression assurance of the subsistence of all active craftsmen), and the professional market (discouragement of standard rates, reliance on what the market will bear), etc. But this does not explain why the ratios of unskilled to semi-skilled to skilled to manager remain much the same throughout industry and commerce, and why the basic or standard pay for these dissimilar job types always increases in that order and usually by a constant ratio.

Undeterred, the economists have made more attempts to establish the applicability of their belief in the fundamental assumption that the labour market governs differentials. Given the inescapable evidence of a wage structure in every firm with a complexity of wage/salary rates, and also a wide variation in inter-firm structures—Kerr [28, p. 176] suggested the variation could be as much as 25 per cent from top to bottom—Dunlop [11] put forward two concepts on which to build a new approach.

He defined a *job cluster* (a familiar term in Job Evaluation) as a stable group of job classifications—types of job—linked by technology, production process and social custom. Each cluster is likely to have changes in pay occur uniformly in the same direction, retaining their internal differentials.

For example, a group of employees in a machine-shop usually form a job cluster as over and against a job cluster in the drawing office, or a job cluster of clerical workers. He believes that in each cluster there are *key jobs*, which are well-defined, do not change much, and whose pay is recognised as fair. These are the rates which employers (and unions where involved) apparently have in mind when establishing the pay structure; and it is those jobs that are affected by the external forces of the labour market, i.e. in terms of comparability, and through them the rest of the jobs in the cluster, and finally through other clusters.

This belief has its basis in the methods of job evaluation described in the preceding chapters here. In the practice of job evaluation such key jobs are chosen as 'anchors' mainly because they are well-known to the job evaluators, *and* are believed to be paid fairly as of the time of evaluation—and so they are *not* changed by the job evaluation procedure, the others are; and, the series having been changed, the cluster alters as a whole to market changes, not first by reaction of key jobs. Where job evaluation methods are not employed, the key jobs are unknown; but what *are* known are the job grades of unskilled to skilled through managerial.

Dunlop's second concept is the *wage contour*. This is, in effect, the job cluster idea writ large. It is defined as a stable group of firms which are engaged in producing the same goods, drawing their labour from the same local labour market and usually allied in some way such as in an employers' association. The firms constituting a wage contour have, naturally, similar occupations and job clusters and are situated in geographical proximity.

There are key firms (like key jobs) which 'set the tone', so to speak, for changes in wage rates. In other words, if one of the key employers changes a rate for a key job (or occupation) the other employers follow, the effect of the change being transmitted from firm to firm through the key jobs. In other words the local labour market has a 'going rate' for different occupations and jobs.

Unfortunately for these concepts the facts are (and these will be elaborated upon below) that the same kind of work in a wage contour, that is, among locally related firms in the same product markets, may have a wide range of pay. The explanations usually given by the economists are lack of accurate information among the labour force about 'going rates' of pay (supported by a tendency among firms to keep their own rates secret from the others, especially in a wage contour perhaps because of competition), widely divergent forms of wage payment (meaning incentive schemes, piece rates, time rates, etc.), restricted mobility and entry of labour (due to tied housing or disinclination to move), and strong trade union activity.

The last-mentioned factor has been seized upon, mainly by Hicks [17] who has suggested a *bargaining theory* to account for differentials, the essence of this theory being that the upper and lower limits of wages are fixed by bargaining power and the final pay is determined by the urgency of the employer's need for labour in production and the urgency of the employee's need to earn wages. This theory has no predictive value [3, p. 49]—there are too many subjective factors involved—and it still does not explain the near constant differential of the pay grades which vary from firm to firm even in the same local labour market in the same kind of industry [34, p. 2].

Some sociologists have suggested that there is an internal bargaining or kind of bargaining situation. Members of the firm become associated in work groups which gain status by reason of their success in work activity or in social activity, and this is reflected in a demand for recognition of greater status by increased pay. This status may be interpreted in terms of, say, departmental importance and the members from top to bottom ranked higher than apparently correspondingly important members in other departments. For example, in the UK the unskilled to skilled members of one occupational, departmental group like lithographers in the printing industry, may be paid more than similar unskilled to skilled members of a technician group. *Or,* more commonly, a horizontally coherent group such as all supervisors, because of their coherence obtain a greater reward than the skilled and semi-skilled people they supervise. This hypothesis has neither been substantiated nor does it explain the facts.

Wootton [74] also moved into the sociological field and suggested that the distribution of grade differentials is due to the statistical differentiation of the required skills throughout the population. Salaries are paid to those who can wield power, and wages are paid to the manual workers, a reflection of the social structure that arises from a stratification because of genetically or socially determined individual differences. The middle class are managers because they are made that way (they are not middle class as a result of becoming managers), a survival of 19th Century social Darwinism. It still does not explain the variation in scales of pay from firm to firm although it may explain the Pareto distribution of income. It has not been substantiated.

Closely allied to the Wootton thesis is the hypothesis submitted by Jaques [23]. He believes that there is a 'normal' distribution throughout the population of a capacity for what he calls 'discriminating expenditure', utilisation of money to the optimum advantage. The capacity is greatest among the few and least among the great number, the distribution being log-normal. Increased capacity is required the higher in the hierarchy of jobs in a firm, an hierarchy determined by the length of time (time-span) that elapses before the result of a man's work is scrutinised by his superior. Since the population distribution of this capacity is log-normal the hierarchy will reflect this, hence the 'pyramid of organisation' in firms. The reward for the job is dependent upon this distribution. This hypothesis is examined in more detail in the next chapter since it is the only one which gives an explanation of the differential distribution of pay grades in a firm. Unfortunately it leads to the thesis that all jobs of the same time-span must be rewarded the same whatever the firm or product or geographical location, and that it matters not how much effort a man puts into a job in terms of hours worked. This is difficult to comprehend.

Few economists have actually removed themselves from their desks piled high with government statistics that cover occupations (designated by doubtful titles) and have gone into factories and offices to discover the reality of wage structures. The late Professor D. J. Robertson was one of the first in the UK [59] and I shall later be referring in more detail to his work, with which I am glad to have been associated. A few have followed suit and lately some data have been published by three economists [60, 34] who have made more intensive and excellent studies, chiefly, it seems to me, in order to validate the economic theory of wages. Like all the others they looked only at wages and not at salaries at the same time, apparently regarding the managerial group as non-competing. This work [60] is most important for the purposes of the study of job evaluation because it puts into proper perspective the effect of the labour market in determining differential reward. I shall begin by quoting from the section *Internal wage structures* by D. I. Mackay [40].

Mackay states [p. 128] "The function of a plant wage structure is to reflect the balance, and changes in it, of the economic forces of demand and supply of labour. Wage differentials demand longer training or peculiar skills and aptitudes and, if the plant wants the correct 'mix' of labour to operate efficiently, theory suggests that such occupational groups must be offered higher earnings than others. So we would expect skilled manual workers to have higher average earnings than the unskilled." He quotes others who have pointed out that the notions of "equity and justice, of equitable comparisons, provide the yardstick by which . . . the fairness of wage increases are judged", and these notions derive from the existing order of payments. Hence, if one group gets an increase "other groups will attempt to re-establish the original relativities", so the wage structure moves bodily upwards through time. These social pressures to maintain "fair relativities" may be particularly intense within the plant. "If this is so, *the wage structure may be inflexible not being particularly sensitive to changes in the demand and supply for different types of labour* [p. 130]. (My italics.)

He shows, as mentioned in the Introduction here, that primary wage drift occurs when pieceworkers' earnings increase, and secondary wage drift follows attempts to restore customary relativities. He then quotes Marquand [42, p. 17] as saying that "drift is largely determined by institutional factors which are not reflected systematically in any of the aggregate series used as independent variables. Even the level of demand for labour, to which a central role in determining drift is frequently ascribed, has no systematic influence at all upon the behaviour of drift at the aggregate level, although there is a weak relationship between drift and changes in the level of demand for labour."

There is doubt as to what produces wage drift whether technological change or productivity increases. What concerns us here is that, if pieceworkers' earnings rise, "to maintain customary relativities, larger national increases are negotiated for timeworkers" [40, p. 144]. But, says Mackay, "national agreements providing larger increases for timeworkers would be inappropriate to compensate for wage drift in pieceworkers' earnings in the plant . . . it is with pieceworkers' in their own plants that timeworkers make comparisons", and the lieu bonus often given "is determined by reference to piecework earnings in the whole plant". Sometimes the adjustment to retain relativities is done by adding "merit payments" which "should show substantial variations between individuals with the same occupation for *in theory* there should be a reward for additional responsibility, special skills or other attributes not adequately reflected in alternative methods of wage payment" [40, p. 146]. The italicisation is mine because the theory cannot refer to the economic theory. It is a recognition that a differential payment may be dependent on other than the relation of labour supply and demand.

After examining wage structures in terms of standard weekly earnings in 'tight' labour markets (high demand, small supply) and 'loose' markets (low demand, big supply), Mackay [40] comes to some general conclusions:

1 "It is not possible to explain the wage structure existing at a given time unless the historical process by which one form of wage payment was added to another to retain workers, to maintain relativities or to satisfy other requirements is remembered". "The overriding impression is that the wage structure develops through a series of *ad hoc* decisions in which one expedient is piled on top of another to raise the earnings of time workers" [p. 149].

2 "This does not indicate that economic forces are unimportant but the result of the system of wage determination is a wage structure which does not always reflect what would arise by the purely economic forces of supply and demand" [p. 149]. "Changes in intra-plant differentials are not wholly, or even mainly, explicable in terms of local labour market conditions. At the very least, changes in intra-plant differentials are not acutely sensitive to ruling employment conditions" [p. 161].

3 "It is not clear that employment conditions have a major impact on the evolution of intra-plant earnings' structure", and "the failure of the internal wage structure to respond to external labour market conditions may, in part, reflect the *strength of equitable comparisons within the plant*" [p. 163]. (My italics.)

4 "There are as many intra-plant earnings structures as plants" [p. 156], and other writers in the same book record 'enormous' spreads of average hourly earnings for the same job. "There is very little uniformity between the standard hourly earnings of members of the same occupation in different engineering plants in the same locality" [p. 263].

5 "There is no 'accepted' relationship between the earnings of different groups which the employee carries with him as he moves from plant to plant" [p. 156]. In other words he does not compare the standard rates of pay for the same jobs in different firms (inter-firm comparability), he compares the rate for his job in any one firm with the other rates in that same firm (intra-firm comparability). That is, he looks at the relativities at his place of work. (Admittedly men are attracted to jobs where it is possible to make big earnings, should they desire to do so, through overtime and incentive/piece rate bonuses, but their attitude to differentials is based on the relativities of standard pay.)

6 Mackay and his colleagues find that if a group of workers in a plant gets a rise low in relation to that in other plants all the other members of that plant get a relatively low increase, and vice versa. There is a scale of high-paying, low-paying firms and increases in pay within a local labour market tend to leave this scale the same.

7 In some cases larger increases in pay are matched by larger increases in numbers employed, but the increases may be lower in other firms with similar increases in numbers—which hardly fits the economists' theories.

8 Some firms, it was discovered, may increase wages at the same time as they are reducing the number employed.

9 "Economic forces are not necessarily irrelevant in the process of wage settlement but nor are they necessarily of primary importance". "The economist's model is, therefore, not adequate by itself to explain the processes of wage determination within the plant" [p. 164]. This is the finding of Mackay's colleagues [40]. Robinson says [p. 273] that claims for increases based on inter-firm comparability "do not in fact rely on economic arguments, based on the working of economic forces through a labour market, but on some *general appeal to equity or fairness* expressed in terms of money wages, with, perhaps, some notion of *ability to pay* lying underneath the claim. They are therefore essentially institutionally-based wage claims, not the result of economic factors". (My italics, referring to propositions in Chapter 11). "These institutional pressures may come from a number of sources" [p. 269], different union attitudes, different personalities acting in bargaining, informal work group pressures, changes in technology, changes in policy, and so on, and so on (see Belcher's list [3, p. 75]).

"One of the problems is that traditional economic theory of labour market behaviour is a sophisticated conceptual superstructure which is built on, and needs a number of assumptions about, rational behaviour and the free working of a market within which individuals are able to exercise a degree of choice. It also contains certain elements which are indeterminate and unquantifiable. Taken as a whole it may be regarded as a beautifully balanced and comprehensive set of interrelated concepts which provide a complete framework for the understanding of how individual workers choose their occupations and places of employment. The finely tuned and balanced part of the theory fit together because it is assumed that the whole theory works, that is, it explains what will happen given the assumptions underlying it. However, from the viewpoint of someone actively involved in determining wage levels and wage structures in the context of a real labour market in which trade unions and informed workgroups exist and operate, it may prove to be not so much a comprehensive explanation as a tautological trap which has little or no operative value". So writes an economist [40, p. 262] with a first-hand knowledge of a real labour market. The theories of the economists on the origin and form of plant wage structures do not hold; it is no wonder that job evaluation has been, for many years, the field of the occupational psychologist.

Nevertheless some economists have tried to explain, on other than the traditional theory, the existence of differentials among the managerial groups, the 'salary structure', which regularly appears to show exponential increases between 'grades' in the hierarchy of the management organisation. There are two theses, by Lydall and by Simon. Lydall [36] starts with the observation of the 'pyramid of organisation', and 'grades' between the bottom and the top. He assumes "that there will be a fixed ratio between the number of supervisors in each grade and the number of persons supervised by them in the grade immediately below", a constant span of control (n). He makes no attempt to differentiate grades and numbers of grades. He then assumes that "the income of a supervisor of any grade is directly related to the aggregate income of the persons whom he immediately supervises. The income paid to a manager depends on the extent of his responsibility; and this can be reasonably measured by the aggregate income of the people whom he directly controls". This 'salary span of control constant' (p) is thus

$$p = \frac{\text{Salary of supervisor}}{\text{Sum of salaries of all those immediately supervised}} = \text{a constant}$$

Since the structure is 'pyramidal' there will be a geometric relation (in numbers) between grades so, if the number of persons in each grade is plotted on a logarithmic scale along one axis, and the income for each grade along the logarithmic scale of the other axis, the result will be a straight-line, and the slope will be given by $\log n/\log np$.

This thesis need not be pursued further because the assumptions are not valid. For one thing a constant span of control does not exist in reality. Thorelli [68, p. 275] writes "spans (of control) will tend to vary not only between executives on the same level but also from one level to the next. Often the number of levels will also differ from one part of an organisation to another." A salary is not dependent upon the 'empire' of a manager, (although some actually believe this to be the case) for one need but point to the specialised jobs where the most senior man, paid a high salary, may have very few staff compared to his colleagues on the production line. Lydall actually admits [36, p. 111] that he has "no empirical evidence for this but it seems to (him) a plausible assumption", that a man's income, which corresponds to his responsibility (not defined) can be measured by the aggregate income of the people supervised. He assumes that titles are indicative of 'grades', but these are obscure, and he does not indicate how he gets his figures or how many grades he finds. In practice it seems he recognises only four, junior managers, middle, senior and top. In any case his equation does not fit the facts as my colleague, Dr Husband has shown [20].

Simon [65] also begins with the observation of the pyramidal structure, and, "each executive has a certain number (n) of subordinates at the level immediately below him, and this number varies within only moderate limits in a given company, and even among a number of companies". He, too, assumes a 'constant salary differential' (p) between grades, without ever defining grades and, again without enquiring into the validity of titles, concludes that this constant "undoubtedly varies from situation to situation, but one can find figures quoted in the range of 1·25 to 2". From this he can calculate the pay (P) of the top manager as

$$P = kN^a$$

where k is a constant, N the number of executives in the firm (including junior managers) and hence size of firm, and $a = \log p/\log n = $ constant.

This apparently corroborates an investigation by Roberts [58] who finds that the pay of the top executive is "related to size of company and to virtually no other variables (in particular, not to profit) after the effect of size has been partialed out", size of company being measured by sales turnover. "It is harder to run a big corporation than a small one." These assumptions of Simon suffer from the same faults as Lydall's and Husband [20] has also shown that the hypothesis does not fit the facts.

Lydall came to the conclusion that his relation between numbers and income was reflected in the total income distribution of the country as expressed in the Pareto 'distribution', that, "in any large organised society there is a definite relation between the income and the number of people having this income" [49]. In other words if the salary distribution of all the firms in a country were totalled the result would be that of Pareto; who found slopes to his curves to vary between 1·24 and 1·89. Lydall finds the Pareto 'law' has its limitations since it applies to only about 20 per cent of all incomes and also to total income of households, but others have thought that this empirical finding of Pareto (it is not a theory or law) should be applied in reverse, to the pay structure of a firm.

The first to do so was K. Adams [1] who introduced the term 'Emolumetrics' for the subject of study of pay. He demonstrated the anomalies of different slopes for different major occupations, teaching and the like, and carried this down into the firm.

Another proponent of Pareto's 'law' is Pearson [56] who, quoting Pareto-type figures from various countries, argued that the salary structure of a company should look the same. "The first job of a salary administrator is to check that the line showing the relationship between numbers and salaries is reasonably straight. If there are deviations the reason should be investigated." To jump from loose nation-wide empiricisms to theoretical, detailed pay structure of a firm is hardly good logic. In any case it still does not explain why the differentials in salary structures are as they are.

Chapter thirteen   **A theory of reward**

The word 'evaluation' according to the Oxford Dictionary, means judgment of value or worth, these two being synonymous, 'value' from the French and 'worth' from Old English. Worth is also synonymous with 'price', that is, worth expressed in money terms. Since the exercise of job evaluation is to arrive at pay (expressed as money) it follows that job evaluation refers in the end to relative money values, the worth of a job; and exercises preceding the establishment of money values, or pay, are essentially job grading (or ranking) where grades express differences that are to be reflected in pay differentials.

First, it is necessary to define what is meant in this book by the word 'pay'. It has already been stated that the word covers what is now distinguished as salaries and wages. It is nearly synonymous with the term 'standard rate' or 'basic rate' which generally implies a scaling or grading of some kind. On the other hand pay must not be confused with 'earnings' or 'take-home pay' which may include money that has no basis in a scaling or grading of jobs.

The wage rate, or *basic pay* is that pay awarded to a member of a firm for work done in a particular occupation, or in a particular grade within an occupation, over a given period of time. The time may be specified as hours per week, or per month, or per annum. There are additional payments such as

Incentives, or payment-by-results,
Merit rates or bonuses,
Overtime,
Rates for conditions of work, and
Fringe benefits.

The basic pay and such additions constitute *earnings*. We are concerned here with the basic pay.

A characteristic of basic pay is its certainty, or near certainty constituting income security. The additional payments can vary. Incentive payments may change because of fluctuations in work flow, merit bonuses can alter as a result of changes in the work organisation or in the feelings of managers, overtime may not always be available because of variations in customer demand, conditions of work change, and fringe benefits are usually at the whim of the directorate, or conditioned by the supply of labour.

Incentives, bonuses, overtime and conditions are extra to the pay for the work itself, fringe benefits are generally inducements to attract and hold labour, but the basic pay is the reward for the work done over the standard period. In the past, basic pay, as negotiated nationally or even locally, tended to be minimal for the needs of men on the shop floor, and a 'living wage' (earnings) was obtained mainly by incentive schemes and overtime. The 'extra' ranged from a third to as much as two thirds of earnings. The fluctuations in earnings, the cost of recording and calculating extras, and the attendant problems of industrial relations has led to the concept of *measured day work*, a standardised unit of work for which the payment is steady. It is sometimes referred to as a time rate.

This 'consolidation' of bonuses and low basic pay produces a higher basic pay for an increased level (or standard unit) of work, but still permits of incentive and overtime payments. Such payments are sometimes calculated as a percentage of the basic pay, hence earnings might be expected to be taken as a new basic pay for a greater unit of work. The calculation is not necessarily logical, however, since the percentage does not imply a proportional increase in the work content. So the basic pay as negotiated or fixed by job evaluation remains the standard as reflecting the *believed* value of the job.

But, according to the economists, as already shown, the value of the job to a firm is not the criterion of pay. (I shall here refer—italicisation mine—to the work of my colleague, the late Professor D. J. Robertson of Glasgow University, who was an acknowledged authority on the subject of shop-floor pay). "Put at its very simplest a wage is the price of labour expressed in *units of work*" and the worker "is selling his services for a period of time, the reward he will be looking for will be a clear promise of a payment based on the length of time for which his services are bought, a wage rate" [59, pp. 230–1]. "A wage is a price, and the relative wages which may be secured by skilled workers depend on demand and supply" [59, p. 160]. But, "Put at its very simplest (the marginal productivity theory) states that an employer will not employ a worker or pay for work if it is not *worth his while* to do so" [59, p. 212].

Undoubtedly there is good common sense in such arguments, especially the way in which Professor Robertson enlarges upon them. Trade union bargaining affects basic pay but an employer does not, cannot employ people at an uneconomic rate, i.e. if the work becomes unprofitable. Undoubtedly the shortage of certain skills will raise the 'worthwhileness' of that skill—but not necessarily its 'worth' as measured in terms of cost. If the skill shortage is reduced its worth-whileness is reduced, but the worth remains constant. To that extent, therefore, the relation of supply and demand affects a changeable element of earnings but not the basic pay, the value of the job. *The labour market element is marginal to the basic pay.*

From the point of view of the employer basic pay is a labour cost, and that cost is calculated, estimated to be more precise, on the "units of work" involved in production or processing. This labour cost, with materials costs and overhead costs, constitutes the first basis of pricing the product. To put it another way the total payroll of a firm, plus materials and overheads, constitute a total cost which, set against sales, represents profitability or value added.

Admittedly this is a simple statement of a complex matter but it is enough to establish the point that the worth of a job is the relative cost of the work put into it and is not established by negotiation or by the movement of the labour market. The operative word is 'relative'. Some jobs are worth more than others—the essence of differentials—and so the work put into them is worth more, i.e. there are more 'units of work' if we assume that all jobs can be compared in terms of one kind of 'unit of work'. If the economists hold that there is no unit of work common to all occupations then the comparable worth of jobs cannot be ascertained, and they are then entitled to conclude that only the labour market and institutional bargaining determine pay. Hence job evaluation as practised by managers and as recommended by governments and consultants has no meaning. On the other hand, if they claim that the labour market effect is only marginal, i.e. additional to basic pay or value of a job, and if, as it seems, institutional bargaining establishes what is regarded as a 'fair' pay (a fair day's pay for a fair day's work) then job evaluation does have meaning, and 'units of work' must be comparable as applied to different occupations and grades within occupations.

An example to illustrate this proposition—at this moment of writing computer programmers are in short supply. The pay offered to them is governed in part by this shortage, in part because of the worth of the job, its value to the firm. The extra over and above the value of the job is, in effect, an inducement to join the firm. It is not part of the worth of the job (though it is 'worthwhile' for the firm to offer this extra in order to get programmers). The worth of the job is comparable to that of skilled tradesmen and when, like them, the programmers are no longer in short supply because of the educational establishments now being set up to answer the demand, it is no longer worthwhile for the employer to offer the inducement allowance, or contingency payment to use a more general term. The programmer's job is still worth the same as the skilled tradesman's and will then be offered the same. In other words *contingency payments of this nature cannot be built into the basic pay*—they remain only part of earnings and are, like the other such payments, liable to fluctuate. The important thing to recognise is that such market contingency payments have been built into the basic pay as permanent non-fluctuating parts—because managers have believed with the economists that the market establishes the value of the job.

As Robertson has pointed out, the nationally negotiated *basic rates* have little meaning at the level of the firm. They are minimal, and most firms have additional payments making their won basic pays. He shows [59, pp. 230–1] how recruitment depends so frequently on contingency payments and concludes "where possible, employers who are engaged in recruitment programmes would be (wise) to reduce the variable element in pay packets, and to provide the best possible offer of a wage rate type of payment", i.e. the basic pay should be the offer.

Despite the economists' observations the question remains, why should jobs be worth more or less, why are they paid differently, why are there differentials? Few economists have tackled this question, and again I take pleasure in quoting Professor Robertson [59, Chapter X, Rewards for Skill). He assumes that the *occupational differential* is most important, but goes on to discuss skill, in terms of its meaning as applied to tradesmen, as over and against semi-skilled and unskilled within the same occupation. He defines skill thus, "in its widest sense (skill) involves knowledge and understanding of difficulties of the type which leads to the ability to take responsible decisions" [p. 158]. (This wide definition has its echoes of the theories of job structure described in Part I.) He also describes the skilled tradesman as "understanding of a wide range of jobs and an appreciation of the way in which one operation fits into a complete series of operations" [p. 158]. (This is comparable to Routine decision-making). "It is necessary to make this distinction so as to clarify the difference between payments for skill and payments for output. In the case of semi-skilled work of the simplest repetitive type there is little gap between the two types of payments since greater repetitive skill means greater output. In more skilled work, skill is the ability to do the job fully, while output refers to rate of performance. Moreover, if the wider type of skill is given due prominence then the gap between skill and responsibility narrows." This, translated into the terms used in this book, means that the greater the skill the greater the ability to take more responsible decisions. The skilled tradesman can decide on process (a cycle of operations), the semi-skilled man decides on operations.

Robertson regards the distinction between the equality/inequality argument about incomes as being essentially political where incomes are seen to be earned or unearned, but earned income is politically and generally justifiable if it is "assumed that work deserves payment" [p. 159]. Pay differentials are not a matter for political considerations but for economic [p. 160].

He recognises that modern technology makes a "simple classification of skilled and unskilled no longer appropriate ... the idea of a range of skilled grades should replace that of a simple contrast between apprentice-trained and unskilled" [p. 163]. Considering the technological changes and educational movements, he concludes that "the more difficult the job the more restricted potential labour supply will be" mainly because of the differential distribution of abilities in the population. "The quantity of workers able to take on skilled work at differing levels of skill declines as the difficulty of the job increases; ... nevertheless the supply of such skill relative to the total of the working population has tended to increase in consequence of more adequate education". Hence there might be a premium placed on "dirty, unpleasant heavy manual jobs, in short the whole range of unskilled manual labour", for which more will be paid, i.e. earnings would be more for 'dirty, unpleasant, heavy manual' referring to payment for conditions, not for basic pay.

This result from the consideration of the demand/supply situation is further complicated by problems of status, the attractiveness of jobs requiring greater skills, conditions of work, satisfaction in taking on 'greater responsibilities', creativeness and the like; and "the most convenient symbol of status in productive work in an economic world is the payment which it receives. It is not precise, especially as there need not be a precise proportional relation between status and remuneration" [p. 168]. He argues that "it is not permissible to assume that an occupation will remain attractive without income differentials which give status" and "it is necessary to provide a ladder of differentials corresponding to the ladder of skill and responsibility." "All that can be said firmly is that a differential is required to separate each occupation on the ladder" and "the differential must be clearly seen to exist and to have permanence. It is not enough to provide that the occasional extra earnings of skill should average out at more than those of unskilled" [pp. 170-1].

To summarise—the supply of people with the requisite ability to carry out jobs with varying degrees of difficulty and responsibility (decision-making) will be contingent upon the status accorded to the job holders because of the degrees of responsibility involved, and status is symbolised in our economy by the money reward. Therefore, it is necessary to have money differentials appropriate to required skills so as to induce the needed supply, and these differentials constitute an hierarchy (ladder) of pay corresponding to an hierarchy of skills.

Implicit in this conclusion is that there is a ladder of skill/responsibility and, as Robertson says [p. 167], "remuneration and . . . variants of it increase as the ladder of skill and knowledge and responsibility in work is mounted". The ladder is accepted as a given fact and is not questioned; just as the phrase 'units of work' is not questioned.

Barbara Wootton in her book *Social foundations of wage policy* [74] throws out this economic thesis and, searching for a theory to account for the concept of inequality in pay, discovers that society is divided into groups of different abilities and these abilities are rewarded accordingly as they are used. In other words, the structure of wages, or hierarchy of differentiated jobs stems from these social differences in ability. At one end there will be hewers of wood and drawers of water and at the other end the top level managers.

A similar theme, as I pointed out earlier, is pursued by Professor Jaques. Quotation is appropriate, the italics being mine [24, pp. 18-19].

"There is an optimum level and rate of consumption for each person, in the sense that consumption at that level and rate is consistent with dynamic psychological equilibrium, and consumption above and below that level and rate leads to increasing psychological disequilibrium.

This optimum consumption is related to the individual's level of capacity for discriminating expenditure.

There is a direct correspondence between each person's level of capacity for discriminating expenditure and his level of capacity in work. There is, therefore, an optimum level of payment for any given level of work: it is that level of payment which will provide a person whose capacity is just up to that work, with an income which matches his capacity for discriminating expenditure and his level of satisfaction consumption.

Individuals differ in level of capacity in work.

Individuals differ also in level of capacity for discriminating expenditure and in level of satisfaction consumption.

The work and income distribution which gives dynamic psycho-economic stability in a society is therefore a differential one, and corresponds with the character of the distribution of capacity to work and capacity for discriminating expenditure among the individual members who compose it."

Jaques calls this 'theory' but later says "it will have to remain a hypothesis". In considering a person's capacity in spending and consumption he rightly concludes that this capacity is characterised by "the psychological work of scrutiny, discrimination, selection and decision. Discriminating expenditure is genuinely discretionary expenditure; and more, it utilises a person's full capacity for the exercise of discretion" [p. 162]. It is "a *possibility* which strongly presents itself that what constitutes a satisfaction level of consumption for any given individual is associated with his capacity to carry responsibility in his work, and that both are associated with his capacity for discriminating expenditure" [p. 161]. He says that "spending behaviour *may be* connected with the use of discretion in work" [p. 163], and two pages later states categorically "the capacity for discriminating expenditure, being a derivative of the individuals' capacity to exercise discretion, *is* directly correlated with capacity for production work as measured in time span" [p. 165].

Similarly, asking the question why hierarchical forms of organisation inevitably occur, he notes "that this form of hierarchy accords with a hierarchy of individual capacity. It is to be suspected, therefore, that the existence of executive hierarchies is a social response to the distribution in society of individual capacities making possible the employment of available capacity" [p. 57]. (See also [26].)

On the other hand, moving from this loose hypothesising, Jaques tackles differentials from a slightly different angle. "The *self-evident* quality of the notion of differential reward *may* possibly stem from the fact that those engaged in employment work are employed in organisations where products and services are the creation of many hands. Differential payment stems from the circumstance of men having to be brought together to produce something. Because of differences in capacity, not everyone can make an equal contribution to the final result. Not everyone should share equally in the rewards." From which we gather that Jaques believes every person's work (that is, his job, his contribution to the achievement of the goal) is his by reason of his capacity, not because he has been allocated it, or has contracted to do it, but because he needs an income to match his capacity for discriminating expenditure. He must assume, for one example, that a skilled tradesman is paid more because, during his apprenticeship, he has developed a capacity for discriminating expenditure and requires a skilled tradesman's earnings to match it.

On the other hand Jaques recognises the difference between a man's capacity and his work when he says "payment is the practical and concrete means of expressing the evaluation and recognition of the *relative value of a man's work*—and in precise quantitative terms" [pp. 152–3]. It is "appreciation of the value of his work which is of such very great importance to the individual" and money is centrally important in creating a "feeling of worth and recognition. Differential financial reward is an integral part of differential . . . recognition and is not separable from it" [p. 154]. It is the work that is evaluated not the capacity, it is the job, it is the 'responsibility', the activities of a man's job which are evaluated not the man himself. The value of his work not his capacity gives to the man relative status, "feeling of worth and recognition", and the status symbol is money, as Robertson remarked. If a man performs his work well, i.e. if he has and utilises capacities for decision-making, he also gains prestige and this may be rewarded by a merit bonus or similar payment in addition to the value payment and the status differential of the work itself. Conversely, a man gets no reward if he does not carry out his work, whether he has the capacity to do it or not.

The belief that differential rewards stem from differential capacities and not from the work in the first place leads to the curious conclusion that "if an employee discharges his contractual obligation by doing in a satisfactory manner the work he is given to do, then in equity that employee is as much entitled to the wage or salary appropriate to that work as an employee engaged on the same work in a more profitable enterprise" [p. 35]. The operative words are 'same' and 'equity'. If we assume that time-span of discretion is a measure of sameness in establishing equity it follows that a man doing the 'same' work over a longer period of time, say 44 hours in contrast to 40, is to be paid the same. Indeed Jaques says that "norms of equity in payment are not affected by hours worked", they "are related solely to the level of work carried" [p. 129]. If a firm is more profitable by reason of extra time worked by its employees it seems peculiar that they would not wish recognition of this extra effort by extra payment. Moreover, firms differ in rates of expansion and contraction and so are prepared to pay differentials in order to attract labour; and differences in product and so organisation of jobs may require variations in the worth of similar jobs, similar that is, in terms of time-span of discretion.

It would appear that Jaques has no theory, only an unsubstantiated hypothesis for the existence of differentials. Yet his empirical observation that the longer the time-span of discretion the more a man earns has in it the seeds of a valid hypothesis. Since time-span is a measure of level of work, of the exercise of responsible discretion, then the more highly paid jobs must require the greater exercise of those capacities apparent in discriminating expenditure, i.e. the greater exercise of "scrutiny, discrimination, selection and decision". These very words reflect the decision-making process as defined here in earlier chapters, information (scrutiny and discrimination), conclusion (selection of alternatives) decision—commitment to action and so responsibility. Hence, the more these capacities are exercised as required in work, that is, the more difficult or complex the decision-making process, the more the man is paid.

The graph for Equitable Work Payment Scale [p. 125] "simply shows the relationships between time-span and felt-fair pay, and does not give any information about levels of executive responsibility and promotion" [p. 130]. However, as we have shown, the decision system theory shows "levels of executive responsibility", in that each decision Band from below upwards in the hierarchy requires progressively more difficult and/or complex decisions. By their very nature the results of higher decisions will tend to take longer to become evident, that is, the longer the time span before results can be examined. The qualification 'tend' is necessary, for much depends on kind of production, organisation, state of market and the like. Hence Jaques' time-span observations can be explained by the theory of decision systems, or, as a corollary, these observations are, in part, proof of the theory of decision systems which also provides 'levels of work' that can be objectively determined by analysis of job structure. But the existence of differentials, the 'self-evident quality of the notion of differential reward', has not yet been theoretically explained.

The key to differentials lies in status and the money symbol attached to it. Both Professors quoted above explicitly and implicitly recognised this. To enlarge on this matter the following quotation is taken from a previous publication of my own [49, pp. 193–4].

"Because the wage earnings are a personal affair in the sense that they belong to the man, and their size depends on him, his capacities and the way he is regarded as an operative, the wage earnings are, in effect a representation of the man in some way or another. His evaluation of his wage is essentially an evaluation of himself. This evaluation is mainly one of worth, and must therefore be concerned with rank and prestige . . .

The factory evaluation of the wage is in three categories:

1 GENERAL OCCUPATIONAL STATUS ELEMENT This is inherent in the basic rate now determined mainly by negotiation at national level. It is the *external* differential by which a man recognises the worth of his function to his fellow man generally. In society his job is valued at so much, therefore, he is valued at so much. The large question of a national wages structure hinges on this evaluation.

2 LOCAL OCCUPATIONAL STATUS ELEMENT This is inherent in all rates paid by the firm to its employees. It includes special payments of all kinds, but mainly rates for work done in the factory. It makes the *internal differential* the worth to the firm of the particular job the man is fulfilling. It is *the worth of his function, and therefore of him, in the eyes of management and of his fellow employees* . . .

3 LOCAL PRESTIGE ELEMENT The third element of the wage-evaluation is concerned with the marginal amount, that is the fluctuating portion which depends upon the effort the man puts into his work. The more he gets the better he has performed his task, fulfilled his function, and therefore the value of him in his (procedure) as well as his function. This (procedure) is that for which he is self-responsible and, accordingly as he operates to better fulfilling of his function so he will be given prestige . . . This is inherent in the marginal wage, what a man makes by variation of his own effort, by reason of how he happens to feel about the job and its environment. It is that element which measures how well he does his job, and symbolises the reward for serving the enterprise through doing it well or not. It is the only element of the wage which is

completely personal in that no others share in it. This does not hold if his job is very much interdependent with others".

"A fair day's wage is one which provides for a balance of domestic needs and occupational ranking ... In general this balance is established by normative decision of the work-group, for the men of a particular work group are almost always from the same kind of milieu with the same kind of domestic needs, and from the same kind of occupation with the same ranking needs". A fair day's work "implies function and the satisfaction in fulfilling function through (procedures)". In doing a fair day's work a man "has given to the general effort by fulfilling his function. In so doing he has received his reward. He is whole, and happily so because he has satisfied both of his *basic needs to serve and to receive*" ... A good day's work is "more than a fair day's work, that is to say men (have) done more than they (feel) obliged to do. Fair implies duty; good here implies beyond the bounds of duty".

Thus the essence of the fair wage lies in fulfilling obligation—duty—that which a man is obliged to do, has contracted to do, his function, his job, that for which he is responsible. It is symbolised by the reward that comes from the contract, the basic pay, the national plus the local occupational status element. He is not obliged to perform beyond that: when he does so it becomes his own choice, and that choice can fluctuate. The stable portion of his earnings, the secure element as Robertson puts it, is the basic pay.

Measured day-work and time rates, which are now becoming popular as a move away from straight incentive schemes for payment, are essentially measures of that work for which the basic pay is given. They are 'units of work'. As Wilfred Brown says [7] "each individual has his own norm of pace of work and application to work and that, given a reasonable physical environment, a level of work reasonably consistent with his capacity and a regular level of pay consistent with such work, he will produce, on average, that quantity of work which is his own optimum contribution. He can spurt for quite short periods in emergency, but he cannot keep it up".

Unfortunately we cannot gauge every man's capacities. We cannot use Jaques' argument that a man's earnings are consistent with his earning capacity as indicated by his discriminating expenditure. A man living in a publicly owned three-roomed flat may be quite capable of living discriminatingly in a private split-level six-room bungalow requiring larger earnings. Therefore we cannot know what a man's optimum contribution is, just as we can never meet the 'average worker' beloved of the work study engineers. What we can measure is the work done or required to be done in a unit of time, a day or an hour, and, if a man does it, pay him what it is worth, that is, worth to the firm.

But that worth is equivalent to status, and that status is related to responsibility, and responsibility is tied to the function which is a member's contribution to achievement of the whole. *Worth is, therefore, to be seen in terms of the whole, and not in terms of the part, that is, not of the man and his individual capacities.* Admittedly capacity must be considered, but only in the sense (as pointed out in Chapter 2) that a man cannot be held responsible for a function if he is incapable of fulfilling it—he is not given a job (and held responsible for it) if he does not have the capacity. We can only assume that we are dealing with firms where men are given jobs they are able to do.

Worth is to be considered in terms of the whole. In more colloquial terms a man's worth is his 'share of the cake', and that 'cake' is the total payroll of the firm. The distributing of the payroll in 'shares' is the function of supporting the parts seen in the light of the organismic theory of the firm—the members (the parts) have to be supported so that the firm (the whole) survives (Chapter 2). *A man's contribution is to the achievement of the common goal, his job is rewarded not priced, where reward is seen to be support. Through the firm he survives, through him and his fellow members the firm survives.* Similarly, we can look at the payroll as not being a cost. Materials are processed and sold, there are materials and overhead costs and selling prices. The difference is value added. From this value added comes support of the parts, maintenance of the members of the firm. The payroll and distributed profits are to be seen as of the same nature. The function of shareholders is the contributing of capital and, therefore, they should be rewarded accordingly. Distributed profits constitute pay (reward), they should not be regarded, as so often they are, as a residual after costs—including the payroll—or, sometimes as a first call, not residual, in order to attract or buy capital, much as contingency payments may be given in order to attract labour to buy it.

As a corollary, or rather as the opposite side of the same coin—a man who is responsible for carrying out a function may be punished if he fails to do so—retributive justice. If he does not fail he is rewarded—distributive justice—we are concerned with what is 'just', 'fair', 'appropriate', 'responsible' and, as we have seen, these are all terms connected with the system of structural authority. *Reward and punishment are part of the same social contract. Moreover, this contract is reciprocal or mutual, as the part is responsible to the whole, the whole is responsible to the part for providing the facilities necessary to fulfil function, and for support and regeneration. Therefore, because of this mutual obligation, there can be no arbitrary decision by one side or the other, of the amount of support. It must be mutually contracted. What can be decided by the firm is the total payroll; its distribution must be agreed.*

If we regard the payroll not as a cost or price but as a reward then we cannot calculate the reward in terms of 'labour costs' as in accounting techniques. In any case that would be impossible, especially for managerial and other jobs not acting directly on the materials being processed.

We can return to the concept of status. (The word implies position so, again, we are concerned with the system of structural authority). We accord status on account of importance of the position. That is, a man's worth is correlated with the status of his job—symbolised by money reward—and so a man's relative worth is correlated with the relative importance of his job. Relative importance can be considered from two (connected) points of view.

IN TERMS OF RESPONSIBILITY

In any one sphere of structural authority the person making the decisions of the highest Band is responsible for all the results of activities in that sphere whether the action is by him or by others in his sphere of authority. He cannot delegate responsibility. Any one in his sphere of authority making decisions of a lower Band cannot be responsible for so many results as he, therefore the senior has 'greater' responsibility, and his decisions, and so his job, are more important than those of the men junior to him. Since his decisions concerning the activities in his sphere can produce results only when his juniors have made their decisions and completed their activities, his decisions cannot be reviewed until after theirs—which explains why he has a greater 'time-span of discretion', to use Jaques' term.

IN TERMS OF EFFECT OF DECISIONS

1 Relative importance of decisions can be judged in terms of their effect on the survival of the firm. From this point of view, in a constantly changing environment adaptive decisions are more important. Policy-making, Programming and Interpretive decisions are clearly adaptive, and Routine, Automatic and Defined are not. The decision that an article be produced is more important to a firm than the decisions on the processes and operations during its manufacture. Or, the idea of a product is more important than the design, which is more important than the drafting of the design, which is more important than the making, i.e. there are *essential priorities* and so importance.

2 In a similar vein of argument—the higher in the decision hierarchy the more difficult and complex the decision process; this difficulty reflects the increasing number of factors to be considered at each stage of the process, these factors being concerned with predictability of outcome at progressively longer ranges in time. The further ahead we can predict the greater the chances of survival, therefore the greater the importance of these decisions.

So it can be concluded that the hierarchy of decision bands represents a hierarchy of relatively more important decisions, and so relatively more status and worth to be appropriately rewarded. But importance is an abstraction for which there are no dimensions. We cannot say that Decision Band E is twice as important as D, or that B is four times more important than A, or, on the other hand, that there is one unit of importance for each Band, that is to say a linear relationship between importance and the decision hierarchy.

To approach this problem from another angle but on the basis of the argument in terms of responsibility—we have already seen that the terms and concepts involved are almost wholly relevant to the system of structural authority. Each decision Grade within this system, is related to those above and below by forms of control, either full or actual, the imperatives being either categorical ('willness') or parenthetical ('mustness invoking willness') and hence rightness, justice and fairness. That is, the 'difference' between each Grade is the same, in that the signal between involves an all-or-none-response, as shown in Fig. 3.2, the Decision-Complex. Hence there is a 'unitary difference' or 'spacing' between each.

So the problem can now be set out in this fashion (see Fig. 13.1). Let the

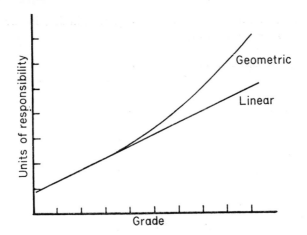

Figure 13.1   Linear or geometric relation of Grade and "units" of responsibility

X-axis represent Grades, the distance between each being the same. Let the *Y*-axis represent the reward in money representing the status/importance of each Grade. We do not know the relation between *X* and *Y*. If one unit difference upwards in Grade is rewarded by one unit increase in reward the relationship is linear; but this may not be the case—the relationship may be more complex.

Since the difference between each Band involves (directly or indirectly) the categorical imperative the human relation between the coordinator and coordinated will be one of the sense of responsibility, meaning mutual obligation. We can say there is one 'unit of responsibility' between each, because it does not matter how many persons are in the Band below a co-ordinator, the relation remains one 'unit of responsibility'—for, the *relation being between one person and another, can be felt or sensed only by these two. Or, since there is only one coordinator, there can be only one 'unit of responsibility'.* (This argument is parallel to the well-known argument as to whether more pain can be suffered by several people together than by one.)

Since responsibility cannot be delegated (as authority is delegated in control) there will be accumulated responsibility upwards, often referred to as 'bearing a greater weight of responsibility.' Thus, if manager L has a relation responsibility to a manager K in his (K's) sphere authority, and M is a third manager responsible to L, then L, being unable to delegate responsi-bility, remains responsible to K whatever M might do. The two 'units of responsibility' M to L, and L to K, remain. K at the top of this line 'bears' or 'carries' two 'units of responsibility' defined by the hierarchy of two Bands; he will bear 'greater responsibility' than L or M. The essence of this lies in the logic of the hierarchy of decisions. A 'higher' kind of decision requires a sequence of 'lower' decisions to execute it, the longer a sequence the 'higher' the decision—and each decision involves responsibility.

Let the relation between each Band be one 'unit of responsibility', then, if the responsibility at Band O be 1, the responsibility at Band A will be

$1 + 1 = 2$ and at Band B $1 + 2 + 1 = 4$. Continuing in the same vein the result will be as in Table 13.1.

TABLE 13.1   *Accumulation of units of responsibility by Band*

Band		Total Band Units
First	O	1
Second	A	$1 + 1 = 2$
Third	B	$1 + 2 + 1 = 4$
Fourth	C	$1 + 2 + 4 + 1 = 8$
Fifth	D	$1 + 2 + 4 + 8 + 1 = 16$
Sixth	E	$1 + 2 + 4 + 8 + 16 + 1 = 32$

That is, if y = reward and x = Band

$$y = 2^x$$

Since each Band (except the first) is divisible into two Grades then when x = number of Grade

$$y = (\sqrt{2})^x = 1 \cdot 42^x$$

The conversion of 'units of responsibility' to units of reward is relatively simple—any one unit of money may be taken as equivalent to one 'unit of responsibility'. Since the relationship of Band and so Grade to 'units of responsibility' is exponential the relationship of Grade to reward (in units of money) will also be exponential and can be expressed as a straight line OA in Fig. 13.2, when the X-axis represents Grades and the Y-axis log money/pay, where pay is given as reward for the content of work expressed in terms of decisions, and the point O is the sum rewarded for the lowest grade of decision, Grade 0. The angle at θ defines the slope, calculated as tan θ, which can be no greater than $1 \cdot 42$ (which agrees with experience).

The slope of the line OA will depend on two factors:

1 *According to the unit of money selected as equivalent of a 'unit of responsibility'.* This will depend on the money available for distribution as reward, that is, the total payroll. Given a fixed amount for Grade 0 pay (point O), the greater the payroll the steeper the line, say OB; the lesser the payroll the less steep the line, say OC. Given a fixed reward for Grade 10, the greater the payroll the greater the amount for distribution to the lower grades, and so the line will be less steep.

2 *According to the policy of the firm.* Given a distribution of the payroll according to line OA an increase in the amount available may be distributed as a percentage increase in reward to every one, say to line $O_1 A_1$. On the other hand the directorate may decide to give a larger increase to the lower-paid members than to the higher-paid. This would mean holding Grade 10 at A and increasing O to O_1 and so a decrease in slope.

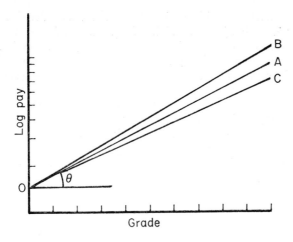

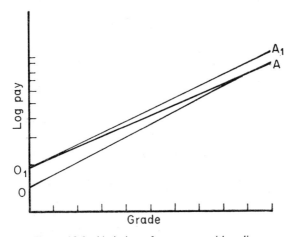

Figure 13.2   Variation of pay curve with policy

The question rightly to be asked is whether there are values intermediate to those for each Grade, that is within the Grade. For instance, the job of one skilled tradesman may be regarded as more important than that of another, both being in the same Grade 3: a tool maker may be doing a job considered more important than that of a production line turner. This is generally expressed in words such 'it is more skilled', 'it is more difficult', 'it is a more complex job' or 'after all the turner depends on the toolroom'. No one would query the validity of these being classed as skilled jobs, and that the basic pay should lie at least at or above the bottom of the basic pay for Grade 3, but the tool maker's job is 'higher'.

The words 'more skilled', 'more difficult', 'more complex' are guides to the theoretical approach. This can be referred to the argument above,

'In terms of effect of decisions', in which it was considered that the more difficult and complex jobs are higher in the hierarchy of decision-making since more factors are taken into consideration, and this is necessary to answer needs for predictability; whence the ultimate criterion of importance, survival, is involved. This argument was there directed towards differences in kinds of decision but the same argument can be applied to difficulty and complexity of jobs requiring the same kinds of decision within the same grade (Chapter 3). The greater the number of decisions of a grade required for a job the more difficult is the job of that grade, and so its importance. The toolmaker's job requires more decisions of Grade 3 than that of the production turner; it is more difficult, it is more important. It can be stated,

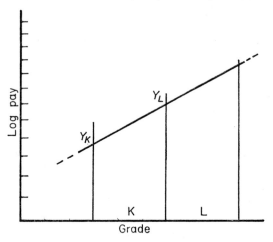

Figure 13.3   Pay and subgrading

in general terms that, in any one grade, those jobs requiring more decisions of that grade are more difficult, so more important, and so should be rewarded more.

This can be put more crudely in more easily understood (and practical) terms. If two men are employed in exactly the same kind of job they will be paid the same, for the number of decisions required in the unit of time is the same. If one of them produces more than the other in the same time he must be making more decisions (of the same kind) and he is accordingly rewarded more. We call it a 'piece-rate' incentive. If a man produces more in this sense, his contribution to the survival of the firm is more important.

In Fig. 13.3 let Y_K be the lower limit of basic pay for Grade K, and Y_L be the lower limit for Grade L. There will be a possibility of a range of jobs in Grade K which have importance justifying distribution of their basic pays between Y_K and just below Y_L. Where these jobs should be placed in this range of basic pays cannot be argued completely logically. The pays for any two jobs, such as those already quoted, may be (in a particular firm) in the upper half, the tool maker's higher than the turner's, there being no other jobs comparable in the number of decisions of Grade 3. In another firm they may be placed lower in the range because of the existence of jobs, such as special maintenance, requiring even more decisions of that Grade. The distribution over the range becomes a matter of non-calculable judgment or of negotiation—though the order in difficulty, and so in basic pay, is logically determinable.

The final problem is the theoretical establishment of basic pay for 'staff', that is for jobs in which only sapiential authority is exercised. (A staff job, say that of an accountant, may be analysed in terms of decisions and placed in the hierarchy as already described.) The job of chemist or operational researcher is typical of the staff job where there is difficulty in recognising kinds of decision, but where sapiential authority is employed, and where status is also conferred. Status considerations are as relevant to such staff jobs as to 'line', for status here, too, is an indication of importance and so worth.

It is again necessary to refer to Fig. 3.2 which represents the Decision-Complex. There the relation of the conclusion unit to the decision is one of advisability, and both are depicted as on the same, horizontal, level. The essence of this horizontality lies in the following theoretical considerations.

A decision requires, and so is preceded by, conclusions. The decision is a selection, for commitment to action, of the alternatives presented as conclusions, so these conclusions must be of the same category of importance as the decision, and equal in 'weight of responsibility'. For example, a metallurgical chemist having analysed the 'mix' from a furnace in the melting shop of a steel works can say to the superintendent of the melting shop that he "must add X in order to get the right steel". That is he is using the hypothetical imperative "You must do so-and-so if you are to fulfil your function", the function being obtaining the right kind of steel. (He could, of course, merely give the result of the analysis to the superintendent and let him draw his own conclusions. That is, he gives only information; and the relation informability implies, at the most, the injunction which can be used upwards as well as laterally and downwards. Whereas the hypothetical imperative can be used only laterally, and then only horizontally and downwards.) The superintendent is entitled to choose one of the alternatives, these being to act or not to act on the advice. If he acts on it and the result is not the right steel he can, and properly so, deny full responsibility since he acted on the advice of one with sapiential authority, entitled by the senior of both to use that authority; or more precisely, the senior has decreed that the sapiential authority of the chemist is such that the superintendent can assume it is adequate, the chemist having been appointed (presumably) because it is so. Therefore 'responsibility' rests as much on the chemist as on the superintendent. In the giving of advice the chemist becomes as important as, has status as high as that of the superintendent.

It can be stated, *in general terms, that where a member of the firm gives advice (defined as that communication involving the hypothetical imperative) that advice is of the same importance as the decision based upon it,* that is, the decision of the person to whom the advice is given. It follows that the reward appropriate to the adviser is of the same grade as the highest grade of decision-maker to whom advice is given, that is 'horizontally'. (The advice, naturally, is on decisions that are part of the decision-maker's job and not for other decisions.)

In the light of the theory of reward just enunciated the relationship of basic pay to Grade (status) should be of a logarithmic nature. But, given the conditions:

1 That the marginal labour market element may be, mistakenly, built into the basic pay.

2 That negotiations with trade unions in what constitutes a fair basic pay may depend on several factors such as negotiating strength and personalities of negotiation.

3 That existing job evaluation methods may take into consideration factors such as conditions and physical effort which have no direct relevance to job content itself, and the methods themselves may be non-logical.

4 That managers and men alike may not necessarily have accurate, far less adequate knowledge of job content.

the relationship, in practice, is likely to be only approximate to the straight logarithmic line.

The application and testing of this theory is given in Chapter 14 and Part 4.

Chapter fourteen   **Pay curves**

The first opportunity to test the theory came in 1961 when I recommended its application in the Southern Rhodesia Public Services [51], following that with a Report [53] on Job Evaluation to be applied in the Services. Some of the observations in these Reports appear in this book and in *The Manual* on method. In 1962 I was able to get the help of several young graduates to go into a wide variety of firms, 64 of them, covering the major industries and commercial houses; and in 1965 and later the subject was selected for postgraduate research by several students in my department. The data for the nine examples given below were collected by them, not by me; it could be said, therefore, that their collection was not biased by my personal interest.

It is worth adding that my young colleagues learned the method of analysis and grading (not assessment) in no more than five days of which at least half were given over to learning the basic theory. (It was at their instigation that the method began to be referred to as the Paterson Method.) For managers who have close knowledge of their firm's activities and having read the theory, the Method can be learned in about three days by the best-of-all learning methods, 'sitting by Nellie' and then trying it out under helpful supervision. In *The Manual* which accompanies this book greater detail will, naturally, be given on how to apply the Method. For that reason only the outline will be set out here. There are three main stages, analysis, grading and subgrading, assessing.

ANALYSIS

An adequate statistical sample is taken departmentally (vertical division) and by Bands and Grades (horizontal division). Titles are misleading—we have found a so-called 'chief accountant's' job of Grade 3 at the very highest. Certainly Bands can be picked out fairly readily, and one then looks for the subdivision into even- and odd-number grades within bands. A job sheet is issued to each of the persons in the jobs so selected, and they are given two or three days to think about and remember their tasks which they enter on the sheet.

Then comes the interview with him. Questions are all designed to focus on his right to make decisions. For example, if he has to go to a senior 'for approval' he is not making the decision, the senior is; and this has to be distinguished from informing his senior that the decision has been made. Or, how did he learn his job, was everything specified or is he allowed to make changes, and what kind of changes, i.e. in his procedure. Another field of enquiry, among managers especially, is to find out if he has a relation of advisability with colleagues. This establishes lateral correlation and has to be used in the case of specialists' or staff jobs. Of course, some interviewees will distort evidence, this is natural if they think their status is higher than it is, or they wish it were—but this is always checked through other interviews, with colleagues and seniors and juniors. But my own experience is that few do so for it is exceedingly difficult to distort the fact that a decision is made or not. This is the essence of the objectivity of the method. The answer in the end is either yes or no, there are no qualifications possible.

For jobs in Bands O and A attention is paid to analysis of operations and elements. In certain circumstances the data provided by MTM studies are helpful and form the basis of the Allan–Paterson (Allpat) Method which is described in detail in *The Manual*. The essence of this approach is that the relative difficulty of deciding a movement of parts of the body can be assessed by the comparative time it takes to make the movement. For jobs in Band B the processes in each task are examined, there is no need to analyse operations and elements. It is often helpful to carry out the interview on the site of the job so that the interviewee can demonstrate what he is doing—some forget items when filling up the job sheet. The higher in the hierarchy, in Bands C and D, the jobs require only analysis of tasks.

[At first I found it surprising, I continue to find it most heart-warming, that people like to talk about their jobs, even the most simple. As I suggested in Chapter 11, a man's job is important to him, for it is him. I might be permitted a purely personal observation here—decision-making, the need for discretion as Jaques puts it, is so much a characteristic of living (it is, literally, vital) that I never tire of listening to and learning from my interviewees what is this reality of life in our industrial society].

The analyst then transfers his notes to a task analysis form which includes not only his opinion of Grade but also much other information, about frequency of tasks and the like that form the basis of subgrading and constitute the data for such possibilities as job enrichment, job structuring (economy of grading), performance appraisal (an analyst must never, but never appraise performance) and incentives.

GRADING

These data go before a Grading Conference which questions the Analysts and concludes on the final grading of tasks and so the jobs. This is relatively easy—it has been found that men from the shop-floor of a foundry can readily distinguish Bands O, A and B, and so Grades, from such descriptions of jobs in an engineering firm [64].

Subgrading does not concern the thesis at this point but in finally setting up a pay structure it becomes of importance and is expanded upon in *The Manual*. In general three subgrades for odd-number grade jobs can be readily distinguished, and two subgrades for even-numbered, much as can be recognised in the US Job Classification scheme. There are three techniques, the Decision-Count where numbers of decisions made are the criteria, the Count-Ranking Technique where adequate sampling of activity is not possible but distinction can be made in terms of difficulty and complexity as defined in Chapter 4, and the Ranking Technique, making use of the Castellion Method, or of the Point Method mainly on the factors skill and alertness, or of the Job Classification Method. Subgrading has a subjective element and I find these last three Methods are most useful. The essential point to be remembered is that Grades are objectively established, and the subjectivity of subgrading is limited within this objective framework.

ASSESSMENT

The last stage is job assessment, the fitting of pay to Grades. Pay curves for Grades are drawn (of which examples are about to be given here); decisions are made on pay policy, the slope of the curve and so distribution of the payroll, on Grade and subgrade overlap; on pay anomalies, what jobs are not being rewarded fairly and how to make the adjustment; and on contingency payments, what extra should be given for special conditions of work, what would have to be paid to bring in the specialised kind of labour needed, and fringe benefits. This is reserved for *The Manual*.

The following three figures are existing pay curves (Grade/Log Pay) of a sample of eight firms—from over 70 analysed—from the radio, food, engineering, tobacco, building, and chemical industries and a commercial enterprise (a building society). None had a strong trade union element. The significance of the correlation of Grade and Log Pay in the first six, A–F, Figs. 14.1 and 14.2, is exceedingly high especially when it is remembered that in none of these firms had job evaluation been used, and differentials had been arrived at by a kind of guess and some knowledge of 'going rates of pay'—but these rates varied from firm to firm just as has been found in the UK [61]. The differential structure does not vary. It seems full confirmation of Jaques' discovery that there is a subconscious knowledge, a feeling of what is 'fair pay', *but in each firm only*, not throughout the whole of industry and commerce, nor even in any one industry.

Figure 14.3, shows two cases, G and H, where the significance is not so high in the sense that two pays (those ringed) are well off the pay curve drawn through the other pays—line of best fit. Curve H is typical of about 25 per cent of the total sample. In all of those firms of this kind there was unrest, relatively poorer industrial relations. I should not like to go so far as

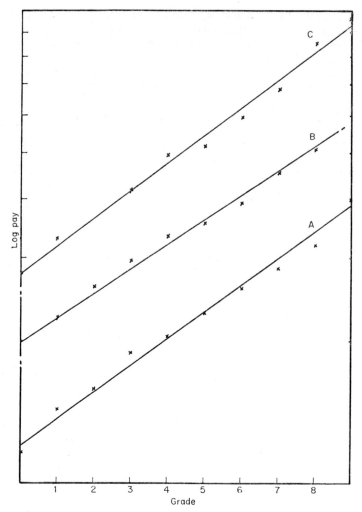

Figure 14.1   Pay curves: Radio (A) and Food (B) Industries, Building Society (C)

to say that the unrest is due to wholly to the unfairness of reward, it may be that the distortion of the curve is due to that unrest. But Jaques' observation that, if pay is more than 5 or 10 per cent away from the 'felt fair' pay curve, a feeling of aggression develops, supports the proposition that the closer to the line of best fit the less the chance of unrest due to dissatisfaction with pay.

However, taken as a whole, the total sample shows that the general theory holds, that differentials tend to be based upon a decision-making grading from unskilled jobs to the board-room, with an exponential increase from Grade to Grade. Below I quote on further corroboration by Dr T. M. Husband; and Dr Boshoff, now at Stellenbosch University has also found the same result (Unpublished PhD thesis). Dr Gouws, one-time Director of the

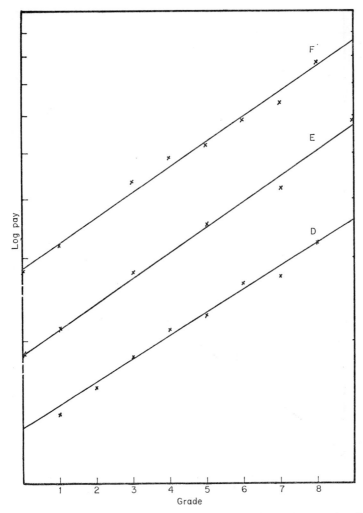

Figure 14.2   Pay curves: Tobacco (D), Chemical (E) and Construction (F)
Industries

National Institute of Personnel Research, delivered an unpublished paper
at a management conference in Cape Town in 1967 in which he demonstrated a similar distribution of pay.

The pay curve can be distorted by trade union activity. Figure 14.4
shows the distribution of pay in a firm in the printing industry where the
printing unions are powerful. The line AB is the pay curve for all shop-floor,
clerical and managerial staff excepting the unions. The line LM is the pay
curve for the printing unions where influence extends from unskilled 'mates'
to the skilled technicians, Grades 0 to 3. The foremen on the shop-floor,
Grade 4, have pay which is in line with the non-union curve. Figure 14.5

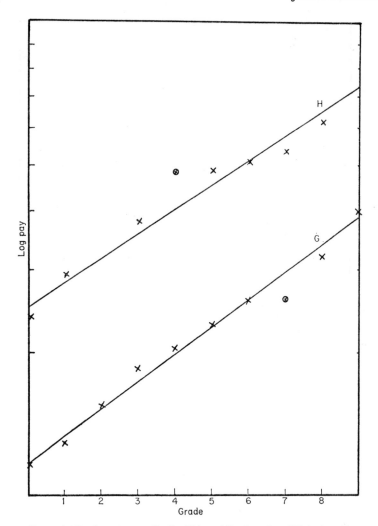

Figure 14.3   Pay curves: Radio (G) and Engineering (H) Industries

is a pay curve from the chemical industry where the combined trade unions on the shop-floor negotiated fixed rates for the four Grades 0 to 3. The female clerical workers were not involved in these negotiations—their pay curve is a continuation of the curve for Bands C, D and E. This represents either the relative weakness of the negotiating body for the clerical staff, or discrimination on account of sex. The same kind of discrimination is encountered in commercial houses where unskilled male employees like sweepers are paid more than unskilled females (who may be doing jobs requiring some training such as in copy typing) and where the semi-skilled and skilled male staff receive pay at the upper end of the pay brackets, grade boxes, for Grades 1, 2 and 3. The curve for the male staff is thus

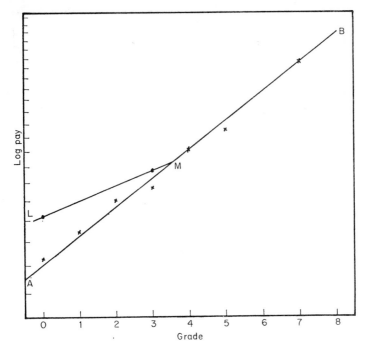

Figure 14.4   Pay curve: Printing Industry, to show effect of trade unions

higher than for female staff. This kind of 'dog-leg' break in the pay curve
has significance in the problem of wage drift.

My friend and former United Nations colleague Mr D. P. Basu of Cobim
(Private) Limited, in Bangalore, India, has kindly provided me with data
on a project in Hindustan Airlines for the purpose of subgrading shop-floor
jobs of Grade 3. The factory has a payroll of about 40,000 and the sample
covered a total population of 3,000 workers. There were two investigations.

In the first case 101 jobs were analysed:

Lathe	37
Grinding	30
Milling	34

These jobs were first analysed by industrial engineers and classified into
two ranks. The supervisors of the operatives on these jobs were separately
asked to rate them by conventional techniques, examining the process sheets
only. They agreed on 27 lathe, 25 grinding and 23 milling jobs and these 75
were then analysed for numbers of Band B, Band A and Band O decisions.
Owing to the absence of a normal distribution of the frequencies the median
value of numbers of Band B decisions was taken as the datum line between
the two ranks. A Yates Coefficient of Association between the grading by the
engineers and foremen, and by the decision-band method was calculated,
being only 0·60 for lathe operatives but 1·00 and 0·83 for grinding and

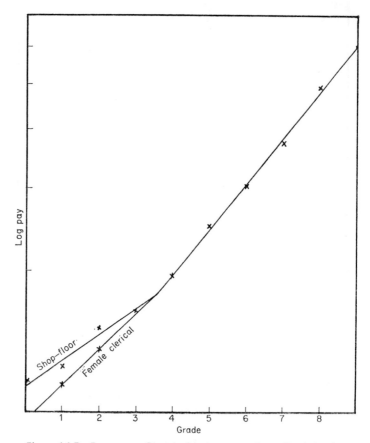

Figure 14.5   Pay curve: Chemical Industry, to show discrimination

milling. The Chi-square tests for the lathe operatives showed no significant agreement but more than 99 per cent for the others. For all the operatives the probability of existence of agreement was high, more than 99 per cent.

This was followed by a much more extensive test. A sample (743) of almost all manufacturing operations was again analysed independently by industrial engineers and separately by supervisors using conventional techniques. Their ratings into three ranks were found to be at considerable variance with each other and correspondence was found on only 443 out of 743.

At the same time each job was analysed for decision content and the ratio $(B + A)/(B + A + O)$ plotted. This graph showed three distinct modes at 0.25, 0.45 and 0.80, and appeared to have the characteristics of a Gamma distribution. Given this distribution three ranges were selected as the basis for a classification of categories, Groups II, III and IV, respectively 0.33 and below, 0.34 to 0.60 and 0.61 and above. These three Groups were then compared with grading of the 443 jobs agreed by the engineers and foremen

TABLE 14.1 *Distribution of kinds of decision in three subgrades of Grade 3*

Subgrade	Percentage of decisions		
	Band O	Band A	Band B
a (Group II)	75	15	10
b (Group III)	55	25	20
c (Group IV)	40	32	28

and the Chi-square test of significance was found to be more than the 99 per cent confidence limit.

Mr Basu concludes "This exercise now can be said to have given us an instrument for determining composition of skill categories throughout the manufacturing activities".

The figures he supplies for the percentage distribution of kinds of decision in each subgrade in Grade 3 are of particular interest in the light of the theory of subgrading by 'difficulty' as specified by numbers of decisions (see Table 14.1). These are depicted graphically in Fig. 14.6.

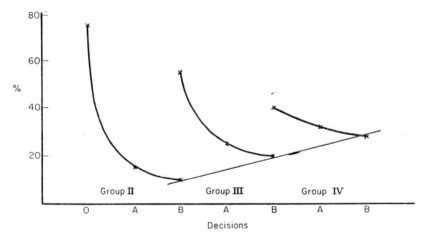

Figure 14.6 Distribution of O, A and B decisions in three job groups of skilled technicians; job composition after Basu

In any one industry the slope of the pay curve appears to vary with size of firm. Figure 14.7 shows the curves for two firms, I and II, in the Glass, Brick and Tile industry, one with 73 the other 547 employees (see Table 14.2). These two firms were in Southern Africa. The low pay for unskilled labour, Grade O, is due to colour discrimination comparable to sex discrimination for cheap labour in the UK. But the coloured labour of Grade 1 is on the same pay curve as the white labour, whereas in the UK the sex discrimination carries on up to Grade 3.

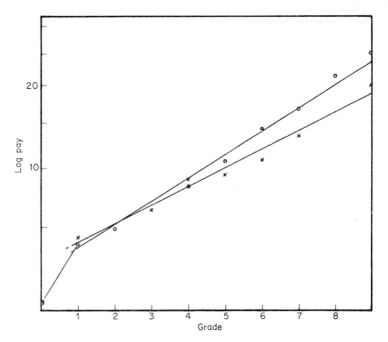

Figure 14.7   Pay curves: large and small firms in Glass, Brick and Tile Industry

The calculation of the slope of the pay curve has several uses. The pay curve can be drawn by eye to give the 'best fit' to the plotted points Grade/ log pay, or it can be calculated (by the method of least squares—see *The Manual*) and then drawn. The slope can be found by a simple mathematical approach.

TABLE 14.2   *Comparison of pay curves of two firms in the same industry*

Bands	Grade	Mean pay I $	Number	Mean pay II $	Number
O	0	1,430	52	1,420	365
A	1	4,320	2	3,820	76
	2	—	—	4,820	10
B	3	6,330	11	6,290	54
	4	9,000	1	8,350	16
C	5	9,360	1	10,800	16
	6	10,800	1	14,400	3
D	7	13,460	3	16,850	5
	8	—	—	21,600	1
E	9	20,100	2	25,200	1
			73		547

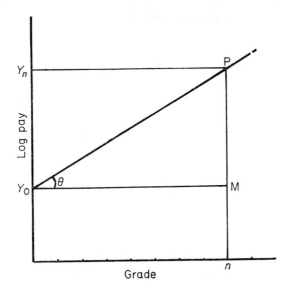

Figure 14.8   To illustrate calculations on pay curves

In Fig. 14.8 let the x-axis represent Grades at equal intervals, let the y-axis represent log pay, and let

n = number of Grade

Y_0 = minimum pay, i.e. for Grade 0

Y_n = pay for Grade n, and

r = the gradient of the curve, i.e. the rate of increase of pay between grades

Then

$$r = \tan \theta = PM/Y_0M$$
$$= (\log Y_n - \log Y_0)/n$$
$$= (1/n) \log (Y_n/Y_0)$$
$$r = (Y_n/Y_0)^{1/n} \tag{1}$$

Similarly

$$Y_n = Y_0 r^n \tag{2}$$

Let k be any number of Grade between n and 10. Then

$$Y_k = Y_n r^{k-n} \tag{3}$$

If N_{0-10} is the number of employees in Grades 0–10, respectively, then the total payroll

$$T = \sum N_i Y_i$$
$$= N_0(Y_0) + N_1(Y_0 r) + N_2(Y_0 r^2) + N_3(Y_0 r^3) \text{ etc}$$
$$= Y_0(N_0 + N_1 r + N_2 r^2 \dots) \tag{4}$$

Calculations can be made in the following fashion:

Example 1: Say the minimum adult pay is $3,500 ($Y_0$) and the pay of the general manager, Grade 8, is $22,000 ($Y_{10}$), then

$$r = (22,000/3,500)^{1/8} \qquad\qquad (1)$$
$$= 1.26$$

Hence there is a constant 26 per cent increase between Grades.

Example 2: Given the gradient (r) and the minimum adult pay (Y_0) it is possible to calculate the pay for any other grade. If the minimum pay is $3,500 and the gradient 1.26 then the pay for a supervisor, Grade 4, is obtained thus:

$$Y_n = Y_0 r^n \qquad\qquad (2)$$
$$Y_4 = 3,500 \times (1.26)^4$$
$$= \$8,825$$

Example 3: Given the gradient 1.26 and the supervisor's pay (Y_4) as $8,825 the pay of the general manager (Y_{10}) is obtained by

$$Y_k = Y_n r^{k-n} \qquad\qquad (3)$$
$$Y_{10} = Y_4 r^{10-4}$$
$$= 8,825 \times (1.26)^6$$
$$= \$22,000$$

My colleague Dr T. M. Husband [20] has applied the theory in an extended fashion by utilising the *Executive salary surveys*, published annually by AIC Consultants Limited. The job ranking in these surveys corresponds closely with Grades 5 to 10, indeed the descriptions are of the same nature (see Chapter 3): Rank 2 is Managing Director (Grade 10), Rank 3 Director (Grade 9), Rank 4 General Manager level (Grade 8), Rank 5 Senior Managers responsible to Rank 4 (Grade 7), Rank 5 Middle Managers responsible to Rank 5 (Grade 6), and Rank 7 Middle Managers responsible to Rank 6 (Grade 5). He followed the example of Roberts [58] who demonstrated empirically that the salary of the top executive tends to be related to sales turnover S, and hence

$$Y_{10} = mS^t$$

where m and t are constants, which Husband found for the UK to be

$$Y_{10} = 144 S^{0.23} \quad (S \text{ in } \pounds\text{m.}) \text{ for } 1965$$

r also increases with sales turnover

$$r = zS^h$$

where z and h are constants, which he found for the UK to be

$$r = 0.94 S^{0.023}$$

Since

$$Y_k = Y_n r^{k-n} \tag{3}$$

$$Y_k = Y_{10}/r^{10-k} \tag{5}$$

Hence

$$Y_k = 144 S^{0 \cdot 23}/(0 \cdot 94 S^{0 \cdot 023})^{10-k} \tag{6}$$

where $S = £$m. sales turnover and $k =$ Grade.

For a firm of about 1,000 employees, using unit production technology, and with sales turnover around £4 million these equations yield

gradient $r = 1 \cdot 33$

Top executive salary $= £4,750$ (basic) in 1965.

For a firm of about 3,000 employees and a sales turnover of around £10m. the

gradient $r = 1 \cdot 36$

Top executive salary $= £5,850$ (basic) in 1965.

The correlation of the pay curve gradient with sales turnover is significant, and the correlation with size (number of employees) is also significant—as expected since, in general, the larger the firm the larger the turnover.

However, Dr Husband has gone still further. He postulated that the correlation would be closer if two other factors were taken into consideration: I, a factor for type of industry (Chemicals and Dyes pay their managers more than Engineering and than Textiles) and R, a regional variation (salary levels are lower in Scotland than in SE England, for example). From statistical tables of the Department of Employment and Productivity of the UK he found I to range from a base of $1 \cdot 00$ to $1 \cdot 20$ and R to range from $1 \cdot 00$ to $1 \cdot 15$. The equation for a managerial salary then becomes

$$Y_k = (Y_{10}/r^{10-k})IR$$
$$= [mS^r/(zS^h)^{10-k}]IR \tag{7}$$

This he tested with a sample of 107 managers attending three different educational centres, from several industries and of mainly middle and senior Grades. 70 per cent of the estimates by Eq. (7) were within ± 5 per cent of the actual pay and only 5 per cent were outside the tolerance limits of ± 10 per cent, that is outside the grade box as calculated from r, which is a good prediction considering that the value of R is not very accurate, and the model tends to underestimate. He concludes:

"The results . . . confirm Paterson's initial findings of a logarithmic relationship between pay and decision level. The model, further, generally shows the strength of the relationship between company size and executive pay". He believes that the model along the lines of Eq. (7) "could have a quite wide-ranging value in modern industry . . . regional and industry-wide pay structures could be developed as yardsticks against which individual companies could match their own structures. Also manpower planning and, more specifically, payroll control could be refined by the use of such data".

Part 4   APPLICATION OF THEORY

The new Method appears to have the requirement of Acceptability on the grounds of simplicity—its fundamentals are easy to understand—of the participation of job holders in the analysis and their agents in grading and assessment, of the sense of justice—equality—and of fairness—equity—of the ability of the firm to pay, of time-saving, of adjustability to technological change, and of control of 'leap-frogging'. The factors of working conditions and the local labour market are catered for as well.

Work Analysis, as the basis of the Method, is to be regarded as also the basis, and logically so, of training and development, merit-rating and promotion, organisation, job re-structuring, management strategies and manpower planning. A new approach to incentives is possible and, with that, productivity bargaining. With job evaluation as well, negotiations on pay are eased and accelerated. Work Analysis becomes a basic technique of all managers, in particular Personnel Managers.

The pay curves of all firms being of the same kind (varying only in slope and total payroll) it is now possible to envisage and to calculate pay curves for industries and, finally a pay structure for the nation based on industrial differentiation (as in the USA) and not on occupational (as it now is in the UK). 'Equal basic pay for equal work' can now become a reality and job security—as career—a possibility. But, because of trade union activity at Decision Bands O, A and B, a 'dog-leg' national pay curve now exists which must lead to more pay inflation and wage drift, that can only be held in check by a national job evaluation scheme.

Chapter fifteen   **Acceptability of the Method**

As the first part of Chapter 11 pointed out, acceptability is a prime requirement of a method of job evaluation; and an aspect of its acceptability is the
actual mechanics of implementation. The technique has not been described
in detail here—that comes in *The Manual*—but references will be made to
such detail in the following remarks, which are expansions of the point of
acceptability in Chapter 11.

1 *Simplicity* is essential, for it means understanding. Because people already
know (and in many cases subconsciously) the difference between semi-
skilled and skilled decisions, between middle management and senior
management, it is relatively easy for them to make the next step of becoming
articulate about these differences. That the Method relies on one factor only,
and this something they already apprehend if not comprehend, is the essence
of the simplicity. Whereas in other methods several factors, degrees of each
factor, weightings, all these are very complex and, being subjective, tend to
confusion and so to raise suspicion. The mere fact that it takes so little time
to learn the principles of the Method and to practise them is evidence of
simplicity.

Scott [64], in an experiment where men from the foundry shop-floor,
with personnel managers and works managers, collaborated on a job evaluation experiment comparing Point, Time-Span and Paterson Methods,
learned that the shop-floor men were quick to recognise the differences in
decision-making in Bands O, A and B, and could distinguish C and D. In
the end, asked which method they would prefer they opted for the last—
and that was, in the main, due to the ease in grasping its principles. In my
own experience I find an hour's talk, illustrated by analysis of jobs with
which the audience are familiar, is enough to convince them of the validity
of the principles. One would not ask shop-floor men to understand clerical
jobs and vice versa, nor to ask them to analyse senior management jobs.

Difficulty arises when grading specialist tasks which are mainly in middle management. The concept of the decision-complex is not easy to comprehend without much preparation, but what does help rapidly are the examples which distinguish the use of the imperatives "You must do X" meaning "if you are to fulfil your function" (and so advice, therefore of the same Grade) and "You should do X" (informability, and so of any Grade). The analyst asks such questions as "Suppose so-and-so came to you and said you must do X what would you do?" And then asks him to explain his acceptance or rejection, not on the technical content but on the imperative. This kind of actual behaviour people understand when it is clarified for them. At times one can have a manager actually grading his own tasks with the help of the analyst. Indeed, as I propose to show in the next Chapter, this recognition is of great use in management generally.

Subgrading, having a higher subjective content than grading, is less easily understood. The analyst's questions about the interviewee's own opinion of subgrading ranks in any one Grade is likely to bring out most useful information for the Grading Conference but, at the same time, if the interviewee is asked to explain why he subgrades in a particular sequence, he finds himself becoming articulate and, having to use overt verbal symbols for what is hitherto impression, he learns.

2 *Participation.* The analyst's interview is the employee's major participation exercise. He is not involved to the extent that he can say what the analyst must do, but he is informing of his own unique knowledge—of *his* job. He is exercising sapiential authority which is vested in himself not in his job, and to that extent he 'is somebody'; and, moreover, it is authority about his job which is partly himself as projected into the society of the firm. His opinions are sought, his information is needed, he is a first source on his own affairs. He does not have to go before a 'committee', as in some schemes, and justify himself, he is giving of his knowledge of facts to another man who, as analyst, is his equal—but doing a different job. (This is part of the justice of the method.) Nor does he need worry about how his facts are going to be treated by the Grading Conference in his absence.

For on that Grading Conference there should be someone who is there to see that justice is done and fairness is applied. It may be a trade union delegate, or, for managers, a managerial delegate, both able to represent the person and to give of their own expertness. (In the Manual it is recommended that, where jobs involve trade union members, a proper official of a trade union should be on the Grading Conference, not a shop steward who, understandably, tends to be biased and has a narrower perspective.)

3 *Justice and Fairness.* The essence of justice, the sense of equality of all members of the firm, is inherent in the Method. There are no 'clusters', no special 'key-jobs', no classes, shop-floor, office and managerial staff, to be treated differently. All their jobs are analysed with the same instrument and by the same people. The constant struggle to eliminate the 'we-they' feeling in industry will be helped by this elimination of differential treatment. There always will be status and prestige differences, of necessity, but the struggle is to eliminate 'class' differences in the firm, differences which are perpetuated

by the concepts of 'clusters', of 'us–them', of the ideas of 'blue-collar and white-collar' and the sense of 'superiority of groups', as over and against the unique differences of all equal persons.

As I write this I can look over the River Clyde in Scotland, historically the 'home' of militant trade unionism, of the Keir Hardie tradition. Just over the hill in the far distance is Ayrshire where the Scottish poet, Burns, wrote "The rank is but the guinea stamp, the man's the man for a' that". (The poets always are the first to tell us of really important matters.) To my mind these are connected. The trade unionists hereabouts are, on the whole, not politically Communist. They are mainly behind the British Labour Party, and their behaviour is conservative (small c), but below all this is a deep-seated belief in the equality of all men. It matters not about their rank, whether they are managers or specialists or whatever—there will always have to be rank—what matters is the individual; as if they were echoing the words of Kant, that every man is an end in himself. Here is the essence of justice. [I shall enlarge on the use of the Method in this context in the next Chapter.]

There is also fairness, the sense of equity in establishing the 'guinea stamp' of rank, distributive justice. Given the Grading the Assessment Committee has the job of deciding the distribution of the payroll. The size of the payroll is essentially a policy decision of the Board of Directors of the firm; it is in the distribution of this 'cake' that the members of the firm participate—for which reason those agents (not just delegates) with the right to *act* for the members, the President or Managing Director, trade union agents and the like, should form this committee.

All the evidence points to the belief that differentials are 'fair' when the Grade/log pay curve is close to linear. Therefore, if adjustments to individual pays are made to achieve better linearity, this is the application of distributive justice in 'sharing the cake'. I have mentioned in passing some of the points in policy of distribution which I need not recapitulate here—they form part of another thesis on *Policy for pay and its administration*.

The activities of the Assessment Committee must be seen in the light of the Theory of Reward (Chapter 13) from which I quote. "Reward and punishment are part of the same social contract", i.e. retributive and distributive justice are the two sides of the same coin. "This contract is reciprocal or mutual, as the part is responsible to the whole, the whole is responsible to the part for providing the facilities necessary to fulfil function, and for support and regeneration. Therefore, because of this mutual obligation, there can be no arbitrary decision by one side or the other, of the amount of support. It must be mutually contracted. What can be decided by the firm", i.e. as a policy decision, "is the total payroll, its distribution must be agreed". This is the function of the Assessment Committee, members of the firm, agents for all the other members of the firm, agreeing on distribution of reward. It should not be bargaining, a quid pro quo agreement, it should not be negotiation, agreement of two or more parties it is an executive committee of the firm agreeing with each other, deciding as a whole. The objectivity of the Grading framework encourages such agreement, it establishes constraints yet allows freedom to manoeuvre within that framework.

4 This freedom to manoeuvre lies in the *subjectivity* of the subgrading procedures. He would be foolish who claims that a method exists which provides an objective method of establishing pay for any job. The Grading structure provides the framework within which variations can take place, a fact of all living Nature [73]. Principles of nonrandomness, a rule of ordered distribution of units, appear in "organisms or even organisms as a group". "This is order without minute precision, order within which there is scope. Therefore, let us not confound rule with fixity, order with rigour, regularity with stereotypism. Each individual is a unique form of expression of general norms and laws" . . . "True organic order, as we know it, sets only the general frame and pattern, leaving the precise ways of execution adjustable and to this extent, indeterminate". This is the *"organic design for living . . . Freedom within the law: responsible freedom to move within an orbit as wide as, but no wider than what is compatible with the preservation of the over-all order that defines the harmony of relationships on which effective living and survival depend"*. A famous zoologist wrote that (but the italicisation is mine). It expresses perfectly what I am trying to say. The firm is an organism, each member is an organism within it, the laws of biology hold here as in the rest of living Nature. Decision Bands and Grades are the framework, the overall order for survival of the firm, the relations of the members are defined by that framework, and are expressed in the system of reward. Within the over-all order of Bands and Grades there is indeterminism that reflects the freedom of the individual—again justice and fairness.

5 and 6 *The need for a pay structure not too far from the existing,* and the *ability of the firms to pay* for changes, are closely related. As I said before the Board will not accept a change it cannot afford—total payroll policy is its decision. But, fortunately, the existing pay structures tend to approach an acceptable differential system, Figs 14.1 and 14.2. The changes required there are slight. But in others, in particular that depicted in Fig. 14.3 H, considerable changes have to be made. In *The Manual* a general principle is stated that "no pay shall be reduced". Any attempt to do so reduces acceptability. The three alternatives for reducing the inequities of non-linearity of curve are:

1 Raising pays that are below—this positive action is acceptable as long as it does not go beyond the curve of equity.
2 Hold pays that are too high until the curve rises to meet them. There is a constant movement upwards as the cost-of-living rises and also because of inflation. If this holding of pay while others are rising to meet it is not acceptable, then
3 The job is re-structured to justify the pay (economy of grading—see next Chapter) or the incumbent is removed to another job with the appropriate pay.

The Method lends itself to clear demonstration of inequities (which sometimes explain otherwise inexplicable behaviour such as high labour turnover) and, at the same time, an indication of how much change should be made.
Much time is wasted in negotiations on 'round the board' pay rises as

distinct from the job evaluation exercise of adjusting inequities of differentials. The total basic payroll can be calculated from Eq. (4) of Chapter 14, and adjustments made for overtime and other payments. The effect of 'percentage' demands can be calculated rapidly and, moreover, the effect of such demands on the total pay curve can be readily demonstrated.

7 *Time-saving*

(a) The inordinate waste of time in conferences and committees for the standard methods of job evaluation stems from their subjectivity as already described. This Method cuts down such time wasting—the grading procedure is fast if the analysts have produced the correct amount of the simple information needed.

(b) Subgrading, being of a subjective nature is slower, but the limits of each Grade are specified by the pay curve and so there is no need to spend time deciding these limits.

(c) One of the difficulties of other Methods is the necessity for very detailed job descriptions on which committees can work. The job description required by this Method is much simpler (see *The Manual*) and analysis of jobs is somewhere in the order of two to three times the speed of other methods (provided the analyst does not become too interested in the interviewees' 'gossip'—it has happened to me!).

8 *Adjustability.* The existence of only eleven Grades from top to bottom means that there is a wide range within each Grade for change in job structure without changing Grade. The Grading Conference keeps records of all its grading and subgrading findings so, therefore, it is comparatively quick for the analyst to analyse the new job, grading the tasks, processes and operations in terms of complexity (if the job remains in the same grade), and comparing the result with the precedent set by the Grading Conference. The employee himself can examine these records—I see no reason why he cannot —and can see for himself the relation of the new job to the old and to others, and so his appropriate subgrade. It also means, as I propose to indicate in the next Chapter, that it becomes easier to re-structure jobs for purposes of training and enrichment. There is no need for committees to meet in order to decide points degrees and weightings of perhaps new factors of importance in a new technology. The Ranking Method is very difficult to use in situations requiring adjustability, the Job Classification Method less so and with it the Point and Castellion Methods. The Time-Span Method cannot deal with new jobs where time-span is still to be discovered.

9 *Leap-frogging* is a technique well-known to good trade unionists doing their job of 'maintaining and improving wages and conditions'. In the absence of any theoretical background to pay differentials, in the belief (however unfounded) that pay is 'according to the going rate' as the economists have encouraged them to do, and because of the subjectivity of job evaluation where it has been installed, managers lose control of the pay structure. The existence of a demonstrable pay curve of equitable payment puts the brake on demands for changes on account of comparability with individual pays

elsewhere. Such a demand then becomes an attempt to move the whole curve and not one or a few pays at a time in the best leap-frogging manner. It means, too, that, in the UK where there is craft unionism, the various unions in one firm have to agree among themselves to act as a body to retain the system of agreed differentials, and to change the curve as a whole, that is, to act as one industrial union at the level of the firm, on the American pattern.

10 *Working conditions* are external to the job and can alter, although the job does not. Moreover, as already pointed out, they cannot be objectively scaled—they can only be the subject of agreement, almost of negotiation between the two parties of the employee (or his agent) and the firm. By keeping conditions outside the job grading and subgrading:

(*a*) The employee, especially on the shop-floor or other place with uncomfortable conditions, appreciates clearly that this factor is well taken into account in determining earnings, it is not immersed in a morass of factors and degrees and weightings, it is a straight forward contractual agreement. It also appears equitable to him in comparing his earnings with those of clerical workers.

(*b*) Since payment for conditions is not built into the basic pay it means that improvement of conditions can be reflected in a change in this contingency payment. If it is built in an employee would then continue to be receiving pay for something that does not exist.

(*c*) Since it is not built in, the differentials in basic pay remain equitable; if they are built in, they may not appear equitable. No one objects to extra earnings of another because of poor conditions of work but he does object to inequitable differentials in basic pay. The consolidation into the basic pay of payment for conditions has been the cause of disagreement on differentials, and so 'leap-frogging'.

(*d*) Trade unions, as already quoted, have the function of 'improving conditions' including physical conditions. The existence of this area for negotiation as a subjective basis means that they have an opportunity for demonstrating their function.

11 *Labour market changes.* Similarly the unions' function of 'improving wages' can be demonstrated by negotiation for changes in pay on account of changes in the labour market—provided the firm has not already acted in reply to such environmental pressures. Extra payment on account of shortage of a particular kind of labour, if built in to the basic pay, distorts the equitable pay curve and dissension tends to develop. Such market payments should be 'contingency'. Otherwise they can become uneconomic. For example, in Southern Rhodesia where I was involved among other matters, in setting pay differentials in the Public Services, the pay of architects in the Ministry of Works was anomalous. In the early 1950's when there was a big building boom, architects were 'expensive' and their commencing salaries were fixed at a rate well above that of their professional colleagues. Ten years later the boom had subsided and there was a 'glut' of architects on the

labour market, willing to take even senior clerical positions. Yet to hire one as an architect the former inequitable, bolstered differential had to be continued. A built-in contingency payment for a former market shortage of supply can be adjusted with little difficulty by holding pay constant until the rising pay curve envelopes it in the appropriate grade box. (Notice that the Method does not require reduction of pay.)

12 The matter of Incentives is discussed in the next Chapter.

Chapter sixteen   **Other Applications of Work Analysis**

At the end of Chapter 11 the requirements of theory were said to be explanatory and predictive—which have been demonstrated; but also, to quote Robinson again, "If the explanation is a good one does it lead to any guide or set out guide lines as to how companies, employers of labour, can improve industrial relations and increase their manpower utilisation". This Chapter sets out guide lines based on the theory, but a *much condensed version*, a bare summary of the possibilities.

Work Analysis has been defined in Chapter 11 as "the analysis of work in terms of the kinds and quantity of the decisions made".

It is my contention that Work Analysis is the basis of all those activities that come under the heading of the primary function of support and regeneration, the personnel function (Chapter 2); and furthermore Work Analysis is a basis of the primary function of management as it is defined in the standard texts, 'planning, organising, staffing, direction, control and innovation'. None of these constituent functions can be adequately fulfilled unless the decision-making system and its potentialities are understood. The key situation of Work Analysis is depicted in Fig. 16.1 showing how the various constituent functions are related. What follows is merely an outline of that system and its implications (clearly, to follow the ramifications of this thesis will require treatment in depth). This outline follows Chapter 11 which indicated the need for a logical approach, for some underlying, some fundamental theme which relates the various activities in a firm, which relates the jobs evaluated to the people performing them.

Work Analysis, as the foundation of this Method of Job Evaluation, separates the job content from the skills, abilities and capacities brought to it by the performer, a separation that is not attempted in any other method except the Time-span. But, having established the jobs and their content, the next logical step is to tie them to members of the firm. It is possible to put down on paper the structure of jobs for a firm, and to show the relations

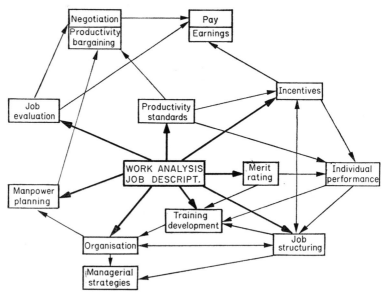

Figure 16.1   Work analysis as central to most managerial activities

of these jobs and hence the roles; but that firm does not 'come into being', does not become a living, social organism until people perform the jobs. Contrarily, the living firm may lose some of its people, the jobs continue and are performed by others, and the firm continues to live—that is the essence of the word social, members are not fixedly part of the firm. Just as the bee-swarm is a social organism which can continue to survive if some members die, so does a business enterprise. Indeed, it may lose many of its members and still survive. Some jobs are eradicated, the others are re-structured, what continues is the system of decision-making; and if that is disrupted the organism dies—however many of its members survive as individuals. Sometimes the system suffers dysfunctions, mainly due to stimuli from the external world (the decision-system is open) and we give crude descriptions to these dysfunctions, such as 'inadequate communications', 'bad human relations' and 'poor industrial relations'. And many researchers —I have been one myself—spend much time looking at these dysfunctions without working out what the healthy business body is, what is its anatomy, what is its physiology, what are the causes of these diseases in terms of the firm's anatomy and physiology.

The anatomist of the modern business corporation is at a stage of understanding comparable to that of the human anatomists of the middle of the 19th century. They had recognised the central nervous system and were beginning to appreciate the involuntary nervous system, the distribution of complexes of ganglia and the like. We know something about the 'formal lines of communication' in an enterprise, we are now beginning to see the functions of the involuntary system, the 'ganglionic complexes' we call 'informal groups' and how these are related to the total system of decision-making. Some writers actually believe that the system should be built around these autonomic complexes. We cannot. I need but repeat the findings of the zoologist I quoted in the previous chapter—there has to be a framework of order within which the indeterminate, the autonomous can act. The framework is the decision-system, men are the unique, the unknown quantities, the mainly unpredictables, who build the informal decision-systems within that framework and need and have the right to exercise that uniqueness. For, after all, it is the individual, of his sapiential authority, which is personal and not social-positional, who generates enthusiasm, who produces ideas, who creates; and these are necessary for survival and growth. The firm has the duty to support and, if necessary, regenerate him, the personnel function. So, within the framework of the decision-making system given by Work Analysis, how is the person so supported in terms of that framework?

In Chapter 11 I made some comments under Operational Principles on such matters as Training, Appraisal and Promotion, etc., the gist of the argument being that this Method of Job Evaluation must be related to such subfunctions, and through Work Analysis which is the basis of the Method. In other words a bye-product, so to speak, of the Method is a new approach to, or at least a help in carrying out these subfunctions. But Fig. 16.1 does not put Job Evaluation as central to them, it puts Work Analysis; so these other subfunctions are not assisted as though a bye-product, Job Evaluation is only one part of that totality centred on Work Analysis.

TRAINING AND DEVELOPMENT

By *Training* I understand the process by which a person learns the way to carry out a job, the technique, the kinds of information to be used and how to handle them. For example, it might be learning how to move machine parts, or how to calculate, or how to work a computer, or how to make designs, how to draw up a balance sheet. All this amounts to learning the 'tools of management', engineering, production, marketing, accountancy, design and so on. They are not management which is a common denominator of all departments which make decisions with these different tools.

By *Development* I understand the learning of the why of these tools (rather than the how), learning principles of approach to problem-solving and decision-making with these tools, learning the principles of utilisation of resources, and particularly of human resources which is the main concern of management. To that extent Development is Education as distinct from Training.

By the very nature of the different kinds of decision, Training is the major activity in Bands O, A and B. The decisions there are not concerned with 'why' but with 'how'. However, Routine Decision-makers (Band B) are better able to understand the 'how' if they know 'why', and by Grade 4, the peculiar grade of 'junior manager', Development begins to play a strong part in the programme. The departmental specialisms of Middle Management still require Training to make Band C decisions, but those making Programming Decisions of Band D require far more Development. The nature of their planning decisions demands a new way of thinking which some years ago I called 'integrative', the capacity to make decisions in breadth (surveying a whole series of different matters) rather than in depth, in looking for solutions in limited fields, in Band C. This integrative thinking reaches its peak in Band E. The definitions of decisions in the Castellion Method are most useful in this context—see Table 8.1.

A Training and Development programme should be based on this clear-cut need to learn progressively more difficult, and different, kinds of decision-making, Training being concerned mainly with the subject matter on which the decisions are made. For example, case studies should be devised, not to solve problems in, say, Marketing, but to solve problems requiring different kinds of decision, Interpretive, Programming or Policy, in Marketing; and there should be a sequence of that nature which thus constitutes Development. (Such a programme must, of necessity, involve Manpower planning.)

In a way this means 'going through the mill' on paper, learning increasingly difficult decisions, and so a new look should be had at the concept of apprenticeship, which is 'going through the mill' in the firm up to Band B. Such apprenticeship is *designed for a job* of decision-making in a specified subject, therefore it is training. Development is not concerned with the subject but with decision, it is *designed for a career* as distinct from a job. At other Band levels there is a similar accent on Training for a job, in Marketing, in Production, in Operational Research and such subjects: training for 'general management' is Development for a career.

One of the major drawbacks in the British craft union system is the accent on apprenticeship, on job rather than career, on the continued belief that certain machine jobs can be done only by 'skilled' men, i.e. with apprenticeship, and not by others, even though the decisions required are semi-skilled. This institution is perpetuated by those job evaluation methods that specify apprenticeship as required "education and experience" for a skilled job, even though that job may have few, perhaps only one skilled decision to be made. (We have a case of a skilled turner who has been working a machine for 23 years, making three process, Routine Decisions *each year* when he re-sets the machine, after which he then operates with Automatic Decisions.) Moreover, craft unions, by emphasising apprenticeship and so job, deprive their members of career opportunities. This demarcation between Bands B and C was the basis of a belief in the UK Civil Service that no person from 'the Executive Class' could enter 'the Administrative Class', and it was eight years between my first pointing out this anomaly and its change by the Fulton Commission on the reorganisation of the Civil Service. I see no reason why a person entering a firm cannot rise to the top if he has the capacities for decision-making and is given the opportunity of a career rather than a job. Which leads to the subject of Promotion.

PROMOTION

1 "No man has the right to promotion purely on the grounds of length of service".

2 "Merit is the sole criterion of eligibility for promotion".
3 "Every man has the right to earn promotion" [57, pp. 90–1].

There still exists, especially in bureaucratic systems, the belief that promotion depends to a great extent on seniority in years of service. There is, logically speaking, only one criterion for promotion and that is fitness for the job, and fitness includes those characteristics which a person brings to the job. It is for this reason that job descriptions (Job Specifications) specifying abilities required, descriptions that are important in the Point and similar Methods which rely on factors including skill and education, are more useful than Work Analysis which does not supply such a description.

However, there is a disadvantage in specifying abilities required, if these are couched entirely in terms of Training which includes seniority, apprenticeship, examinations passed and the like.

1 Such Training criteria do not guarantee a person's capacity for performing a job with which he has had no contact. Industrialists know that the holding of a university degree, even in business administration (which is a Training programme mainly), does not guarantee the capacity to manage well—although the intelligence inherent in the capacity to pass examinations is useful in management; and so some graduates 'get by' but seldom rise. Similarly an apprenticeship is not necessary to guarantee capacity to make Routine Decisions—there are many skilled jobs (as defined here) which can be and are carried out by persons without the standard apprenticeship.

2 Such job descriptions lend themselves to discriminatory practices. For example, to say that a job requires a graduate will cut out of the list of eligible candidates some who are capable of making the decisions of that grade having learned to do so without academic education. Again, in parts of USA the opportunities for further education are limited for coloured people or, to put it another way, there is a greater percentage of coloured population who do not have some of the higher educational qualifications through no fault of their own, yet they are capable of making the decisions required. The situation is exacerbated in South Africa and India.

Some definitions may be appropriate here. *Eligibility* (in the context Promotion) means the possession of those characteristics which befit a man for promotion. *Efficiency* is proved competence, and there may be more than one type of competence involved, although, in general, efficiency marks competence and capability, as distinct from *proficiency* which marks expertness and adeptness in a particular function. *Qualification* means the possession of competences which are necessary for fulfilling a specific post towards which promotion is possible. It may include efficiency and proficiency and it may include a competence which has not yet been proved in experience, that is to say it may be a qualification which has been tested by examination but not in practice. An examination may qualify a person for a particular post requiring those capacities tested by the examination. But it does not necessarily follow that he is eligible for the job, for he may not have proved himself in terms of efficiency and proficiency. For example, a man in Grade 2 may have passed examinations which are necessary for qualification for a post in Grade 5, but, since he has had no experience of decision-making in the intermediate Grades he is not eligible.

The criteria for Promotion lie in Development, the learned capacity for making decisions—in other words proven capacity for doing a job. Undoubtedly the inclusion of paper *qualifications* that are helpful in making decisions is most useful in showing certain capacities but they do not specify *eligibility* for promotion, earned right to promotion. The 'proof of the pudding is in the eating' is a pragmatic dictum of considerable importance in business.

Development is part of the function of managing.

1 In order to bring those in his sphere of authority to the highest efficiency —and this is his duty, responsibility 'upwards' to the firm, to get the best possible decisions—he must so organise the Development of his staff that they learn progressively more difficult decision-making, usually more complex decision-making.

2 He must develop subordinates, or one subordinate, in order to take over in case of emergency (no man is indispensable) or for translation to another part of the firm where a crisis demands help.

3 Every man must be given his chance, his right to earn promotion. This is part of responsibility 'downwards.' (I prefer to think of it as a relation between equals and so horizontally.) It is not a matter of sending a junior 'on a course' of training. Development is primarily 'on the job'.

The prime consideration in Promotion is whether a person has learned to make the necessary decisions for the job or has shown himself capable of making these decisions—and Work Analysis provides the information on the decision-making content of a job. This leads to Merit-Rating for promotion and Performance Appraisal which is closely related.

MERIT-RATING AND PERFORMANCE APPRAISAL

By *merit* I mean that quality combining qualification, efficiency and performance, wherefore a man showing such a quality is eligible for reward. By *performance* I mean the application of competencies to the achievement of the purpose of the enterprise through carrying out a job.

A man may be efficient at a job but, unless he applies that efficiency over a considerable period of time, he has not shown performance. For instance, a turner may be highly efficient on a lathe, perhaps proficient on a particular lathe, but, if he uses this efficiency erratically and inconsistently, his performance may be lower than that of another turner who, less efficient, nevertheless consistently applies what efficiency he has. It may be said that the word 'diligence' implies performance in this sense.

As in job evaluation, how is performance in one kind of a job, say in production, to be compared with performance in another, say in sales? The opportunities to show a high standard of performance in the sense of overt quantifiable results vary from job to job. A skilled turner may be very diligent in producing one item, a salesman may 'hit' a soft market by chance and sell a lot. We have come back to the problem of distributive justice, and again Work Analysis can help, though not completely.

There is one item common to all jobs, decision-making and, following that, differentiation by kinds of decision. In reporting on a junior a senior can give a subjective but certainly useful opinion on diligence after the junior has gained a standard of efficiency. Thereafter merit lies in performance demonstrated by ability to learn more complex decisions. If the senior is giving opportunity to earn promotion, to merit promotion, he is providing opportunity to show performance in this manner measured against a standard established by experience—is the junior slow, average or fast in learning more complex decisions? The faster he is in learning the more he will be contributing than the slower person—and so he should be rewarded. (But he will not necessarily be contributing more unless he exhibits consistently as well, diligence.) So by analysing the work in terms of decisions the progress in decision-making can be gauged, and in a near quantifiable fashion.

Similarly, the performance of the senior can be near quantified if appropriate records are kept of how he re-structures the jobs of his section or department so as to give opportunity to his juniors and also to make his department more efficient (1, 2, 3 under Promotion above). This re-structuring is a regular process and cannot be done haphazardly (job structuring under Organisation below) and if done properly must, by its very nature, lead to high performance of his unit. Thus Training, Development, Merit-Rating and Promotion become integrated through the application of Work Analysis.

ORGANISATION

The theory of decision-systems requires that organisational structure be composed of decision-complexes with the appropriate relations of the decision units and so of the persons in these units. Poor organisation means a misuse of human resources, of men in decision-making. In the main this stems from a misunderstanding of the basic principles of *delegation* which consists of the normal

    1 Assigning of functions ('delegating responsibility').

    2 Delegating authority ('authority commensurate with responsibility'), and the least recognised but most important

    3 Specifying kind of decision.

The extensive literature on the difference between delegation and decentralisation hinges on failure to recognise this third aspect.

Seniors keep to themselves decisions that should be delegated to juniors of a given Grade. Not making decisions of that Grade these juniors then feel they have lost status, their jobs are not so important as their titles indicate.

They become dispirited or rebellious or show other signs of frustration. Given the decisions appropriate to their Grade, and increasing the difficulty and complexity as well, they feel the propriety of their grading so their status and so themselves. *Job enrichment*, about which so much is made of in the literature these last few years, is merely the essence of good organisation according to decision-system theory. It follows that job enrichment cannot be readily undertaken as part of normal good managerial practice unless the managers know Work Analysis.

The *economy of grading* is a process akin to job enrichment and depending on Work Analysis. If a man's job contains but a few of those decisions of the Grade for which he is being paid this is not only wasting his talents (if he has them) but also misuse of the reward structure. If there are few decisions of the senior Grade the job can be *re-structured* so that the tasks or processes requiring these decisions can be used to enrich another job, and the tasks requiring decisions of a lower grade used to enrich jobs in that lower grade. The payroll is being better used and men are being better used. What is more, since the re-structuring is based on Work Analysis, which is also the basis of the assessment of reward, there is an immediate and easy way to establish the change in reward with the change in structure—which is not possible with any of the other Methods of job evaluation.

This is an actual example of re-structuring in practice several years ago [53, p. 66]. I discovered a Grade 10 member of staff overwhelmed with so much work, a bulging brief case over the weekend, because, so he said, his Grade 9 people were in the same trouble. In fact he had asked for the addition of one Grade 8 and two Grade 7 men to his staff. On examining his brief-case I found only two papers that required Grade 10 decisions, the rest were Grade 9 and Grade 7. The next day I found the same thing in the brief-case of one of the Grade 9 staff who was making some decisions of Grade 5. One of these Grade 5 staff was making decisions of Grade 1 as well as of Grades 5, 4 and 3. Within one month, with the aid of a few bright young people seconded to me, and applying the principles of the economy of grading, the whole of this enterprise was re-structured. Twelve Grade 0 clerks were brought in (not Grade 8 and Grade 7) and the system of decision-making 'pushed upwards'. The Grade 10 member and his immediate staff now found themselves with time to do the job proper to their Grades and so were earning their reward justly and more effectively—what is more, they liked it.

By structuring on the basis of Decision Bands the *use of meetings*, as part of the decision-making system, becomes logical, confirming the empirical observations of Lickert and others [54, Chapter 14]. All meetings in an enterprise fall into four categories according to their function in a decision-complex, Informative Conferences, Conclusive Conferences, Directive Committees and Executive Committees. There are no other kinds of meeting. The composition of these meetings is established by the kind of decision to be made and the appropriate sapiential authority required. This logical and optimum use of meetings and so of human resources in organisation cannot be achieved without Work Analysis.

Managers who complain about the waste of time on committee work are also those who are unaware of the times and situation to use particular forms of *management strategies*. There is much facile talk about consultative and participative management as 'ideal' strategies to suit all purposes. But there is little clarity in definition. 'Managerial grids', '3-D Management', MBO, all boil down to the matter of involvement and commitment of men to the immediate purpose (not necessarily the broad goal—so many writers confuse purpose and goal). Men are not involved far less committed when they are 'consulted' only at the Information stage of the decision-complex. When they are consulted at the Conclusive stage in Conclusive conferences they become morally involved because their conclusion is concerned with 'goodness' of the decision. Forming part of Executive committees they are literally committed, more than just involved. Proper consultative management involves men at the Conclusive stage, proper participative management commits men at the Executive stage. 'Organic' structures are those that involve and commit people in the use of sapiential authority (which is personal and is not structurally defined); 'mechanistic' structures are autocratic or bureaucratic, with accent upon structural authority with neither involvement or commitment.

Under this heading of Organisation falls another useful addition from Work Analysis. It is now possible to represent organisational structure in a new and more accurate fashion as a *Matrix of Decision Band and Function*. Table 16.1 is an example from a chemical plant. Apart from the advantages that come from showing the relations in terms of kind of decision the illustration of difference of decision kind in 'horizontality' instead of in 'hierarchy' gives expression to the late-20th Century philosophy that stresses equalitarianism. I have never met in industry any one who has not recognised, and certainly agrees to the necessity for coordinative decisions, and so senior and

TABLE 16.1   *A decision structure in a chemical plant*

Band A Automatic		Band B Routine		Band C Interpretive	
A1	A2	B3	B4	C5	C6
Process Opers.	Process Coord. Inv. Exptl. Chem.	Prop. Planner Process Sup.	.... Invest. Chem. Senior Inv. Chem.	Plant Mgr. (P-product)	
? Colour Matchers		Shift Exptl. Chemists	Colourist (Plant) Colourist (Admin.)	Development Chemist	Sect. Mgr.
Process Opers.	Process Coord.	A-prod. Planner Process Sup.	.... Suptdt.	Plant Mgr. (A-product)	
Inv. Exptl. Chem.	....	Invest. Chem. Skilled Techs.	Senior Inv. Chem. Senior Asst. F. Asst. F. (Mtce)	Plant Engr.	
		Tng. Sups.	....	SDP, WSA. Coord. Tng.	
Lab. Exptl. Chem.	Shift Exptl. Chem.	Plant Lab. Sup. Asst. Pl. Inspect.	Plant Inspector Electr. F.		
		Skilled Techs.	Electr. Sup. Instr. Sup. Designer		
		Cost Clerk	....	Plant Acct.	

junior. But I have met those who object to 'superordinate/subordinate', 'superior/inferior', 'boss'!

INCENTIVES

On this subject I have already noted, in Chapter 11, that there should be some logical relation between job evaluation and incentives. Of course we accept that, if a person works harder or longer, he should be rewarded more—but how is this reward to be measured? (The Time-span Method of job evaluation does not permit of such measurement since time-span, according to Jaques, corresponds to earnings whatever the hours worked, and not to basic rate). Criticisms of incentive schemes is rampant but none of these criticisms, at least those I have read and heard about, distinguish between the scheme and the method of implementing it. Again definitions are needed, especially because of the interconnections of incentive and differential payments—I shall be considering only monetary incentives.

An *incentive* "is a money reward for bettering some aspects of performance; efficiency, stability of output, labour turnover, absenteeism, accidents, better industrial relations". Here, we are concerned with job content, output [49, p. 145]. It is intimately related to Grade differentials, as shop-floor staff see them, because a piece-rate, or payment-by-results (PBR) incentive scheme, can bring about a situation where extra reward (bonus) gained by extra effort may be built into the basic pay, the difference becoming regarded as a differential which, thereafter, has to be maintained. The trouble is that some people, for instance managers, may continue to see the reward as earnings—basic pay-plus-bonus—and the staff see it as basic pay only. At that point of recognition the incentive scheme no longer works as such.

It is possible to understand the staff point of view in this way: Since in unit time, say one shift, the incentive stimulates the men to greater output, the number of decisions per unit time is increased, therefore the difficulty or complexity of the job increases and so its importance, for which they are rewarded by extra payment. But this is exactly the same as a subgrade differential awarded on account of greater difficulty or complexity decided by the techniques of Decision-Count or Count-Ranking. A new subgrade comes into being, higher than the previous one, and on this new basic pay subsequent incentives have to be calculated, not on the original basic pay— otherwise the staff will not react to the incentive.

The same kind of thing happens when bonuses given as incentives to greater output become built into basic pay, when basic pay-plus-bonus is transmuted into 'measured day work' pay calculated on average output over a period of, commonly, a year. The result is a differential in basic pay as over and against other staff of the same Grade, and they, mindful of the previous differential, demand that the status quo be re-established. Leap-frogging has commenced and wage drift. A way to prevent this is to demonstrate that the consolidation has, literally, increased the complexity of the job and the differential is justifiable. This can be done only by Work Analysis and assessment on decision-grading.

Of course if the incentive reward is very large, and if it has been calculated as a percentage of the original basic rate, that rate must have been too much for the worth of the job—it must have been determined either by guess or by poor job evaluation and the original differentials were awry. *For that reason it is essential that differentials be established on the basis of Work Analysis before incentive schemes are instituted.* (Years of trouble in the British docks had its roots in failure to recognise this principle.)

This cannot be done on the basis of any other method of job evaluation. An incentive reward is given for something extra. Consider the Point Method as typical and the factors used. The work does not involve extra skill in terms of experience and education which remain constant. The conditions of work do not alter. There is no extra responsibility since machines and other facilities are not altered. There is only extra physical and mental effort, more movements have to be made, more equations have to be solved, but the same kinds of movement and equations, the same kinds of decision only more of them. Hence a basic pay founded on all these factors cannot be the base for a calculation of incentive payment; nor, if the job is subsequently assessed will the result alter, for the kind of movement and the kind of mental effort do not change, as the other factors do not change.

It seems to me that primary and secondary wage drift (see Chapter 1), as arising from the use of piece-work, and then incentives, can be explained as in the third paragraph above. And, given this explanation which is based on the logic of Work Analysis, measures can be worked out on operational principles in order to counteract and control wage drift. The first essential is job evaluation by the Method described here. Which leads me to the final Chapter.

Chapter seventeen **A National Pay Structure**

The difficulties in setting up an industry-wide pay structure have been outlined in Chapter 1 with special reference to Swedish experience. The greater difficulties facing the institution of a national pay structure were illustrated by the case of Holland. The sources of these difficulties, I can usefully recapitulate, seem to be:

1 Use of a job evaluation method which has no theoretical validity, either explanatory or predictive.
2 The failure of the method in adapting to changing technology, changing labour supply and changing conditions of work.
3 The failure to recognise ability to pay and the incentive of reward for efficiency.

It is my contention that this new Method avoids these sources of difficulty; it has proven theoretical validity both explanatory and predictive, it fits the facts; the summation of the pay curve is dependent upon the payroll and so ability to pay; the slope of the pay curve is dependent upon the agreed distribution marking efficiency of staff; the Method permits of rapid restructuring of jobs in answer to changing needs; pay for conditions of work and related labour shortage, being based on subjective criteria, is separately agreed or negotiated. The Method can be applied to all jobs, not just manual, throughout any one industry, and Dr Husband's indices for industry (Chapter 14) establish a differential based on existing structures. Similarly he provides an index for regional differences. A national pay structure can then be formulated.

Indeed, such a structure, expressed in other ways and terms, already exists. If the slopes for all the firms in a nation were summed the result would be a distribution curve of pay of the exponential kind theoretically postulated. Since there is, in general, a natural reduction in number of persons in each decision grade—for a decision of one grade coordinates several decisions in a lower grade—there will be over the whole nation an approximation to an exponential decrease in numbers of people in each grade. Therefore, the higher the income the fewer the people receiving it; and the result is Pareto's well-known income distribution curve. This was first referred to (at least as far as my reading goes) by Zipf [76]. The Pareto curve does not occur by chance, it is the summation of a subconsciously determined process of differentiation.

There is a movement in the national pay curve, which I first referred to in 1961 and two years later [51 and 52]. Figure 17.1 shows the change in

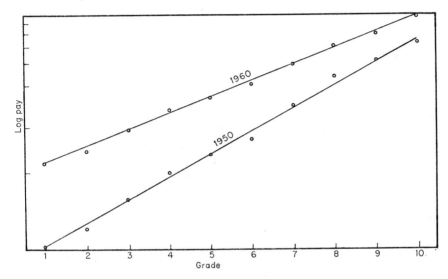

Figure 17.1 Pay curves, UK Civil Service, 1950, 1960

the pay curve of the UK Civil Service, as one industry, over a period of ten years. The significance of this movement is best explained by macro-economics, which is not my field, but I hazard a guess that it stems from an egalitarian change in a more affluent society coupled with rising cost of living, and alterations in ways of living because the nation is more affluent. But which factors are eggs and which chickens I do not know.

The rest of this Chapter is in the form of notes; their amplification would require as much space as all the chapters of this book combined, but such notes will indicate the potentialities of this Method on the national scale.

1 Such a *national pay structure* is not based on occupational differentiation but on industrial. It follows that the traditional British craft unions are structurally incompatible with such a pay structure. There is a reflection of this difference in changes occurring in the USA, where there is widespread industrial job evaluation, a movement away from plant bargaining (which is expanding in the UK at present) and concentration on industrial. It is happening, however, in the UK where unions combine, as in the automobile and chemical industries, to negotiate industry-wide bargains. The problems

of inter-union disagreement over occupational differentials and consequent leap-frogging can be softened by use of the Method—job content can be more objectively compared. In one experiment described by Husband [20] the introduction of the Method into a firm in the printing industry brought together all the unions, general and craft, and they now work in concert— an industrial union in miniature. Recognising the difficulties facing re-organisation of trade union structure in the UK towards industrial unionism this kind of activity at the level of the firm is a half-way stage which can be acceptable.

2 One of the most important needs of today's industry and commerce is *flexibility* (the capacity of the firm to change structure) and *adaptability* (the capacity of the individual to adopt a new job structure). Demarcation arising from craft trade unionism is one of the inhibitory factors. If jobs are evaluated on the basis of kinds of decision and not on skills or on techniques, or on the subject for decision-making, the way to easing demarcation is open. Trade unions can be assisted in such a change from the *insecurity of jobs* (hence demarcation) to the *security of careers* in decision-making. For example, in a chemical plant the craft engineering union would not agree to a chemical process worker, normally making Routine Decisions (skilled), using a spanner for the simple, unskilled operation of removing the nuts from an autoclave shield. The justification was insecurity of the craft jobs. Yet by giving up unskilled tasks and operations the skilled craftsman would be enriching his job and so raising its subgrade, hence getting more pay. And, reciprocally, the skilled mechanic could learn tasks belonging to other occupations, he would become more adjustable, capable of taking on jobs not of his trade when that trade was less in demand. We certainly need more specialists in the new technologies but correspondingly we need more 'generalists' and the old specialisms with their traditional apprenticeships are not adaptable.

3 Because job content can now be compared on a logical basis the phrase '*equal pay for equal work*' becomes a reality. Sex, colour and class discrimina-tion can be wiped out on the basis of a coherent statement of fairness and justice. The arguments put forward by some protagonists of this theme are distorted, comparing the 'average woman's pay' with the 'average man's', or the 'average coloured man's pay' with the 'average white man's', without reference to equality of work. Only the basic pays for grades can be compared. And some interesting results emerge. In the automobile industry the cry for equal pay for women would require that the unskilled seat-cover seamsters should be paid the same as the unskilled man on the production line who is receiving the highest unskilled pay in the country. But this pay is essentially in two parts, a basic unskilled pay and a contingency payment for the conditions of work on the line. His quoted pay is earnings. By building the contingency payment into the basic pay the employers have produced just that confusion that has brought about pay inflation. The rightful demand for equal pay has become an unfair demand for equal earnings.

4 The pay structure for some firms and industries shows a 'dog-leg' up to Grade 3 as a result of trade union bargaining, Fig. 17.2. This is not uncommon. The result is that staff, of Grade 3 itself up to Grade 6, are 'feeling' the sense of inequity. The supervisors and middle managers of our society (shaded area) are restless and, as a consequence, there is a growing move towards trade unionism in order to restore the differentials they feel are their

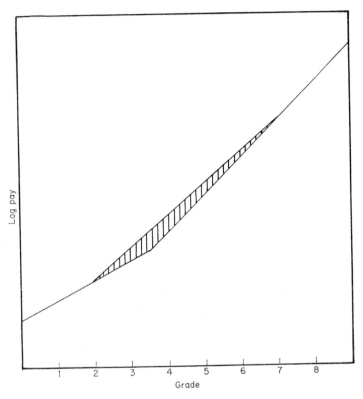

Figure 17.2   To illustrate effect of 'dog-leg' pay curve

'natural' right. It is not to be wondered at that, in the UK, the trade union called Association of Scientific and Technical and Managerial Staffs is fast gaining membership. Firms, industries and government should take note; here is another source of pay inflation. For a firm the first stage in restoring an equitable pay curve is to peg Y_2 and Y_7 and raise the Grades between; then peg Y_1 and Y_8 and raise again, a sequence to be contemporaneous with the general rise shown in Fig. 17.1. (See *The Manual*, Chapter 13.)

5 *Comparability* of occupational earnings is not possible on a national scale. The only basis for comparability is slope of the pay curve coupled with minimum basic pay. It is not logical to compare, say, the earnings of dockers with the pay of local government clerks. The high earnings of the unskilled

automobile industry staff cannot be compared with the pay of school teachers. It is the amount of payroll and its distribution in the form of basic pay that forms a solid platform for comparison, not earnings. The automobile industry can afford a big payroll and can afford big contingency payments to the unskilled drudge on the line—his earnings are mainly a recognition of his reduction almost to being an automaton; and said one steel foundry middle manager to me, "I wouldn't work as a blast furnace bricklayer for twice my salary". Equal *basic* pay for equal work!

6 The slope and the minimum basic pay is dependent upon the firm's and the industry's *ability to pay*. That ability has its roots in the efficiency of the firm, the greater the output–input ratio the greater the return and so reward. A payroll and its distribution geared to efficiency is better than the Scanlon or Rucker techniques.

7 The greater the efficiency and so the greater the reward the more attractive the firm or the industry is to staff who are themselves efficient. The higher the minimum wage and the steeper the slope the better a firm or industry can handle *labour market changes* attracting the ambitious skilled and managerial staff.

8 But this aspect of *industrial differentials* requires a deeper analysis. As a person contributes to a firm, a firm contributes to industry, and industry to the nation. The obligation of a firm, meaning responsibility, is not first to shareholders, it is first to the nation. A firm is part of a living social organism, the nation, and as a part it survives through survival of the whole. Its first obligation is to the whole. The saying, "What is good for General Motors is good for the USA" should be, "What is good for the USA is good for General Motors". If the nation requires for its survival expansion of exports, as does the UK, then firms, if they can, must make the effort. The world is now the market, no longer just the nation. There should be a reward for firms who fulfil their obligations in this sense, a premium of some kind based on controlled contingency payments where the firm considers it justifiable.

After its first obligation to the nation the firm's second obligation is to its members, including staff and shareholders alike, who have to be rewarded for their contributions of work and capital. I use the word reward advisedly for I am of the opinion that a major change in attitude is required (apparently simple but in reality difficult). For too long we have believed in the economic man, that figure beloved of the economists, a man who reacts only to external influences, who is activated only by economic motives, maximising profits or advantages, selling his labour, a reactive man. Yet the psychologists tell us that man, at least in a society where his physiological needs are satisfied, have other needs that are not economic but social, the need for status and prestige, for belongingness, for the chance to help shape his destiny, a self-actualising man. And whatever the economists may say about Marshall's theory of net advantages being an economic theory, it is an understanding of man as a self-actualising man. He does not sell his labour he gives it for, giving, he is rewarded, not only by pay, but by these other intangibles, the net advantages. He gives, the firm gives; he does not sell, the firm rewards. His labour is not to be bought at a price and regarded as a cost, but regarded as his contribution—and the greater the worth of that contribution the greater the reward.

And distributed profits are reward as well. Of course shareholders want to get a money return for their capital; but they do not just lend it they risk it; and for this risk they are rewarded. If the firm makes no profit the shareholder gets no reward, but the staff continue to receive theirs. If the firm prospers both have a share of the prosperity, that is, if the payroll is increased with increased ability to pay, both benefit. I would argue that, pay and distributed profits being reward,

> if change of pay is dependent upon payroll and slope of the pay curve then change of distributed profits is also dependent upon payroll and slope of the pay curve.

Using Eq. (3) of Chapter 14, if P is pay and S is distributed profits, the relationship can be expressed mathematically thus:

$$\frac{d\sum_{0}^{10} n_1 Y_1}{dr} = aP = bS$$

where a and b are constants. The ratio a/b is the expression of distributive justice.

Since justice of any kind depends ultimately on the sense of 'we-ness', that is since distributive justice in the firm depends on the sense of staff and shareholders all being members, then the ratio a/b, the 'share of the cake', cannot be negotiated as between two sides. It can only be agreed—by the Job Assessment Committee of the firm. (See *The Manual.*)

It is my opinion that part of the trouble lately confronting the British Government's introduction of its Industrial Relations Bill, especially the opposition of trade unions, stems from a misunderstanding, a confusion of distributive and retributive justice, the two sides of the same coin. Retributive justice is concerned with the use of power in imposing penalty for failure to fulfil obligation, distributive justice is concerned with reward for fulfilling obligation. The Government is arguing about retributive justice, trade unions have, traditionally, fought for distributive justice. My contention, in introducing this Method of job evaluation in this fashion, is that distributive justice sets the framework for retributive justice—it would have been better for the Government to have solved the problem of the 'share of the cake' before introducing its Bill.

Bibliography

1 ADAMS, K., 'Industrial emolumetrics', *Ind. Rev. Africa* (August 1960).
2 BARTLETT, F. C., *Psychology and the soldier*, Cambridge University Press (1927).
3 BELCHER, D. W., *Wage and salary administration*, Prentice Hall, New York (Second edition, 1963).
4 BENGE, E. J., BURKE, S. L. H., AND HAY, E. N., *Manual of job evaluation*, Harper, New York (1941).
5 BENGE, E., *Job evaluation and merit rating*, US National Foremen's Institute (1944).
6 BRENNAN, C. W., *Wage Administration*, Irwin, Illinois (1963).
7 BROWN, W., AND JAQUES, E., *Glacier project papers*, Heinemann, London (1965).
8 CHAMBERLAIN, N., AND KUHN, J., *Collective bargaining*, McGraw-Hill, New York (Second edition, 1965).
9 CHESLER, D. A., 'Reliability and comparability of different job evaluation systems', *J. appl. Psychol.*, V32, pp. 465–475 (1946).
10 CLARK, J. B., *Distribution of wealth*, Macmillan, London (1899).
11 DUNLOP, J. T., *The theory of wage determination*, Macmillan, London (1957).
12 ELLIOTT, A. G. P., Job evaluation: science fiction?, *Personnel Mgt.*, V42, pp. 36–47 (1960).
13 FOGARTY, M., *The just wage*, Chapman, London (1961).
14 GRAY, J. S., AND JONES, M. C., 'Ready-made versus custom-made systems of job evaluation', *J. appl. Psychol.*, V35, pp. 11–14 (1951).
15 HAY, E. N., *AMA handbook of wage and salary administration*, pp. 56–65, AMA, New York (1950).
16 HAY, E. N., 'The application of Weber's Law to job evaluation estimates', *J. appl. Psychol.*, V34, pp. 102–104 (1950).
17 HAY, E. N., AND PURVES, D., 'A new method of job evaluation—the guide chart profile method', *Personnel* V28, pp. 162–170 (1951); V31, pp. 72–80 (1954); V35, pp. 63–72 (1958).
18 HICKS, J. R., *The theory of wages*, Oxford University Press (1935).
19 HUSBAND, T. M., *Job evaluation and the decision process*, Unpublished MSc Thesis, University of Strathclyde (1966).
20 HUSBAND, T. M., *Pay and organisation structure*, Unpublished PhD Thesis, University of Strathclyde (1970).
21 INBUCON LIMITED, *The direct consensus method of job evaluation*, London (1969). (Circulated privately.)

22 INTERNATIONAL COMMITTEE FOR SCIENTIFIC MANAGEMENT, *Report of international conference on job evaluation*, Geneva (1950).

23 JAQUES, E., *Measurement of responsibility*, Harvard University Press, Cambridge, Mass. (1956).

24 JAQUES, E., *Equitable payment*, Heinemann, London (1961).

25 JAQUES, E., *Time-span handbook*, Heinemann, London (1964).

26 JAQUES, E., 'Speculations concerning level of capacity', in Brown, W., and Jaques, E., *Glacier Project Papers*, Heinemann, London (1965).

27 JOHNSON, F., BOISE, R., AND PRATT, D., *Job evaluation*, John Wiley, New York (1946).

28 KERR, C., *Wage relationships—the comparative impact of market and power forces in theory of wage determination*, edited by J. T. Dunlop, Macmillan, London (1957).

29 KERSHNER, A. M., *A report on job analysis*, Office of Naval Research, Department of the Navy, Washington, DC (1955).

30 KNOWLES, K. G. J. C., AND ROBERTSON, D. J., 'Differences between the wages of skilled and unskilled workers, 1880–1950', *Bull. Oxf. Inst. Stats.* (April 1951).

31 LANHAM, E., *Job evaluation*, McGraw-Hill, New York (1955).

32 LAWSHE, G. H., AND SATTER, G. A., 'Studies in job evaluation: I—Factor analyses of point ratings for hourly paid jobs in three industrial plants', *J. appl. Psychol.*, V28, pp. 189–198 (1944).

33 LAWSHE, C. H., DUDEK, E. E., AND WILSON, R. F., 'A factor analysis on two point rating methods of job evaluation', *ibid.*, V32, pp. 118–129 (1948).

34 LERNER, S. W., CABLE, J. R., AND GUPTA, S., *Workshop wage determination*, Pergamon Press, London (1969).

35 LOTT, M. R., *Wage scales and job evaluation*, Ronald Press, New York (1926).

36 LYDALL, H., 'The distribution of employment incomes', *Econometrica*, V27, pp. 110–115 (1959).

37 LYTLE, C. W., *Job evaluation methods*, Ronald Press (1954).

38 MCBEATH, G., AND RANDS, D. N., *Salary administration*, Business Publications, London (1964).

39 MACHLUP, F., 'Marginal analysis and empirical research', *Amer. Econ. Rev.* (September 1946).

40 MACKAY, D. I., *Internal wage structures in local labour markets and wage structures*, edited by D. Robinson, Gower Press, London (1970).

41 MCNEMAR, Q., 'Opinion attitude methodology', *Psychol. Bull.*, V43, pp. 289–374 (1946).

42 MARQUAND, J., 'Wage drift: origins, measurement and behaviour', Woolwich Economic Papers, No. 14, *Pol. Dept. Bus. Studies*, London (1967).

43 MATCHETT, G. J., 'Wages', *Encycl. Brit.*, Chicago (1956).

44 MEIJ, E. (Editor), *Internal wage structure*, North Holland, Den Haag (1963).

45 MICHEL, H., *The economics of Ancient Greece*, Cambridge University Press (1940).

46 NATIONAL BOARD FOR PRICES AND INCOMES, *Job evaluation*, Report No. 83, HMSO, London (September 1968).

47 NATIONAL BOARD FOR PRICES AND INCOMES, *Job evaluation (supplement)*, Report No. 83, HMSO, London, Cmnd. 3772 (December 1968).

48 OTIS, J. L., AND LEUKART, R. H., *Job evaluation*, Prentice Hall, NJ (Second edition, 1954).

49 PATERSON, T. T., *Glasgow Ltd., a case study of industrial war and peace*, Cambridge (1960).

50 PATERSON, T. T., *Morale in war and work. An experiment in the management of men*, Max Parrish, London (1956).

51 PATERSON, T. T., *First Report of the Commission of Enquiry into the Organisation of the Southern Rhodesia Public Services*, Rhodesia House, London (1961).

52 PATERSON, T. T., 'The Jaques System: impractical', *New Society*, V19 (December 1963).

53 PATERSON, T. T., *Job evaluation: Third Report of the Commission of Enquiry into the Organisation of the Southern Rhodesia Public Services*, Rhodesia House, London (1963).

54 PATERSON, T. T., *Management theory*, Business Publications, London (1966).

55 PATTON, J. A., *Job evaluation in practice*, AMA Management Report No. 54, AMA, New York (1961).
56 PEARSON, H., 'How to pay', *Management Today* (January 1967).
57 REYNOLDS, L. G., AND TAFT, C. H., *The evolution of wage structures*, Oxford University Press, London (1956).
58 ROBERTS, D. C., *Executive compensation*, Free Press, Illinois (1959).
59 ROBERTSON, D. J., *Factory wage structures and national agreements*, Cambridge University Press (1960).
60 ROBINSON, D., *Wage drift, fringe benefits and manpower distribution*, OECD (1968).
61 ROBINSON, D. (Editor), *Local labour markets and wage structures*, Gower Press, London (1970).
62 ROGER, J. E. T., *Six centuries of work and wages*, Unwin, London (1919).
63 RUPE, J. C., *Research into basic methods and techniques of Air Force job analysis*, US Air Force Human Resources Center, Lackland Air Force Base (December 1956).
64 SCOTT, D., *Job evaluation: technique, practice and potential*, Unpublished MSc Thesis, University of Strathclyde (1969).
65 SIMON, H. A., 'The compensation of executives', *Sociometry*, V20, pp. 32–5 (1957).
66 STIEBER, J., *The steel industry wage structure*, Harvard University Press, Cambridge (1959).
67 TAYLOR, G. W., AND PIERSON, F. C. (Editors), *New concepts in wage determination*, McGraw-Hill, New York (1957).
68 THORELLI, H. B., 'Salary span of control', *Jour. Mgt. Studies*, V2, pp. 269–302 (1965).
69 TRATHNER, M. H., AND KUBIS, J. F., 'A comparison of value requirement ratings by reading job descriptions and by direct job observation', *Personnel Psychol.*, V8, pp. 183–194 (1955).
70 UNITED NATIONS, *Economic Survey of Europe in 1955*, Research and Planning Division, Economic Commission for Europe, Geneva (1955).
71 US DEPARTMENT OF LABOUR, *Industrial job evaluation systems*, Washington (1947).
72 WAR MANPOWER COMMISSION (DIVISION OF OCCUPATIONAL ANALYSIS), *Training and reference manual for job analysis*, Washington, Govt. Ptg. Off. (1944).
73 WEISS, P., 'Beauty and the beast: life and the rule of order, *Scientific Monthly*, p. 286 (December 1955).
74 WOOTTON, B., *The social foundations of wage policy*, Unwin, London (1955).
75 YODER, D., AND HENEMAN, H. G., *Labor economics and industrial relations*, Southwestern Publishing, Cincinnati (1959).
76 ZIPF, G. K., AND RUCKER, A. W., 'How to set salary brackets that spur achievement' *Mod. Mgt.*, pp. 1–4 (November 1949).

Index

education, 94–5
experience, 95
numerical computations, 91–2
pressure of work coefficient, 90–91
vigilance, 92–3
Categorical imperative, 13
Chamberlain, N., and Kahn, J., 133
Chesler, D. A., 77, 132
Civil service
see UK Civil Service,
Clark, J. D., 132
Classification (job) method, xii, 45–60
difficulties, 59–60
IOM scheme, 45–9
US Public Service Scheme, 50–9
act, 50, 59, 161
Clerical job grading:
IOM manual, 47–9
Clusters, job, 45, 62, 73, 76, 117, 134,
175–6
Collective bargaining, 2
Comparison scale job, 84
Compatibility of schemes, 117
Compensable factor, 45–62
Complexity, 8, 156
job structure, 39
Comprehension ability:
Castellion method, 92
Conclusion:
decision-making, 9–11
Conditions, working, 119, 143, 179
factor-comparison method, 83
point method, 71
Consequences of errors:
Castellion method, 93–4
Content, job, 120, 122
Contingency payments, 144–5, 161, 179,
180, 194, 196
Control, 17
Cortis, Dr L., 86
Count-ranking technique, 161
Craft unions, 4
Currie, R., 24

Decision bands, 24–30
guide-chart profile method, 109–15
Decision-complex, 11, 22 (Fig.)
Decision-making, 7–8, 9–20
Castellion method, 86–90
effects on pay, 148
production management, 9–10

Decision process, 9, 10 (Fig.), 22 (Fig.)
Decision structure, 21–30, 187–90
Decision system, 11
Decisions:
kinds of, 23–4
relative importance of, 152
sapiential authority, 157
specific to function, 31
Defined decisions:
decision bands, 26
Delegation, 194
Department of Employment and Pro-
ductivity, 171
Description, job
see Job description
Development, 125, 183–4
Differential rewards, 2, 4, 5, 12, 9,
131–41, 145, 147, 196, 162
job clusters, 134
net advantages, 132
wage contours, 134
Difficulty, 8, 28, 95, 156, 167
clerical work, 46
job structure, 37–9
Direction, 20
Discretion:
time-span method, 97–8
Discriminating expenditure, 136, 146
Discrimination, 164–7
Dostoievski, F., 121
Dunlop, J. T., 134
Dutch standardised method, 5

Earnings, 142
see also Pay
see also Wages
Economy of grading, 34, 49, 160, 188
Education:
Castellion method, 94–5
point method, 66
training, 125, 183–4
Efficiency, 185
Effort, 123
Element, 8, 24, 33, 35
Eligibility, 185
Elliott, A. G. P., 76
Employers Association, 4
Enlargement, job, 34
Enrichment, job, 34, 160, 188
Equality, 117, 175
Equipment, responsibility for point
method, 69